THE Family LEGACY

Shaping Culture from the Inside Out

How to lead your family, live your legacy,
and shape culture in the process.

RANDALL W. BIXBY

Copyright © 2020 Randall W. Bixby
All rights reserved. No part of this book may be used or reproduced in any manner whatsoever without prior written consent of the authors, except as provided by the United States of America copyright law.

Published by Best Seller Publishing®, Pasadena, CA
Best Seller Publishing® is a registered trademark
Printed in the United States of America.
ISBN 9798600405820

This publication is designed to provide accurate and authoritative information with regard to the subject matter covered. It is sold with the understanding that the publisher is not engaged in rendering legal, accounting, or other professional advice. If legal advice or other expert assistance is required, the services of a competent professional should be sought. The opinions expressed by the authors in this book are not endorsed by Best Seller Publishing® and are the sole responsibility of the author rendering the opinion.

For more information, please write:
Best Seller Publishing®
1346 Walnut Street, #205
Pasadena, CA 91106
or call 1(626) 765 9750
Toll Free: 1(844) 850-3500
Visit us online at: www.BestSellerPublishing.org

Cover designed by Joel Rodriguez and Steve Fata

Praise for The Family Legacy

This world is missing tools that shape our families to live a full journey of relational health, and Randy Bixby is offering a full tool set that is so complete that I think it needs to become a new handbook for families, counselors, and pastoral care providers.

There is gold in every family relationship but we need emotionally intelligent language to equip us to walk in the full value of these relationships. I haven't seen another book quite like this. I would encourage you to make an investment into your family and read through The Family Legacy- Shaping Culture form the Inside Out! It will change the way you think.

SHAWN BOLZ
www.bolzministries.com. Author, Speaker, TV Personality, Prophet

★ ★ ★

There are only a handful of educators I work with for our training programs and Randy Bixby is my hands down favorite. His focus is transformation and that's exactly what he creates. Like few others he has the unique ability to put his finger on the exact issue and what it takes to create lasting change. The Family Legacy- Shaping Culture from the Inside Out, is his greatest work, his Magnum Opus! A must read.

DR. LANCE WALLNAU
Founder Lance Learning Group. Author, Speaker, Strategist, Futurist, Consultant

★ ★ ★

The Family Legacy: Shaping Culture from the Inside Out should be mandatory reading for anyone that feels called to influence the Family Mountain. This is the type of book that not only will transform your own family; it can also help shape culture and reposition families into the role Father intended them to provide in society. Kingdom leaders at the gates of culture need paradigm-shifting approaches like this for every sphere of culture. Randy Bixby has tapped into something we must all learn from and apply right away.

JAMES KRAMER
Founder/CEO Commissioned and Pneuma33 Creative

More than any human institution, family is clearly heralded as the most significant in bringing meaning and fulfillment to our lives. Yet the very existence and notion of family has suffered more injury, abuse, hostility, neglect, failure, reinterpretation, reengineering, rejection, and reappraisal in the last century than ever before. In spite of all, family remains the most celebrated and significant institution in the formation of multi-generational human relationships. Marriage and family books abound, but none deliver the depth of integrated information and insightful experience with pragmatic application like The Family Legacy- Shaping Culture from the Inside Out.

Randy Bixby has spent decades interpreting the details of individual behavioral patterns through the lens of character development and looking deeply at the DNA of individual responsibility and family dynamics built on lessons in emotional intelligence. The trust-building process comes from truly understanding who we are and why we do what we do as we do it together. It's no overstatement to assert that this book is essential reading for rebuilding our families today. Used in combination with the experiential learning modules, workbook material, and workshops available, Bixby's book provides the foundation for a social, psychological, and spiritual architecture that will help rebuild our families and our culture. Given the challenges we face today as families, it couldn't be more timely.

GORDON RIDDLE PENNINGTON
Founder, Burning Media Group

★ ★ ★

Heaven's government is family. There is a generational move of the spirit that is restoring family on earth as it is in Heaven. I've had the great privilege of travelling the world for more than 20 years and have experienced God's Kingdom family movement first hand. It is changing the world! My friend, Randy Bixby, has written a book called The Family Legacy that will teach you how to transform culture from the inside out starting with your family.

LEIF HETLAND
President, Global Mission Awareness. Author, Called To Reign

★ ★ ★

By the creative utilization of authentic ideas, data and personal life experiences, my dear friend Randy Bixby, has masterfully explained why our society has been plagued with the debilitating contemporary cultural challenges we are currently facing.

As I read The Family Legacy- Shaping Culture from the Inside Out, I could clearly see that it provides a biblically based roadmap that's designed to equip and empower families to comprehensively navigate through the challenges of relativism, decadence and apathy, while simultaneously unveiling a worldview for family life. No matter what families may go through, we know that ultimately, Jesus is the answer, but what are the questions?

This book succinctly addresses every question centered around the biblical narrative for family life. As Christianity is grappling with the negative implications of cultural trends of society at large, this skillful writing gives spiritual insight, biblical clarity and practical step by step actions built on the revelation of our Father's heart for family. I emphatically recommend this book for families, churches, small groups and especially leaders.

ELLIS L. SMITH
Apostolic Leader, Jubilee City Church- Detroit

★ ★ ★

The family is in crisis today. What can we do about it? Randy Bixby has provided tools to help us restore the family in his new book, *The Family Legacy: Shaping Culture from the Inside Out*. You will find this a roadmap to restore the family. I encourage you to read it and apply the steps Randy outlines in this great book. Well done Randy!

OS HILLMAN,
author, Change Agent and TGIF Today God Is First

★ ★ ★

From the moment I began to read The Family Legacy- Shaping Culture from the Inside Out, I was gripped with an overwhelming sense of urgency and responsibility. Randy paints a clear picture of the ailments that plague our nation. With prophetic insight and a tremendous amount of research, Randy cuts through the thicket of confusion and delivers a simple, yet profound solution that will reroute the moral decline we see all around us.

The Family Legacy reveals how to transform culture through God's prescription, the family. While reading it I was reminded of a story told in 1 Kings 16:34. "Hiel the Bethelite built Jericho; he laid its foundations with the loss of Abiram his firstborn, and set up its gates with the loss of his youngest son Segub, according to the word of the Lord..." Like Hiel, many times our contribution to society comes with the greatest sacrifice of all, our families. Randy shows us how we can have strong and healthy families that transform culture together. I cannot recommend this book highly enough

SAMUEL BENTLEY
Director Ramp School of Ministry

★ ★ ★

Inspiring, practical, and compelling!

Randy Bixby's work is an indispensable resource for such a time as this. The Family Legacy- Shaping Culture from the Inside Out displaces the confusion, chaos, and dis-ease that permeates almost every area of our lives while, simultaneous inspiring, instructing, and motivating us to address the most compelling challenges we face in both private and public life. This book is AMAZING!!!!! I plan to dispense it to every single person I work with - I will be purchasing cases!

VIRGINIA DIXON
Director of Inner Healing at The Center for New Medicine
CEO of Tender Hearts Enterprises

★ ★ ★

From the first time I met Randy Bixby, I loved the man. His sincere passion to make a difference coupled with his humility to love well challenged me. I knew I wanted to get behind him and push.

Although he has experienced tremendous success in various fields, Randy's life has not been easy. I have watched him walk through some of the most challenging experiences a man can face and not only maintain his integrity, he maintained love.

It has been in the context of these very challenges that Randy hammered out real solutions. Perhaps his greatest contribution however is the methods he uses to pass those truths on to the rest of us. Randy has developed extremely insightful processes designed to orchestrate personal epiphanies, those life changing realizations which result in true and lasting change.

I for one am grateful Randy has distilled his life work into book form. Take this book, grab your family around you and utilize this material. Better yet, take the next step and utilize the many other tools Randy has developed. You won't be disappointed.

DAVE OLSON
Senior Pastor- Heartland Church Ankeny, IA

★ ★ ★

Everything in the human experience flows from the foundation of family. The state of our culture reflects the state of our families. Randy Bixby has done an excellent job of creating practical tools to steward the family as designed that will ultimately shape culture from the inside out. In *The Family Legacy: Shaping Culture from the Inside Out*, you will find six core protocols and more than sixty exercises, tools, and experiences that will lead you and your family into experiencing:

- A deep understanding of the real problem, the real solution, and a pathway to determine your family legacy.

- The empowering truth and practice of life flowing from you not to you.

- How you have the choice to be a cultural architect, or not. Choosing to architect your family experience intentionally will influence everything around you AND teach your children to do the same for generations to come.

- A thriving family, an enduring legacy, and a transformed culture.

I encourage you to make a generational and life-changing choice to put the protocols into practice. You will change the trajectory of your family legacy and the trajectory of our culture forever.

REV. MARK L. GURLEY,
CLU, CHFC, CLTC, CAP, COSJ

★ ★ ★

Randy Bixby's book; The Family Legacy, Shaping Culture from the Inside Out, is an authentic life-changing practical guide that speaks to the problems of brokenness in this generation and the step by step process of restoration and real cultural transformation that happens from the inside out beginning with your family. As a mentor and lead pastor with the Open Bible Churches for the past 42 years, this is a must read for all who appreciate and value leaving an enduring family legacy.

DR. J. RANDY GRIMES,
D.Min., Pastor, Open Bible Christian Church
Professor, United Theological Seminary, Dayton, Ohio

Dedication

To my grandson, Sage Thomas Tobin-Bixby, whose forty weeks in utero and seven days in the Neo Natal Intensive Care unit profoundly impacted our family legacy. In his brief yet profound life, Sage changed all of us from the inside-out. His legacy lives on not only in us, but in the lives and families of his organ recipients. We will never be the same. Everyone we touch will be touched by Sage. He so powerfully exemplified our family legacy, to transform people, families, and culture from the inside-out. September 5-12, 2019.

You can help bring this transforming work to families by giving to Sage's Legacy. To learn more and give to this scholarship fund for families in need, visit our website www.culturalarchitects.org

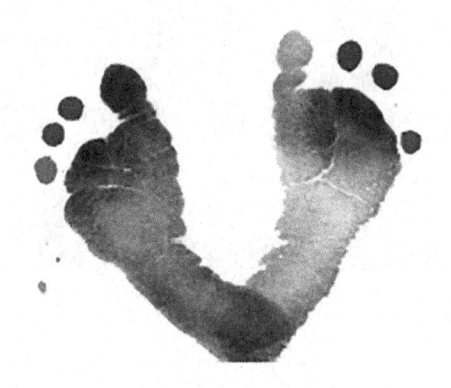

"There is no footprint too small that it cannot leave an impact on this world."

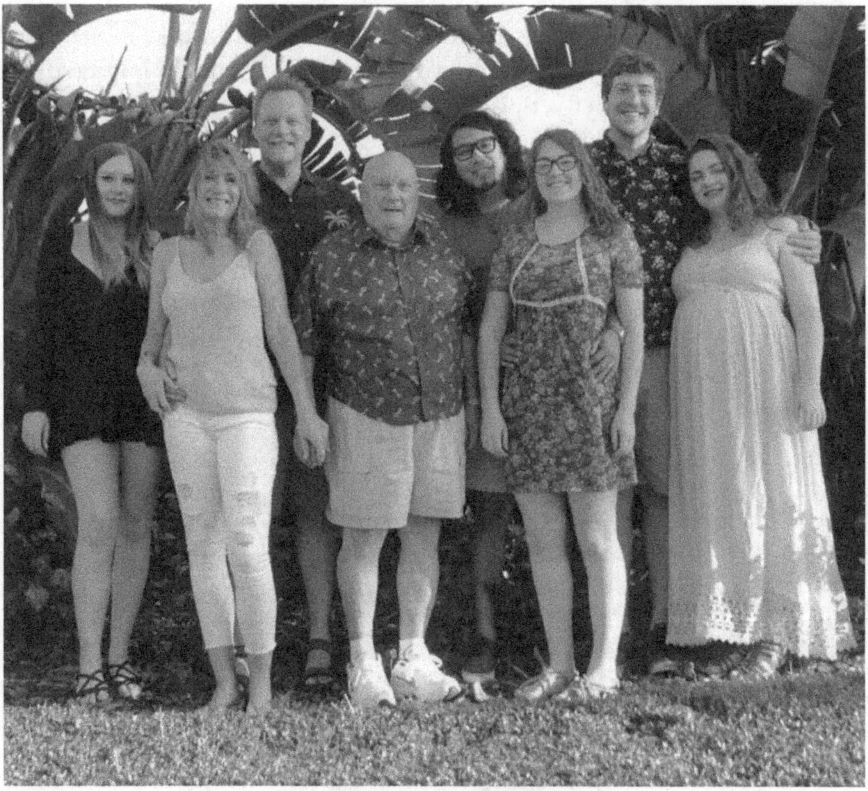

Acknowledgements

To my parents, Garry and Jan Bixby, thank you for your authentic love for God, each other, and your children. Your sacrificial examples of integrity, empathy, leadership, and wisdom are the riches of my inheritance and your legacy. I love you.

To those whose choices changed the eternal trajectory of my family line and mission, Carlyle and Dorothy Bixby, Theresa Larson, Suzanne and Paul Roberts. I am forever grateful for your courage and perseverance in wholeheartedly loving and serving God and those He entrusted you to steward. Your rewards are great. I love you.

To my children, Garrett, Kara, and Miranda, in your DNA flow the identity and purpose of God's design for our family line expressed in our Bixby family motto: "love…learn…lead". This book is for you above all others. Together, we have been deeply wounded and are being graciously healed. Thank you for your willingness, participation, and input in creating the Family Legacy Protocols. Live them with your families. Equip your children to do the same. You are magnificent! I love you.

To my wife, Lesli, you were worth the wait! I couldn't ask for a better woman and partner to journey with me into oneness. You carry Father's "mother heart" like no one I've ever known. What you have overcome with God has given you great authority as we continue to be about our Father's business together. Thank you for your indispensable partnership in healing our family, writing this book, and developing the training for families. I love you, infinity!

To my Heavenly Father, Thank You for calling me at age twelve. You are my delight and my all in all. I am in awe of You. Being one with You is the most amazing life journey possible. When I was broken and uncertain if I could go on, You said, "just love your family." I said, "I can do that." Three years later, You are healing my family. We have written this book together for families, for Your Family, and for Your glory. May Your kingdom come, and Your will be done on earth and in families as it is in heaven! It's Yours to do whatever You want with it for Your glory. I love You!

BIXBY
HONOR ~ FAITH
ARTS ~ EMPATHY
AUTHENTIC ~ VISION
JUSTICE ~ HEALING
ABUNDANCE ~ PERSEVERANCE ~ COURAGE
Love Learn Lead

Contents

Chapter 1: The Problem. The root cause of why civilizations fall and how you and your family legacy are at risk. **17**

Chapter 2: The Solution. Shaping culture from the inside out and the Family Legacy Model. **49**

Chapter 3: My Story. My family journey through childhood, wounding, healing, and the unique formation of Family Legacy tools, modules, workshops, coaching, and training. **73**

Chapter 4: Preparing for Your Journey. Definition, value, scope, motivation, and how to get the most out of the Family Legacy Protocols for generations to come. **85**

Chapter 5: Protocol 1: Family Legacy EQ. Creating an environment of safety, trust, support, forgiveness, love, purpose, and fun. **109**

Chapter 6: Protocol 2: Family Legacy Identity. Discovering together your family identity and uniqueness: past, present, and future; establishing family character, values, and purpose; creating a family coat of arms. **139**

Chapter 7: Protocol 3: Family Legacy Ritual. The regular family meeting framework: food, fun, story, wisdom, and a supportive coach approach. **165**

Chapter 8: Protocol 4: Family Legacy Venture. The annual family learning adventure trip or vacation with maximum legacy benefit. **185**

Chapter 9: Protocol 5: Family Legacy MISSION *(Momentary, Intentional, Specific, Supportive, Intervention,* as *One,* in Response to a *Need)* **217**

Chapter 10: Protocol 6: Family Legacy Impartation. How to intentionally impart the most important things so your legacy endures. The wisdom, blessing, stuff, unfinished business, and the Family Legacy Generational Covenant. **235**

Chapter 11: Family Legacy Toolbox. A complete listing of the sixty-plus Family Legacy tools available free online. **283**

Chapter 12: Family Legacy Solutions: Training, Coaching, Subscription, E-courses and Resources. A listing of the Family Legacy solutions offered through Cultural Architects. **287**

Preface

This book is for you if ...

On a Personal Level

- You love your family and want them to thrive in every way together no matter how old they are now, what they have been through, or how impossible that may seem.
- You want to see your family reconnected, healed, and successful.
- You want to create a safe, loving, fun, supportive, and healthy environment in your home.
- You want your children to know their identity, values, and purpose and be equipped to live them successfully.
- You are looking for a better way to "do family" with greater emotional intelligence and a coach approach that transforms family dynamics.
- You want a practical blueprint and tools to follow that will ensure a significant and enduring legacy.
- You are committed to building a legacy of character in your family along with a legacy of true wealth.
- You want a process for passing on the most important things in life—wisdom, understanding, and blessings—while teaching your children how to do the same.

On a Leadership and Strategic Level

- You resonate with the calling to influence culture for the better by raising leaders in your family line with character, emotional intelligence, leadership insight, and authority at the gates of culture.
- You are looking for an answer to equipping families in your church to thrive and impact culture.

- You are responsible for equipping pastors, leaders, organizations, or movements to build families, businesses, communities, and culture.
- You resonate with the seven-mountain cultural transformation movement and are looking for a comprehensive, practical, and effective equipping strategy (family, government, business, education, media, arts and entertainment, and religion).
- You understand that, in the end, whoever wins the family wins the culture.

What Is This Book About?

The Family Legacy: Shaping Culture from the Inside Out is a practical guide to a thriving family, an enduring legacy, and a transformed culture.

This book is written through the lenses of leadership, personal responsibility, intentionality, simplicity, a biblical worldview, emotional intelligence, and a coach approach to family, and it is experiential practice by design. In other words, the way to benefit from the contents of this book is to put them into practice, do the exercises, experience its concepts, and use the tools and protocols that will bring about the answers and results you are seeking.

This book is not information first. It is revelation, practical experiences, and tools first—along with plenty of valuable information. Contained in these pages are the experiences you can have with your family that will result in you living and leaving a powerful family legacy for generations to come!

The Family Legacy Model is a simple, enduring, transferable framework to do family. The six protocols and practices that follow intentionally build the family as designed while teaching our children and grandchildren to do the same.

The protocols provide a simple process that families can use to transform individuals and families from the inside out so the generations downstream can experience healing, growth, and success in life while imparting these practices to their children and grandchildren.

The six effective protocols empower families to:
- treat one another with kindness, love, respect, and forgiveness to create a family environment that is safe, loving, trusting, fun, supportive, godly (faith-filled), and purposeful.

- discover the unique (providential) history, true identity, and purpose both individually and as a family.
- establish family rituals that are life-giving and supportive in empowering the entire family to succeed.
- enjoy family adventures together that are packed with purpose, fun, learning, storytelling, good food, and a deep emotional implantation that establishes the family legacy into the family genetic code.
- come together as one in times of family crisis to bring clarity, comfort, and shared responsibility.
- effectively impart the most important things so the legacy endures: the wisdom, the blessing, the stuff, the unfinished business, and the family legacy generational charge.

Practicing these protocols will cut off the power of negative generational influences. Practicing them will preempt the toxic indoctrination of our godless public and university education systems. Living the protocols will empower our children to think critically and objectively beyond the smoke and mirrors of the deceptive mainstream media and keep them connected to the God of their faith, working with Him to succeed in a long and prosperous life.

The culture that has the most successful families will have the most successful civilization and will endure.

The most important focus for a healthy world is truly healthy families who are producing healthy children who become healthy leaders at the decision centers of culture while equipping their children to do the same.

How is this book different? In a few words, it's more than theory and concept. It is a practical how-to book with more than sixty exercises, experiences, and tools to equip families.

Important Distinctions of the Family Legacy Model

- biblically based and designed
- integrates emotional intelligence into the context of family
- use of a coach approach in the family
- transferable process for generational impact
- experience-based training methodology
- intentionally designed for maximum legacy benefit
- more than sixty experiences and tools to equip families with a step-by-step how-to framework

The Family Legacy Model provides a meaningful blueprint for cultural transformation from the inside out. I am writing from a lens of a lifetime exploration of truth and principle, character and leadership, failure and success, and healing and helping. I am writing as a grateful son and as a father and grandfather who is passionate about empowering my family with an enduring and influential family legacy. I am writing from the lens of an authentic believer, follower, and lover of Jesus Christ with a biblical worldview.

I am not writing from a religious, self-righteous, know-it-all, judgmental lens on top of a soapbox. My lens has been tested by loss, failure, abuse, trials, and pain of all sorts. Thankfully, I am also writing from a perspective of healing and restoration and a viewpoint of searching for, finding, experiencing, and equipping others with solutions!

Over the past three decades, I've had the pleasure of serving in professional roles that include pastor, missionary, denominational executive, a house of prayer and nonprofit director, legislative chaplain, trainer, business owner, speaker, author, and ICF-certified coach. My professional career has been all about empowering, training, and coaching leaders of leaders to govern themselves well and shape culture from the inside out! I have invested my life in equipping people to know and love God by partnering with them to demonstrate maturity and fruitfulness individually, in their families, in their churches, in their businesses, and in their communities.

This book is about *action, process,* and *results.* While I think theoretically and strategically, my passion has always been to take action and live what I say I believe and not lower the bar to settle for the impotence and arrogance of only "thinking and knowing." Information and knowledge alone are just not enough to bring about transformation.

My training methodology is experiential and active for this reason. I give people tools for how to live and get the results for which they are committed. I show and equip more than I tell. I focus on an inside-out transformation framework and the individual first, followed by their family, business, church, community, nation, and so on.

I equip and empower cultural architects—leaders who are skilled in inside-out cultural transformation. These brave people are willing to work on themselves, lead by example, and show others how to do the same in their function as decision makers in key power centers of culture. My company, Cultural Architects, focuses on leadership, communication, and the development of human capital at the "gates of culture."

- the gate of family
- the gate of religion
- the gate of education
- the gate of business
- the gate of government
- the gate of media
- the gate of arts and entertainment

Why This Book Now?

Bottom Line

It's now or never. Our families are hurting, and the falling dominoes are picking up speed. We've got to get ahead of this now—before it's too late. The time for a book and equipping system is both long overdue and right on time!

In my urgency to empower people to respond effectively to the cultural collapse that is upon us, I spent several years bringing the transformative protocols and training primarily to people at the gates of government, business, religion (church), and family. While the reports of personal transformation, growth, and exciting results in the lives of thousands of people have been encouraging in proving the validity of the work, another discovery drove me to write this book and shift my primary focus in this season to the family.

In working with leaders at the gates of culture, I experienced over and over that the challenges facing leaders—the deep issues that had them stuck, afraid, broken, and ineffective in their leadership roles—were due to unresolved issues rooted back in their family of origin and their experiences as a child through their specific and unique family experiences.

Through an intense season in my own life, I awakened to this priority and the necessity of focusing on my own family, leading them through the wreckage we've experienced into a brighter and more meaningful future.

My family has been through the challenges of pain, brokenness, early death, divorce, addiction, and recovery. We have faced the challenges of slander and shame, guilt and isolation, the fears of rejection and failure, conflict and abuse, lack and debt, the sleeplessness of anxiety and depression, mental illness and the pursuit of mental health, the uncertainty of job and home moves, and disconnection, isolation, purposelessness, insignificance, and more.

We have also experienced the gratitude of healing and unconditional love. We have tasted the power and freedom of forgiveness. We have encountered the joy of abundance and surplus. We have known the humble confidence of overcoming and the faithful strength of a loving heavenly Father. We have persevered to growth and the maturity of wisdom. We have felt the safety and security of trust, the sweet and refreshing sleep of peace, and the camaraderie of belonging. We have experienced the power of purpose, focus, support, and intentionality.

Through our faith, a relentless pursuit of growth and healing from various modalities including spiritual, psychological, scientific, biological, emotional, therapy, leadership training, and trial and error, we have discovered practical ways to be healed and to bring that healing to others. Moreover, we've taken it several steps further into shaping the lives and culture of families for greater success, joy, satisfaction, and significance.

My family has begun living the protocols contained in the following pages. We are practitioners of the Family Legacy Model. Not perfectly, but faithfully. We are a different family as a result. Our work continues as we persevere through life's challenges together.

The big difference is that now we have a how-to framework for doing family. The Family Legacy Model and six core protocols represent that framework.

What you are holding in your hands in this Family Legacy book is a practical guide to doing family powerfully. This framework for how to do family successfully will help you reconnect and energize your family for success. However, you have to take action!

It does no good to only know what should be done—or what could be done to experience and pass on a powerful and successful family legacy. While knowing what to do is admittedly more than most people possess, it is not enough. We must be able to activate and experience a regular rhythm of intentional principles, practices, and protocols with our families and train them in how to do the same with their families in every generation.

On a personal note, I'm writing this so my wife, children, and grandchildren have the lasting codified benefit of the wisdom we have fought for and so they can take what we have learned and use it as a foundation for putting them into practice and building even more for their children and for their children's children.

Preface

In addition, whenever I share with leaders what we are doing with our family and the effects that the protocols are having on us, they wanted to know, "When will the book be finished and where can they get a copy of it?" They say, "There's nothing like this out there," "This would be amazing for the families in our church," and "Will you come to do this with my family and me?"

People I trust and respect have told my wife and I that they sensed this Family Legacy work would become the dominant focus and practice of the rest of our lives. We shall see. My heart tells me they're right. I will continue to work with all those sent my way.

The insights and practices we've discovered and implemented in our family are working! We are still in process for sure, but we are making noticeable progress! We have a core value in our family: "We have to live it to give it!" We are practitioners of these tools and experiences, and we continue to learn along the way with every lesson.

My heartfelt desire in this work are twofold. First, to obey God and to partner with you by building in your family a revelation of true identity, deep purpose, real healing, lasting joy, long life, abundant prosperity, and the know-how to equip your children and grandchildren to do the same. In short, to make your family experience better now and in the future. Second, I desire to partner with you to create healthy families who build healthy leaders who lead wisely at the gates of culture as kingdom cultural architects.

I trust that you will have the courage to engage in the Family Legacy Protocols so that you can reap the rewards that they offer! Each of the chapters in this book is a keynote speech and a module in training. Each of them includes hands-on experiential exercises, tools, and activities designed for maximum learning, growth, and generational sustainability.

The Family Legacy Protocols can be accessed in various ways if you would like to put them into practice in your family. From the do-it-yourself book and toolbox to the guided video journey and workbook, to one of our Family Legacy workshops or conferences for leaders, congregations, and families, we are here to help you live an enduring family legacy. Our Family Legacy coaches and facilitators are available to you and your family for direct support and facilitation of the protocols. You may also find great value as a Family Legacy network member, a monthly subscription for those who want special access to everything we've got to support you in your journey.

Finally, many of you may be interested in our premiere Family Legacy Encounter Workshop, where we take your entire family through a weekend encounter facilitated by our family. If you want to change things fast and in a way that will last, this is for you!

Whatever you decide to do with the Family Legacy journey, do something. The fact is, you will live and leave a legacy for your family. It is unavoidable. What will it be? What difference will it make?

From our family to yours, we bless your family with revelation knowledge on how to do family in a new and better way filled with more love, laughter, purpose, prosperity, power, presence, and wisdom. Because wise people build families, businesses, and communities—and it is an inside-out job.

Introduction

Our families are struggling, our culture is faltering, and our future is staring history in the face while standing on the slippery edge of a cliff. Will we learn that the fall of the family ensures the fall of a civilization and fix it before it's too late? What's at stake if we do not? Beyond conceptual and theoretical answers, what can practically be done to produce thriving families, enduring legacies, and a transformed culture?

Fix it? What exactly is *it*? What is the real problem?

Marriages are in trouble, and families are going down in flames. We are losing our communities, our churches, and the culture that our founding fathers set in place at the cost of all they had: their wealth, their reputations, the spilled blood of their sons and daughters, and even their life breath.

The word *crisis* comes to mind. We are in crisis as a nation.

Individuals are in crisis as mental illness and suicide strike at large and growing numbers of our population. There is a crisis in marriages with high divorce rates and increasing numbers of adults choosing not to marry … a crisis in families with many children facing murder before birth, various abuses, poverty, food insecurity, fatherless or motherless homes, and generations of the nearly "walking dead." We have a racism crisis in communities and a moral crisis in government as we overspend into debt while deception, corruption, and ideology divide our population fiercely.

We have a crisis in leadership that is ill-equipped, overwhelmed, and blindly leading us over the cliff. A crisis in the church of identity drift (not knowing who we are) as it shrinks in relevance, attendance, and influence. A crisis in education as free speech is being threatened while indoctrination has replaced discovery—a crisis in health with staggering numbers of substance abuse, addiction, overdose deaths, and obesity.

I go into more depth of the current state of our nation in chapter 1. Tragically, all the wreckage is not the *it*. The pain-riddled statistics are the fruit of a deeper problem, a deeper *it* that is the root.

The Root Problem: Identity drift coupled with an individual failure to self-govern well and the choice to not steward the family as designed.

This starts the flywheel of pain, trauma, and dysfunction in the family in motion, which leads to the social, moral, and cultural degradation of our homes, our businesses, our communities, and our culture.

The choices made knowingly or unknowingly not to agree with our true identity, not to self-govern well, and not to steward the family as designed are the root of the problem. Many other calamitous choices that deprioritize the family and devalue the protocols (practices) required to live and leave a powerful family legacy above more selfish pursuits are at the root of our problem. In addition to our own choices are the choices of our generations past that have been hardwired into our genetic legacy and influence our subconscious thinking.

If not addressed adequately, hurt people continue to hurt people. The pain and devastation continue to cascade from one generation to the next, inflicting more wounding, more anxiety, more depression, and more destruction, which leads to fewer and fewer families producing healthy leaders who are entering places of influence at the gates of culture.

Moreover, the cultural fall continues from the inside out to topple the power structures and systems of our families, our businesses, and our communities. As our broken generations take the baton for their leg of leadership at the gates of culture, their internal brokenness further degrades our cultural institutions—even as their own children's wounds ensure the legacy of hell on earth will be passed on.

Individuals and families suffer, trapped in a downward spiral, and are falling further and further away from their true identity and design as our culture rots from the inside out.

The Solution: An inside-out transformation that reveals true identity while restoring proper self-governing and the stewardship of the family as designed.

Leaders positioned at the gates of culture govern or direct the flow of decisions, laws, and resources. Leaders at the gates of family, government, education, arts and entertainment, business, media, and religion choose what is allowed and disallowed in the sphere of their authority. Their decisions are made based on the character of their leaders. Their core thinking and values determine the results of the decisions that determine and shape the culture they architect. (Culture is our deepest-rooted assumptions about what is true or right.)

An unhealthy culture is the result of unhealthy character in leaders at all of the gates of culture. Unhealthy leaders are the result of generations of unhealthy families. Unhealthy leaders will shape an unhealthy culture. Healthy leaders from healthy families will shape healthy cultures. We reproduce the culture that agrees with our character.

This inside-out character crisis in leaders is the challenge of the hour. It is the reason for Cultural Architects, along with my focus on equipping families and, ultimately, leaders of leaders at the gates of culture. Training families to get healthy and produce healthy children, who in turn become healthy leaders for generations to come, will alter the trajectory of our nation from the inside out.

"Well, of course," you may say. "Individual transformation leading to the healing and revitalization of healthy families yielding healthy leaders generationally is the way to get things on track."

But How?

What do I actually and specifically do to transform my character? What practices do I follow to have a revelation of who I am? Of why I'm here? How exactly do I self-govern well and powerfully steward my family as designed? How precisely do I teach my children and those I lead to do the same and shape culture together?

The answers to these questions are what *The Family Legacy: An Insightful and Practical Guide to a Thriving Family, an Enduring Legacy, and a Transformed Culture* address. While each family has its uniqueness, the principles, practices, and protocols contained in this book equally apply to families of all shapes, sizes, values, and configurations.

The Family Legacy Model is a simple, enduring, transferable framework to do family. It contains a set of protocols to follow to intentionally build the family while teaching our children and grandchildren to do the same.

The Family Legacy Protocols are a mechanism that facilitates a revelation of true identity that empowers individuals to govern themselves and steward their families well. The protocols are simple, effective, generational, fun, accessible, and enduring.

These protocols provide a process that families can effectively practice to transform individuals and families from the inside out so the generations downstream can experience healing, growth, and success in life while imparting these practices to their children and grandchildren.

The six effective protocols empower families to:

- treat one another with kindness, love, respect, and forgiveness creating a family environment that is safe, loving, trusting, fun, supportive, godly (faith-filled), and purposeful.
- discover the unique (providential) history, true identity, and purpose both as individuals and as an entire family.
- establish family rituals that are life-giving and supportive in empowering the entire family to succeed.
- enjoy family adventures together packed with purpose, fun, learning, storytelling, good food, and deep emotional implantation to establish the family legacy into the family genetic code.
- come together as one in times of family crisis to bring clarity, comfort, and shared responsibility.
- effectively impart the most important things so the legacy endures: the wisdom, the blessing, the stuff, the unfinished business, and the family legacy generational charge.

The protocols empower people to transform the culture from the inside out, properly govern self, generationally steward the family as designed, and teach the next generation to do the same.

Introduction

The Family Legacy Model

Six protocols (practices) for leading your family, living your legacy, and shaping culture in the process:

- **Protocol 1:** Family Legacy EQ. Creating an environment of safety, trust, support, forgiveness, love, purpose, and fun.
- **Protocol 2:** Family Legacy Identity. Discovering together your family identity and uniqueness: past, present, and future, establishing family character, values, and purpose, creating a family coat of arms.
- **Protocol 3:** Family Legacy Ritual. The regular family meeting framework: food, fun, story, wisdom, and a supportive coach approach.
- **Protocol 4:** Family Legacy Venture. The annual family learning adventure trip or vacation with maximum legacy benefit.
- **Protocol 5:** Family Legacy MISSION *(momentary, intentional, specific, supportive, intervention,* as *one,* in response to a *need)*
- **Protocol 6:** Family Legacy Impartation. How to intentionally impart the most important things so your legacy endures. The wisdom, blessing, stuff, unfinished business, and the Family Legacy Generational Covenant.

Practicing these protocols will cut off the power of negative generational influences. Practicing them can preempt the toxic indoctrination of our godless public and university education systems. Living the protocols will empower our children to think critically and objectively beyond the smoke and mirrors of the deceptive mainstream media and keep them connected to the God of their faith, working with Him to succeed in a long and prosperous life.

I believe it's not too late to engage in these practices and send our children back into the gates of culture as leaders who are healthy cultural architects who can create a better future for all.

As I go, so goes my family ... so goes my business ... so goes my community ... so goes my government ... so goes my school ... so goes my church ... so goes the media ... so goes the arts ... so goes the world ...

Whoever wins the family wins the culture in the long game.

The most important focus for a healthy world is healthy families who are producing healthy children who become healthy leaders at the decision centers of culture and equip their children to do the same.

Here is wisdom. Listen and hear one of the wisest men to ever live weigh in on this:

> Wise people are builders. They build families, businesses, communities. And through intelligence and insight, their enterprises are established and endure. Because of their skilled leadership, the hearts of people are filled with the treasures of wisdom and the pleasures of spiritual wealth. (Proverbs 24:3–4 TPT)

> Those who find true wisdom obtain tools for understanding the proper way to live, for they will have a fountain of blessing pouring into their lives. (Proverbs 3:13 TPT)

> As wisdom increases, a great treasure is imparted … it is a more valuable commodity than gold and gemstones, for there is nothing you desire that could compare to her … Wisdom extends to you long life in one hand and wealth and promotion in the other. (Proverbs 3:14–16 TPT)

The wise words of a Father written to his Son thousands of years ago are the bedrock foundation of the *why* behind this book and the Family Legacy Protocols, training, coaching, and resources.

Take some time with these questions.

- What exactly are you building with the life you have been given?
- How are the building projects coming along?
- How about your family?
- How about your business?
- How about your community?

Prologue

A Tale of Two Families

This amazing story of two families spanned several generations. Both trace their lineage back to two men who lived in colonial America. One called himself Jukes, but his name isn't so important. He was constantly coming up with a new alias to stay a step ahead of the law. Jukes was, according to his neighbors, "a shiftless, lazy no-account." The little that he managed to scrape together was mostly gained by his marginal skills as a petty thief. However, Mr. Jukes was never clever enough to outwit the local sheriff. He was constantly in and out of jail. His wife was a woman of low morals who spent too much time in a drunken stupor.

At the turn of the twentieth century, a series of sociologists managed to uncover 1,200 descendants in the Jukes family tree. Some three hundred were professional beggars. More than one hundred were convicted criminals. Sixty were thieves and pickpockets. At least four hundred of them were drunkards or drug addicts. Another seven were convicted murderers, although several more were suspects. More than fifty of them spent time in mental institutions. Of the 1,200 descendants discovered by educators, only twenty had ever learned a trade. Half who did learned their trade in prison. Fewer than two hundred of Jukes's descendants finished high school, and none attended college. The Jukes's family record was one of pauperism, prison, imbecility, insanity, prostitution, panhandling, drunkenness, and drug abuse.

One sociologist also studied the family tree of a colonial contemporary of Jukes. He was a preacher, as was his father and grandfather. Scholars say that he was the greatest theologian and philosopher ever produced by America. His dynamic preaching sparked a great spiritual awakening that birthed the American Revolution. Maybe you remember this third president of Princeton, the Rev. Jonathan Edwards, and his famous sermon "Sinners in the Hands of an Angry God," but you may not have ever shaken his family tree to see what fell out.

A total of four hundred descendants have been traced to Jonathan Edwards and his wife, Sarah. Among them was a US vice president, three US senators, three governors, three mayors, thirteen college and university presidents, and thirty judges. Around sixty-five of Edwards's progeny were college professors. Another hundred were ministers, missionaries, or seminary professors. Eighty were public officeholders. In his family tree, there were one hundred lawyers and sixty medical doctors. Several descendants had written books, published newspapers, or been editors of journals. Until the beginning of the twentieth century, every major industry in America had as its founder or promoter an offspring of Jonathan and Sarah Edwards.

Most families are mixed bags of success and failures. Few are as dismal as Jukes's descendants or as stellar as Edwards's progeny, but the contrast cannot be missed. The lesson cannot be dismissed. Parents have a profound impact on their world for generations to come. The story of two families shouts a message!

Chapter 1
The Problem

It isn't that they cannot find the solution. It is that they cannot see the problem.

—G. K. Chesterton

So, what exactly is the problem?

This is what the current problem looks like in the United States:

- Families are broken, with a 50 percent divorce rate; two-parent homes are in decades of decline.
- Fatherlessness, abandonment, and single-parent homes abound.
- Communities are grappling with poverty and food insecurity. In 2017, an estimated one in eight Americans was food insecure, equating to 40 million Americans—including more than 12 million children. The US Department of Agriculture (USDA) defines food insecurity as a lack of consistent access to enough food for an active, healthy life.
- Record opioid overdose deaths in the US were more than 49,000 in 2017.
- More than 21.5 million Americans suffer from substance-abuse addictions.
- Approximately every fifteen minutes, one baby is born suffering from opioid withdrawal, according to the National Institute on Drug Abuse.
- San Francisco is littered weekly with tens of thousands of used and discarded drug syringes along with piles of human feces.

- Record increases in death by suicide reached 47,173 in 2018, according to the CDC, making it the tenth leading cause of death (and the second leading cause for individuals between fifteen and thirty-four).
- States have legalized the murder of the innocent unborn right up to full term.
- Approximately sixty million unborn children have been murdered to date.
- Deadly gangs like MS-13 have expanded and brought violence, crime, and devastation.
- The US leads the world with 2.3 million criminals incarcerated, according to Prison Policy Initiative.
- 1.2 million high school students drop out per year, which means one every twenty-six seconds.
- There has been an increase of all kinds of sexual perversion.
- According to the American Association for Marriage and Family Therapy, nearly 12 million Americans struggle with sexual addiction in the United States.
- 47 percent of internet users view pornography.
- One in four girls and one in six boys will be sexually abused before they turn eighteen years old.
- There has been an increase in homelessness in cities such as Los Angeles, with the resulting reemergence of once-conquered diseases like typhus.
- There have been increases in weapons, drug and human trafficking, assaults, and financial crimes.
- There is rampant and devastating child and human sex trafficking.
- There is a growing drain and strain on welfare and safety nets.
- Record numbers of people are leaving religion and the church.
- Public trust in the government remains at historic lows. Only 18 percent of Americans today say they can trust the government in Washington to do what is right "just about always" (3 percent) or "most of the time" (15 percent), according to Pew Research.
- There is a sharply and dangerously divided political environment.
- Our nation is roughly $22 trillion in debt.
- Our sons and daughters have been engaged in more than eighteen years of war.
- Our nation's crumbling infrastructure is demanding immediate investment in the trillions of dollars.

The Problem

- According to Common Sense Media, teens spend an average of nine hours a day online, compared to about six hours for those aged eight to twelve.
- There are 4,599,100 disconnected youths in America today, or about one in nine teens and young adults (11.7 percent). Disconnected youth are teenagers and young adults between the ages of sixteen and twenty-four who are neither working nor in school and are cut off from the people, institutions, and experiences that would otherwise help them develop the knowledge, skills, maturity, and sense of purpose required to live rewarding lives as adults, according to the Social Science Research Council.
- There is a loss of communication and emotional connection with our families, our neighbors, and our nation.
- We are isolated from others, and people are existing more and more in a world of their own online.
- Law enforcement officers are being attacked, killed, and criticized like never before.
- One in five adults in America experiences mental illness, according to NAMI.
- There are 133 million results when searching the internet for "leadership crisis in America."

The problems we face as a nation are deep and wide. Behind every bullet point are untold millions of wounded and hurting people. Behind every number are families in crisis, legacies in question, and a culture in desperate need of change.

The devastation listed above is the fruit of a tree that must have an ax laid to the root. The problems listed above are merely the fruits naturally being produced and harvested from a root source. The root problem is the origin of all the death and destruction above. The price tag is impossible to accurately calculate: trillions of dollars, lost lives, destroyed families, squandered wealth, failed businesses, unsafe communities, damaged relationships, and on and on and on.

> *If you are unable to understand the cause of a problem, it is impossible to solve it.*
>
> —Naoto Kan

> *A problem clearly stated is a
> problem half solved.*
>
> —Dorothea Brande

The real problem—the root cause—is *identity drift* coupled with an individual failure to self-govern well and the choice to not steward the family as designed.

We don't know who we are. There is a drift from our *true identities* both as individuals and families. We continue making choices to self-govern poorly because of our own deep brokenness, deception, and lack of awareness. We aren't even aware of the genetic legacy of wounds, weaknesses, and mind-sets that are currently influencing us locked into the genetic code of our DNA.

As a result, we fail to steward our families as they were designed, inflicting more pain on our generations. We send our wounded and degraded sons and daughters into leadership at the gates of culture where they govern out of their increased woundedness and deception. The culture falls, and the next generation repeats the cycle, thus starting the flywheel of pain, trauma, and dysfunction in the family. This leads to the social, moral, and cultural degradation of our homes, our businesses, our communities, and our culture.

The bottom line is we currently lack the will to seek wisdom, to get understanding, to humbly and faithfully accept it, and to take action that agrees with the Designer to shape culture from the inside out by building families, businesses, and communities.

Instead, we are enticed by any and every other venture, whether good or bad, that promises an easier, more comfortable, more prosperous, and more instant journey to what our hearts actually treasure more than family.

The root of the problem is the following:

- the choice to remain unaware and out of agreement with our true identities
- the choice made knowingly or unknowingly to self-govern poorly
- the choice to not steward the family as designed
- the choice to deprioritize the family and the protocols (practices) required to live a powerful family legacy

That these choices are perpetuated generation after generation is why we are in the predicament we are in as a nation. Several other choices add fuel to this fire, including the following:

- the choice to not live and do family "as designed"
- the choice to do something else—anything else—but work on me and my family
- the choice to do nothing
- the choice to know and not to act
- the choice to pursue riches, fame, or pleasure apart from the nurturing of the family generationally
- the choice to seek instant gratification over self-control, purity, and proper discipline
- the choice to not forgive, to remain stuck, and to not heal relationships within the family
- the choice to let days evaporate without intentional and fruitful investment into the family
- the choice to abdicate building our children's values, identities, intellects, and purposes to others
- the choice to not discover and practice a set of family protocols that provide identity, purpose, healing, vision, support, and success generationally
- the choice to believe that it is impossible, too hard, too emotional, or too uncomfortable to face
- the choice to blame anyone and anything else to avoid personal responsibility

The consequences of these choices and the devastating physical, emotional, relational, and spiritual fallout they create are enough to deeply and permanently wound a person to their core. The trauma is enough to alter the genes in our DNA and give birth to disease. The mortal blows deeply ingrain destructive patterns of thinking that demand attention and coping mechanisms, both healthy and unhealthy. They simply overwhelm our emotional and mental capacity to thrive. In some cases, they overwhelm our resources to even survive. If not healed appropriately and in a timely way, the consequences are horrific to individuals, families, communities, and nations over time.

If not addressed effectively, hurt people continue to hurt people. The pain and devastation continue to cascade from one generation to the next, inflicting more wounding, more pain, and more destruction, which leads to fewer and fewer leaders entering places of influence at the gates of culture who are:

- whole and stable
- moral and ethical
- selfless and self-controlled
- kind and good
- loving and pure
- wise and principled
- trusted and respected
- leading well from a place of health, character, and wisdom

In cities like Detroit, decades of entrenched corruption due to the lack of character and integrity among government leaders have bankrupted the city. I traveled the streets of Detroit in early 2013 and 2014. Several neighborhoods looked like war zones with burned-out homes, blown-out windows, and junglelike overgrown foliage. Garbage and trash litter the landscape, and homes and entire neighborhoods were being bulldozed and made into green spaces.

The cultural fall continues—from the inside out—to topple the power structures and systems of our families our businesses and our communities. As our broken generations take the baton for their leg of leadership in culture, their internal brokenness further degrades our culture as their children's wounds ensure the legacy of hell on earth will be passed on.

And we further produce families, businesses, communities, and cultures void of agreement with design that are:

- not engaged in the intentional, sacrificial loving investment of a moral and practical legacy into the lives of our children and grandchildren of identity, purpose, love, wisdom, success, significance, and influence that must be experienced and passed on generation after generation to shape culture from the inside out!
- disconnected and disengaged from the education of our children. When was the last school board meeting you attended, curriculum meeting you gave moral input to, or donation to a university with a biblical worldview or a commitment to the US Constitution?
- passive in civics and government local, state, federal. When was the last city council meeting you attended, office you ran for, election you volunteered in, or vote you showed up for?

- blindly trusting of the media. When the blind lead the blind, both fall into a pit.
- declining in church and religious involvement. Powerless and no-effect churches run programs but don't transform lives and don't equip people to shape themselves, their families, their communities, their nations, or their cultures at any level.
- consumers of morally bankrupt arts and entertainment instead of creators of moral and inspirational art and entertainment.
- lawless (calling right wrong and wrong right).
- selfish (doing what is right in their own eyes).
- lovers of money (at the very root of all kinds of evil). People are in business for a buck and not a greater purpose.
- unaware of their own family history and their roots of influence and contributions to the leadership of communities and nations of origin.
- unintentional in passing on the most important stuff in life: identity, history, purpose, character, wisdom, influence, and contribution.
- in desperate need of a personal transformation experience, a blueprint for success, and a vehicle to help them complete their journeys.

Does any of this sound familiar? Of course, it does! This is exactly what has been happening in America and many other nations around the world for the past sixty years.

This has resulted in lost destiny and legacy of families for generations. The redemptive purpose of any given family line is snuffed out: Innovations will never be introduced. Songs will never be sung. Books will never be written. Businesses will never be started. Problems will never be solved. Love will never be experienced. Peace will never be enjoyed. Grandchildren won't be nurtured. Life will not be fully lived. Legacies will not be powerfully left. And that cycle will continue.

Be honest. Has this cycle gotten you and your family legacy caught in its spin right now? Perhaps, just as I found myself and my family included in the statistics above, you do too.

Ask yourself some questions about yourself:

- Have you experienced the emotional wounds of broken families, crumbling communities, or corrupt culture?

- Have you experienced the loneliness, financial strain, sadness, betrayal, fear, stress, and pain of a divorce personally? Your parents? Your children?
- Have you experienced the grief, anger, and emptiness of a loved one lost before their time from a sickness, an accident, or suicide?
- Have you been pinned down by the weight of abuse and violence in the home as a result of alcoholism or addiction?
- Have you experienced the fear, humiliation, and shame of false public accusations?
- What were the wounds of your mother and father? Of their parents? And theirs?
- How were you and your children affected as a result of all of this?
- How have you intentionally forgiven, healed, and grown from those wounds and others?
- How have you taken your family through a process to do the same?
- Have you instructed your children how to follow these processes in their lives and to teach their children to do the same for their children?
- Have you rediscovered your family line's identity and purpose?
- Have you equipped and empowered your children with tools to succeed in living powerful legacies?

The gates of our culture are crumbling. Our families, businesses, churches, schools, arts and entertainment, media, and government are beginning a free fall toward destruction.

The status quo isn't enough. Doing nothing is worse. Believing, praying, and hoping without taking new, bold, innovative action is empty. We need a wake-up call! We need a blueprint with a practical set of protocols for personal and family transformation that is simple, effective, sustainable, and generational!

Until we wake up, I fear our families will not thrive, our legacies will not endure, and our culture will not be transformed. We will not be able to turn things around and begin living powerful family legacies that can shape and transform culture from the inside out for the better until we decide individually I've had enough, the time is now for me, and I take personal responsibility to be and do differently.

This is the passion of my life's work with Character Genetics and now with Cultural Architects. This is the focus of the Family Legacy message, book, training, coaching, and experiential workshops.

Why Civilizations Fall

Individuals fall first, which results in *identity drift*. When an individual makes a choice to disagree with the truth of who they are and how they are made, with what is good and just, lawful and right, selfless and loving as set forth by our Creator in His divine design, they launch an inertia of pain, depravity, and consequence that accelerates into a momentum of destructive cascading effects on families for generations.

As families fail, the wounds concealed in the hearts of children who become adults and take their inherited and childhood programing (mind-sets, values, wounds, and weaknesses) with them into their leadership at what I call the gates of culture. From those gates, decisions are made by leaders with wounded character, and the destructive momentum increases and erodes the foundations of businesses and churches, governments and systems of education, media and entertainment, the economies of nations, and beyond to the most devastating impact: the next generation … and the next … and the next.

When one human being missed the mark in the biblical account of Adam and Eve, the entire human race fell with them. Likewise, when the one God/man, the Christ, made things right, the entire human race was given access through the choice of faith to rise with Him. Individuals and their choices impact countless others in a similar way.

The choices of an individual have lasting—even eternal—effects on our children, our families, our communities, and our civilizations.

It's like the butterfly effect articulated by Edward Lorenz. In chaos theory, the butterfly effect is the sensitive dependence on initial conditions in which a small change in one state of a deterministic nonlinear system can result in a large difference in a later state. In other words, the butterfly effect is a phenomenon that has evolved from chaos theory. In metaphorical language, it means that a small change can give rise to a big tidal wave. He concluded that a simple movement like the flapping of a wing by a butterfly can give rise to a tornado somewhere else.

An inside-out disintegration of character in the individual gives rise to a depraved culture whose impending collapse is predictable, proven, and well documented historically, but I believe it is preventable if we solve the actual problem.

Culture is shaped from the inside out by the most powerful beings walking the face of this earth: human beings. Men and women make choices, and their decisions affect no one more deeply than their children and their generations.

Individuals shape the family, and the family has the primary opportunity and responsibility to shape sons and daughters who eventually shape businesses, communities, cultures, and nations. Children grow up to be adults and carry into the future the family name and all that comes with it: the belief systems, the values, the patterns, the wounding, the dysfunction, the honor, and the character, good and bad.

As our children reach adulthood and take their places in culture, their collective inside-out influence will shape the gates of culture. They will govern there until the children they raise take their places—and the cycle continues, always shaping culture from the inside out.

The family is the most fertile and perpetual seed for transforming and shaping culture and all that comes with it. The family precedes education, government, religion, business, arts and entertainment, and the media.

It is not a question of *if* your family will impact the world but of *how* you will choose to "do family." How you choose to do family will inevitably impact the world and shape culture from the inside out, for good or bad.

While no secret to some, to most in the church, this is a blind spot, a conveniently ignored reality, or a poorly executed response. Radical Islam understands this. The LGTBQ community understands this. The New Age movement understands this. The progressive far left understands this. Win the young and families, and in the long game, you win the ideological battlefront and gain the power to shape culture.

History teaches us many important truths, among which these two are preeminent in their power to build and to destroy individuals, families, cultures, kingdoms, and civilizations:

- The poor stewardship and failure of the family as designed by God from the inside out is more destructive than the biggest armies, the greatest invasions, and the deadliest plagues in bringing civilizations to their knees.
- The faithful and intentional stewardship and success of the family as designed from the inside out is more constructive than any form of

religion, government, education, or thriving economy in building civilizations and the cultures that drive them.

*Those who don't know history are
doomed to repeat it.*

- Edmund Burke

It is no mystery why civilizations fall. We know exactly why. We have studied and analyzed myriad empires, kingdoms, and civilizations and have conclusively determined and verified the causes. It is not hidden. It is not difficult to understand. We know.

Unfortunately, knowing history alone is not enough to keep us from repeating it. If only knowledge were enough—we would all be rich, famous, wealthy, and healthy and experts in all fields. The truth is there is more knowledge available now in the information age than has ever been in the history of humanity. In the palm of our hands, there is a mobile device not long ago viewed as a science-fictional aspiration that delivers a world of knowledge to our fingertips instantaneously. Nevertheless, wars continue, divorces remain, children suffer, poverty and world hunger persist, racism and class warfare abound, terrorism strikes fear in the masses, nuclear war remains a viable threat, and our planet groans under the poor stewardship of those who know better.

Knowledge alone is simply not enough to transform individuals, communities, businesses, churches, nations, and cultures. It's not. While knowledge, specifically *revelation knowledge*, is critically important and a necessary first step toward learning from the past and moving ahead in the process of transformation, by itself, it is impotent.

If we persist in knowledge through its distilling process on to understanding and eventually, to the experience of wisdom, we can learn to take personal responsibility, strategic action, and be transformed from the inside out! If we persist, we may be able to escape the damnation of history's failures in our lives, our cities, and the world.

Why do civilizations fall? It is a fact of history that all world-ruling empires have collapsed. But why did they collapse?

There is a cause for every effect. The great historian Edward Gibbons wrote about the fall of the Roman Empire, the greatest empire of all the world-ruling empires. In his historic masterpiece, *The Decline and Fall of the Roman Empire*, Gibbons identifies five major causes that contributed to the fall of the Roman Empire:

- the breakdown of the family
- increased taxation
- an insatiable craving for pleasure (hedonism)
- an unsustainable buildup of armaments
- the decay of religion

Gibbons was showing us how and why Rome fell. Don't the conditions surrounding Rome's fall sound very similar to the conditions present in the world today? Certainly, they are present in the United States.

History shows that the strength of any nation depends upon the strength of its families. Family is the rock-solid foundation on which a country's culture is erected.

The Modern Romans, a booklet produced in 1975 by Ambassador College, stated the following:

> Largely forgotten today is the fact that the home is the basic foundation of any society. It is the most influential element in national character. It lays the first groundwork for learning individual character, values, goals, morality, self-control, and loyalty.

We reproduce the culture that agrees with our character. Our character is forged in the family.

Furthermore, a brief look at eight world empires shows there are three factors that always precede a civilization's collapse.

Social Decay

Social decay is evidenced by a society's loss of economic discipline, which is often brought about by a rising bureaucracy that instills so much red tape that the civilization is mired in inefficient processes. The bureaucracy's resulting loss of power often gives way to a crisis of lawlessness.

Cultural Decay

Cultural decay results in a loss of respect for tradition, a weakening of the cultural foundations of the society, and an increase in materialism as the civilization's successes provide riches beyond what is needed. This rise in materialism shifts important factors, such as education and innovation, to the side.

Moral Decay

Moral decay occurs as excessive materialism produces a rise in immorality. As traditions are pushed aside, religion is often neglected and, in some cases, restricted by the civilization's leadership. Violence increases as the civilization's worth of human life is devalued. In nearly all cases, the decline in morality goes unrecognized as citizens see the degradation of moral values as an emancipation from the constraints of morality placed on them. Sexual immorality and divorce along with lust for unbridled pleasure doom individuals and their families.

The Roman Empire (800 BC—AD 400)

As Greece collapsed, the Roman Empire began its surge toward dominance. Since Rome's system of government became the framework for modern republics such as the United States, its history is quite relevant as a guideline for modern civilizations. Rome produced a profound impact on the development of language, art, religion, architecture, philosophy, law, language, and of course, government.

Rome's first two centuries were times of peace and prosperity. Romans became excellent engineers and political administrators and possessed an exceptional military structure. Religion was widespread, and citizens possessed high morals. Romans believed in honesty, discipline, frugality, and self-sacrifice.

When Julius Caesar took office in 50 BC, Rome had reached its peak. Immigrants moved into the empire, bringing new religions and cults, and leaders began spending the nation's riches on large palaces, monuments, and public entertainment venues. An emphasis on sports and entertainment exploded as work became second to pleasure. The government supplied grain to its citizens with as much as one-quarter of the citizens' food requirements being supplied by the government.

As riches grew, the people became greedy, self-indulgent, lazy, and complacent, and arrogance and luxury infected the Roman people. Morals and manners fell away, and entertainment became bawdier and more violent. Homosexuality and adultery became the norm, and soon afterward, it became acceptable for bestiality to be practiced in the open. Roman families began to dissolve as Romans sought instant gratification. Children became a needless burden, and contraception, abortion, and infanticide became common and, in some cases, encouraged in order to control population growth. Violence continued to grow, and gladiators were worshipped by the citizens.

To fund the extravagant spending and consumption, Rome raised taxes and began requisitioning property from the citizens to make ends meet. As oppressive taxes were imposed on the people to fund the massive public expenditures, resources began to dwindle. Rome began attacking other countries for their grain, metals, and timber, and farmers were forced to sell and move into the cities. The cities quickly became crowded.

As resources tightened, citizens lost respect for religion and began stripping churches and temples of their brick to use in building homes. Citizens began to revolt, and civil wars began to erupt in various regions of the empire. A weakened government had to fight off external invasions amid a climate of political chaos.

As the historian Edward Gibbon noted:

> Leaders of the empire gave into the vices of strangers, morals collapsed, laws became oppressive, and the abuse of power made the nation vulnerable to the barbarian hordes.

Subsequent rulers—Galba, Otho, Vitellius, Vespasian, Titus, and Domitian—allowed the decay of Rome's morals to continue while spending vast amounts of money on extravagances. The lavish gladiatorial games accelerated, and Rome's leaders took many lovers; their wives often joined them in large-scale orgies. Homosexuality ran rampant, and pedophilia soon followed as rulers kept young boys with them at all times for their sexual pleasure.

It goes on and on and gets worse and worse. The collapse of the family robbed any future hope for reform, and the great Roman Empire came crashing down.

What lies ahead for the United States of America and the great nations of the future?

In *The Closing of the American Mind*, Professor Allan Bloom said,

> This is the American moment in world history, the one for which we shall forever be judged. Just as in politics the responsibility for the fate of freedom in the world has devolved upon our regime, so the fate of the philosophy in the world has devolved upon our universities, and the two are related as they have never been before.

The example above demonstrates the path a civilization takes from birth to collapse. It is easy to align America's path with the example of Rome, the civilization we have the most in common with (and which in many cases, was used as the "blueprint" for American society). Morals continue to decline, slowly, sometimes unnoticed, as generation after generation become more desensitized to the dangers brewing. Given the past historical record, it is quite easy to predict the ultimate outcome.

Without clear, effective, intentional, disruptive, immediate, and enduring action taken now to transform individuals and families from the inside out, the United States and the world will follow these civilizations over the cliff to our demise.

Like the respected NBC political journalist and host of *Meet the Press* for many years, Tim Russert, said of the hotly contested 2000 presidential election that would determine the next president and leader of the free world: "It's Florida! Florida! Florida!"

History is shouting at us: "It's Family! Family! Family!"

In 1952, a California appeals court touched on the fulcrum of history, the family:

> The family is the basic unit of our society, the center of the personal affections that ennoble and enrich human life. It channels biological drives that might otherwise become socially destructive; it ensures the care and education of children in a stable environment; it establishes continuity initiative that distinguishes a free people.

> From antiquity, the family has served as the basic building block of free societies. Likewise, we find a strong emphasis on the high estate of parenthood and history. Wherever we turn in the ancient world, to Judaism, to Greece or to Rome, the family structure has been revered. And long before foreign invaders toppled any of those great societies,

they collapsed from within, due largely to the deterioration of their family structures.

In 1840 when French historian Alexis de Tocqueville had completed *Democracy in America,* he concluded that an individualistic society depends on a communitarian institution like the family for its continued existence. This is because the family unit serves as the seedbed for the virtues of the society.

The family, not the state or the school, therefore, has been primarily responsible for teaching lessons of independence and proper conduct, which are essential to a free, democratic society. If, as we now see, these family functions begin to break down, then everything else we cherish is in peril."

Individuals fall first, then families, then generations—and then everything else.

Addressing this problem is the purpose of this book along with the speaking, training, coaching and experiential workshops that provide the tools and protocols for families to succeed.

Our Families Are in Trouble

On one hand, this book is not directly addressing how be a good father/mother or how to have a healthy marriage. There is little question that being a good parent and having a healthy marriage are essential to a flourishing family and a lasting legacy. Healthy parents are at the core of the family.

On the other hand, the Family Legacy Protocols, especially the EQ (emotional intelligence) protocols, are an extremely effective way to grow as a human being and grow in any role that your being fills, including the role of a father or a mother or a husband or a wife. The exercises are experiences with tools that, by design, deliver personal growth and big ah-has that lead to real transformation and improved performance in all aspects of life, work, relationships, faith, and health.

With that said, in my research for this book, I discovered the following statistics of fatherlessness in the United States. I was moved with deep emotion by the wreckage, pain, and grief of great loss to so many dreams, the loss of so much potential, so much suffering outside of a father's loving care, and all of the costly consequences to society that are rooted here in the broken family.

I reviewed the lessons of history in the previous section and questioned if there was any true spark of hope that humans could learn from this and build something better for all. If fathers go down, families aren't far behind. When families go down, businesses, communities, cultures, and nations are about to go down next. We know this, but what is being done about it? What am I doing? What are you doing?

If something doesn't happen immediately to shape the course of how we do family, transform parents and marriages, and immediately disrupt the way things are heading for the family, we are in a lot of trouble—perhaps irreversible and terminal. We need some kind of miracle, and I believe God is sending those miracles.

Empathy tenderizes me, and hope gives me purpose.

Please take a moment to study the findings slowly and from the heart. Feel the pain. Imagine the tears, the sleepless nights, the fear, and the generational devastation.

Fatherlessness

- Sixty-three percent of youth suicides are from fatherless homes, five times the average (US Department of Health/Census).
- Ninety percent of all homeless and runaway children are from fatherless homes, thirty-two times the average.
- Eighty-five percent of all children who show behavior disorders come from fatherless homes, twenty times the average (Centers for Disease Control).
- Eighty percent of rapists with anger problems come from fatherless homes, fourteen times the average (*Justice & Behavior*, vol. 14, 403–426).
- Seventy-one percent of all high school dropouts come from fatherless homes, nine times the average (National Principals Association Report).

The Father Factor in Education

- Fatherless children are twice as likely to drop out of school.
- Children with fathers who are involved are 40 percent less likely to repeat a grade in school.

- Children with fathers who are involved are 70 percent less likely to drop out of school.
- Children with fathers who are involved are more likely to get As in school.
- Children with fathers who are involved are more likely to enjoy school and engage in extracurricular activities.
- Seventy-five percent of adolescents in chemical abuse centers are from fatherless homes, ten times the average.

The Father Factor in Drug and Alcohol Abuse

Researchers at Columbia University found that children living in two-parent households with poor relationships with their fathers are 68 percent more likely to smoke, drink, or use drugs compared to teens in two-parent households. Teens in single-mother households are at a 30 percent higher risk than those in two-parent households.

- Seventy percent of youths in state-operated institutions come from fatherless homes, nine times the average (US Department of Justice, September 1988).
- Eighty-five percent of all youths in prison come from fatherless homes, twenty times the average (Fulton County, Georgia, Texas Department of Correction).

Father Factor in Incarceration

Even after controlling for income, youths in father-absent households still had significantly higher odds of incarceration than those in mother-father families. Youths who never had a father in the household experienced the highest odds. A 2002 Department of Justice survey of 7,000 inmates revealed that 39 percent of jail inmates lived in mother-only households. Approximately 46 percent of jail inmates in 2002 had a previously incarcerated family member. One-fifth experienced a father in prison or jail.

Father Factor in Crime

A study of 109 juvenile offenders indicated that family structure significantly predicts delinquency. Adolescents, particularly boys, in single-parent families were at higher risk of status, property, and person delinquencies. Moreover, students attending schools with a high proportion of children of single parents are also at risk. A study of 13,986 women in prison showed that more than half grew up without their father, 42 percent grew up in a single-mother household, and 16 percent lived with neither parent

Father Factor in Child Abuse

Compared to living with both parents, living in a single-parent home doubles the risk that a child will suffer physical, emotional, or educational neglect. The overall rate of child abuse and neglect in single-parent households is 27.3 children per 1,000, whereas the rate of overall maltreatment in two-parent households is 15.5 per 1,000.

Daughters of single parents without a father involved are 53 percent more likely to marry as teenagers, 711 percent more likely to have children as teenagers, 164 percent more likely to have a premarital birth, and 92 percent more likely to get divorced themselves.

Pause. Breathe.

I am not singling out fathers and pinning the blame on anyone here. In fact, we all have some level of personal responsibility around the crumbling state of the family in America. From the long line of our familial ancestors and their life choices to our clergy, government leaders, educators, and business leaders, all of us have experienced the consequences of poor stewardship of the family over generations—and then there are our own life choices, past, present and future.

- How have I chosen to show up in life and family in the past?
- How am I choosing to show up in life and family today in the present?
- How will I choose to show up in life and family every day forward that I have the breath of life?

All of our combined generational journeys have brought us here. This is what we have today. If this is *our* country, then this is *our* challenge and opportunity. This is *our* problem and our solution to find.

We declare in our Pledge of Allegiance that we are "*one* nation under God." We are *one* American family—one nation of many citizens. This is a larger truth for us to embody as we address the challenges our families face today in America. We are one, and we are individuals; both are true.

This reality of oneness is present from our earliest origins. God Himself is one, and He is one family of three individuals (Father, Son, Holy Spirit). Remember Jesus's prayer in John 17 was that we would be one "just as" He and the Father are one. One human race with many individuals. One family with many members.

This is in part why the choices and actions of one person so directly impact the many. This is both an aspect of our problem and our solution. It just is. everyone matters to everyone.

In light of this, I want to make one final important observation from a biblical perspective in regard to husbands and wives in a marriage covenant, the core unit of the family. In God's design of "oneness," He has ordained a man and a woman to leave their father and mother and to be joined in marriage and to become "one flesh." He said, "The two shall become one."

There is so much pointing of fingers and blaming one another for our problems in the family. Husbands blame wives, wives blame husbands, children blame parents and then each other, on and on. Blame is a part of our fallen nature. Blame is a hiding from our personal responsibility. Blame is often a response to avoid the shame of personal failure. Blame only postpones solving the problems we have created together in marriage and family. Blame wounds. Blame separates. Blame inoculates us from taking the proper personal responsibility to be and act differently in ways that heal and solve our problems.

Ever since the first married couple sinned in the Garden of Eden, out of shame, they began blaming one another. Because God is just, He rendered consequences to the couple brought on themselves by their sin. They included man having to toil and work the land and bear the responsibility of being head of the woman. Woman would be subject to the man and have pain in childbearing. Adam and Eve's choice to disagree with being one with God resulted in a loss of oneness with each other. Oneness was broken in the Fall.

From that moment to the end of history, this oneness is broken. However, out of love, Father God refused to allow this to continue. He sent His Son Jesus to restore humanity's option to choose to be *one* again: oneness again with God in three persons through the cross of Christ, oneness again with husband and wife, and restoring His divine design to marriage and to the family.

What clear differences I now see as I compare how much of the world views and experiences marriage under the curse and consequence of sin. They aren't yet aware of the restoration of oneness that is available to them in Christ.

Under the curse and consequence in marriage:

- men ruling over women
- men primarily responsible for making decisions
- men primarily responsible for providing leadership
- men responsible for the provision of the family
- men receiving higher pay for equal work
- women being ruled by men
- women not primarily responsible for making decisions
- women not primarily responsible for providing leadership
- women not responsible for provision of the family
- women receiving lower pay for equal work

With Christ's finished work and oneness restored to the marriage and the family no longer under the curse and consequence:

- Women were taken out of man and are now restored back to being "as one" with man as in the Garden.
- The primary responsibility rests on both because both are one. The two are one.
- Who dominates? The one.
- Who gets the credit? The one.
- Who gets the blame? The one.
- Whose responsibility is it? The one.
- Who makes the decisions? The one.

Many religious doctrines work to pollute the purity of God's design for oneness through *proof-texting* and ignoring both cultural and historical factors in interpreting scripture regarding the roles of men and women in marriage. I am experiencing this revelation of oneness in marriage and family like never before in my half century of life. I am profoundly grateful for God's design of oneness in marriage.

I am not focusing on marriages directly as a part of the Family Legacy Protocols, but the protocols will absolutely empower you to grow toward oneness in your marriage and family.

So much more can be said and done here. I recommend two resources that I found particularly helpful in my journey.

Danny Silk and Loving on Purpose

Jimmy and Karen Evans and Marriage Today Ministries

My father taught me as a kid that every great challenge presented a great opportunity. He said that the way to look at things was to see and to explore both the challenge and the opportunity and to understand the problem and focus on the solution. He said, "God works all things for the good of those who love Him ... so, son, look for the good."

I thought, *we have a big mess on our hands for sure when it comes to families and everything that's shaped by them. Where is the good?*

I was filled with hope and conviction that God is changing things, and one of the ways He is doing that is by bringing the Family Legacy Protocols into being for just such a time as this. He chooses the broken things and the despised things to show He is strong. He chooses the simple things to confound the wise and the weak things to shame the strong so that He alone can get the glory, which He fully deserves! I believe the heart of God is to heal and restore fathers and mothers, families, and generations—and the businesses, communities, and cultures that families influence.

The protocols are deeply transforming for individuals and families. As the family changes, the legacy changes. The culture also changes. Now is the time to take action. Heaven and earth agree.

What if God wanted to heal you? Heal and restore your family, give you the tools to do family a whole new way, to enjoy doing it—well, at least most of it, ensure the legacy in your children, and show you they know how to impart it to their children so the legacy lives on and on. What if He wanted you to help other families find their way as you did? What a difference that would make.

An Impotent Ecclesia

Let's suppose for the moment that what I'm suggesting is a moment of clarity and that "identity drift coupled with an individual failure to self-govern well and the choice to not steward the family as designed" has led to the fall of the individual from the inside out. That has led to the collapse of the family, and the collapse of the family is causing the fall of our businesses, our communities, our nation, and our culture.

Then what? Well, I have a ton of questions. There are too many to cover entirely here, but let's briefly address a few of the most important ones.

What does this mean?

Well, truly, it depends on what each person makes it mean. Our worldview and life lenses will give individualized meanings to this. My original meaning as written was that if we as human beings truly understood and agreed with our identity, from a biblical perspective, we would follow the Designer's thoughts, ways, plans, and heart. We would understand and be empowered to self-govern well, according to His wisdom, and become builders instead of destroyers from the inside out. We would not succumb to the very decisions that destroy us on the inside. We would love one another. We would value and prioritize our families the same way He does and steward our families as He designed them.

How did we get here?

Important question. I see the answer as both simple and complex. It is a paradox. It is simple in that we have been deceived. It is complex in that the deception is robust, containing so much smoke and mirrors that it clouds our ability to pinpoint which lies are responsible for our condition. Also, the deceptions for each individual are variable and personalized.

It's simple because the chief deception from a biblical worldview in Genesis was to trick us into choosing to agree with the enemy and his lies instead of agreeing with our Creator, Designer, and Father. What lies? That God isn't good. That He is keeping the best from us. That His words don't matter. That humanity can somehow enjoy the same quality of life on our own as we could as *one* with Him.

The core deception was to get us to choose to disagree with God. Simply put, it was unbelief.

This is the taproot of the problem. If we choose to disagree with God, we lose everything. We lose the ability to know our true identities. We lose the ability to self-govern well. We lose the ability to steward our families as they were designed.

It's complex because once we enter unbelief by choosing to disagree with God, who is by very nature *Truth*, we are vulnerable to any and every other lie that can be told. And there are too many to list.

Here are some deadly lies that rot us from the inside out and eventually cause a great fall:

- I'm not enough: smart enough, rich enough, good enough.
- It's all about pleasure. If it feels good, do it.
- I can do it on my own apart from God.
- Seeking treasure and money is what life is about.
- It is fun to be lawless, immoral, hurtful, and intoxicated.
- I can do whatever I want to without consequence.
- I am the God of me, and I decide what's true.
- Truth is relative.
- I'm not that important to God.
- I'm not powerful enough to overcome temptation, fear, poverty, hate, or abuse.
- It's too late.
- I don't know how to change—or I can't learn to change.
- I don't know how and can't learn to govern myself well.
- I don't know how or can't learn how to steward my family as designed.
- I don't have what it takes to leave a powerful family legacy.
- My efforts to change from the inside out and be better won't matter.
- If I don't act, it's no big deal.
- Someone else will do it.
- I don't have the time.

Who is responsible for this?

Directly and succinctly, there is plenty of responsibility to go around:

1. The enemy of our souls.
2. The human race (except One).
3. Every individual has some personal responsibility for their own choices.
4. The Body of Christ here on the earth has responsibility as His ambassadors and governing body on the earth. Since the church has failed to stand in the fullness of her identity and not effectively make disciples, many remain in deception.

Who is responsible for helping people find their true identities?

1. The Holy Spirit.
2. Every individual has a personal responsibility and must choose what they agree with or believe about their own identity and whether they will help others or not.
3. Mothers and fathers.
4. The Body of Christ is responsible for helping people know the Truth since they are the sons and daughters of God and have access to true identity.

Who is responsible for helping people know how to self-govern well?

1. The Holy Spirit.
2. Every individual has a personal responsibility and must choose how they will self-govern and whether they will help others self-govern well or not.
3. Mothers and fathers choose for themselves and how they will engage with their children.
4. The Body of Christ is responsible for equipping people with how to self-govern well. Equipping people to live and walk in agreement with the Truth. More than telling, we must *show* and equip!

Who is responsible for helping show us how to steward our families as designed?

1. The Holy Spirit.
2. Every individual has a personal responsibility and must choose how they will steward their family.

3. Mothers and fathers choose of themselves and how they will engage with their children.
4. The Body of Christ is responsible for equipping people to steward their families as designed by our Creator.

Who is ultimately responsible for me and my family? I am. And you are ultimately responsible for you and your family.

What needs to be done to turn this around? I will address this more fully in chapter 2, but let's follow through on this thought for a few moments. To answer this question, let's look at those who are responsible for the change. Don't confuse responsibility with blame. They are different. Responsibility, as I am using it, means those who have the power, ability, and charge to determine an outcome.

The Holy Spirit

The Spirit is here with us always. He is the one who draws us to Jesus. He is our Teacher, our Comforter, and the Revealer of Truth. There is no one more qualified, more effective, or more committed to teaching us our true identities. No one is more able to empower us to have self-control and self-govern well. There is no one who knows more clearly than He does how the family is designed and how to properly steward them. There is no one more interested and engaged in bringing all of humanity's bloodlines to Jesus as a pure and spotless bride than Him. That is the ultimate family legacy. I believe we get to partner with Holy Spirit while we are on our watch to build a better, purer, more loving, more healed, more joyful, more peaceful, more prosperous, more free family line through our Family Legacy partnership. I believe that what we do in our family matters—forever and profoundly.

I believe the Holy Spirit is working on the earth. He is also waiting for each of us to partner with Him in this most important work. Becoming more like Jesus on the inside and governing on the earth with Him on the outside of us was God's original design for us and our families. That we would all be one family in Him and that we would govern the earth as it is in heaven (Genesis 1:28).

Clearly, any effective turnaround will require partnership with the Holy Spirit. He is ready—are we?

Every Individual

Every individual has personal responsibility. By our Creator's design, each person has individual agency and holds great power along with great responsibility. I choose for me, you choose for you, and creation pays attention and relates to us in compliance with our choices of what we agree and disagree with and what we believe.

Bottom Line

Each of us has the power, ability, and charge to live in agreement with God or not. That responsibility is profound and is able to transform ourselves, our families, our businesses, our communities, and our culture.

Mothers and Fathers

We are entrusted with children, and while they have their own responsibilities, as flesh of our flesh and bone of our bone, parents have been given the responsibility to properly steward them. We are to protect and nurture them in the truth and teach and equip them to know their identities, to know and live in wisdom, and to see that we have done our part in equipping them to be successful in life as they take their shift of leadership at the gates of culture. Finally, we must ensure that they will teach their children the same things for generations to come.

The Body of Christ on Earth

From a biblical worldview, God's solution for this was to live inside of human beings as one. He designed us in the beginning and wants to have us be His sons and daughters on the earth. He wants us to be His governing body in culture. He wants us to be His ambassadors here. He wants the church to be His hands and feet here on earth. He had to send His only Son to die on a cross and overcome death, the grave, and the deception that messed everything up in an ancient garden. It cost Him deeply. He is good. He is holding nothing back from us. His words matter and will never lose power.

Bottom Line

Jesus said the he was building his church (ecclesia). That word means his governing officials. It's taken from the Roman culture of the day. Leaders at the gates of culture were elected to govern in the sphere they were given. They would go in to hear the heart of the king or ruler and then go back to their place in culture and make it the same there as what was in the king's heart. They governed. They directed the flow of resources and laws. They directed the processes of farming and military conquests. They determined how the roads would be built, how the crops would be grown and sold there, how they would educate the children, and what forms of art and entertainment would be permissible. They would make decisions and exert influence so that the culture looked like and agreed with the heart of the king.

I am convinced that this is exactly what Jesus is building on the earth when He said, "I will build my church, and the gates of hell won't prevail against them." If we are not building what Jesus is building, we are laboring in vain. Honestly, the church as a whole is not *building* what Jesus is building. If we were, the nations of the world would be very different than they are now. Our culture would be dramatically different than it is now. Our families would be so different than they are now.

I'm not beating up the church. I am concerned for her. I believe we all have a part in presenting ourselves as His bride and to govern well during our watch while teaching our generations to do the same. Fundamentally, we are not equipping effectively; otherwise, things would be different. How we equip and how we do church both matter! Telling people what to think or believe or know is not getting the job done! We must shift the fundamental way we teach, equip, and empower. We must live this stuff in action. We must lead by example—not in how big our church is or how relevant it is.

Instead, we must lead in governing on earth like it is in the King's heart. We must make disciples who know and live from their identities as children of God and as part of a family of governing officials ruling their sphere on earth as it is in heaven. I'm not talking about a political, military, or social movement. I'm talking about showing up in life, releasing the flow of heaven, and stopping the flow of hell as priests who self-govern well by living and walking in the Spirit. As parents who steward the family like the King wants, equipping our children to do the same, and sending them into the gates of culture to govern there.

Part of the reason our families, businesses, communities, and culture are in crisis is because as leaders in the church, based on results, we have failed.

And if you can accept that, then we can repent. We can change our thinking and agree with God. We can start new building projects with Jesus and join Him in what He is building: a family of governing officials who are ruling the earth like heaven. We can change the way we equip people. We can transform the way we make disciples. We can turn our agreements into energetic action that is focused on equipping families and leaders who influence from the gates of culture for the glory of our King!

I am passionate about changing the way that the church is defined, the way the church equips believers (cultural architects), and the way the church shapes culture from the inside out for real. This is undeniably a partnership with Holy Spirit. This cannot be done with human strength alone. We must join Him in what He is doing by bringing what we have to what He has to transform ourselves, our families, and our culture.

Deception and Lack of Awareness

There is another subtle aspect of the problem that remains hidden in plain sight outside of the awareness of leaders working to address the collapse of culture from the inside out. It's what my wife refers to as a "BFO" or a blinding flash of the obvious.

Simply stated, what we are currently choosing to do and not do isn't working. We are unaware of it, and we haven't accepted it.

I have no doubt there are some good people with pure intentions giving it all they have with a measure of effectiveness. There is a remnant of forerunners out there who resonate with this message and are taking action as well. However, from a biblical worldview and an honest look at the state of our culture, for the most part:

- How most people come to understand their true identity and design isn't working.
- How people are choosing to self-govern isn't working.
- How parents are choosing to steward their families isn't working.
- How spiritual leaders are choosing to do church isn't working.
- How we are choosing to equip people for living life isn't working.

- How we are choosing to engage government and politics isn't working.
- How we are choosing to educate our children isn't working.
- How we are choosing to tolerate the direction of the arts and entertainment industries isn't working.
- How we are choosing to tolerate the current state of the media isn't working.
- How we are choosing to engage in business isn't working.
- How we are choosing to govern isn't working.

Whether we know it or not, we are designed to govern. Human beings were made to direct the flow of virtually anything you can think of in one way or another. Through our choices of agreement and disagreement, we allow and disallow how things go from the inside out. Whether in us, in our families, in our finances, in our emotions, and our relationships, or outside of us, in the family, the government, education, business, the arts, media, and the church, our choices have power.

This is by design. We govern laws, resources, ideas, science, technology, and medicine by our *choices*. We govern our appetites, our flesh, our emotions, our values, our priorities, and our families by our *choices*.

If this is true, I have some questions.

Q: Why would anyone knowingly make choices that lead to the destruction of their lives, their families, and ultimately their culture?

A: Deception and unawareness. People are deceived, but they don't know it. We are deceived into thinking our choices will yield certain results, only to find out they don't—or that they have other consequences that are costly and damaging.

Q: What choices are we making that have produced what we have? Too many to list. Here are a few.

A: The choice to disagree with God's design and do things my way.

A: The choice to keep doing what we are doing expecting a different result (the status quo).

A: The choice to become an expert critic and cynic (a problem expert void of a solution).

A: The choice to blame anyone else but me and avoid personal responsibility and personal transformation.

A: The choice to make a thousand excuses instead of changes: "I don't know what to do," "I'm overwhelmed," "It's too complicated," "I don't have time," "It's too late," "I can't change anything," or "It's too uncomfortable."

A: The choice to wait for someone else to fix it.

A: The choice to wait for God to fix it.

A: The choice to treat symptoms instead of the cause (abortion, poverty, divorce, mental illness, etc.).

A: The choice to be distracted by bigger buildings, better media, better music, cooler spaces, and coffee shops instead of building people, families, businesses, communities, and culture.

A: The choice to pray more without listening and taking action to do our part.

A: The choice to be proud and do things differently than God.

A: The choice to not strategically invest in my family by teaching them who they are, why they are here, and how to succeed in life

A: The choice to do nothing.

Q: What choices can we make to change what we have?

A: Make the opposite choices listed above, take action, and teach your children and grandchildren to do the same. Make sure they are also equipped and committed to do the same and require the same for the generations to come.

There is so much at stake. We must fix this before it's too late—but how?

Chapter 2
The Solution

An inside-out transformation that reveals true identity while restoring proper self-governing and the stewardship of the family as designed.

If the fall of an individual starts the process that leads to the fall of culture and civilizations, then the transformation and rise of the individual starts the process for the restoration of the same.

Real cultural transformation happens from the inside out. Starting with the individual and then on to every aspect the individual influences: the family, the business, the community, the schools, the media, the government, the church, and the culture.

Inside-out transformation is the solution for our disintegrating culture.

Important Note

Perhaps the big idea of shaping culture is beyond your current vision—or you are one of the millions of people who just want their own family to heal, grow, and thrive to ensure a family legacy of significance for generations to come.

The solutions set forth in this book and the Family Legacy Model with the six protocols will absolutely equip you to transform your family. This is a practical guide to doing family that will cause your family to thrive today. The Family Legacy practices will ensure an enduring legacy for generations to come. As a result, I believe that businesses, communities, cultures, and nations will be transformed from the inside out as well.

The Gates of Culture and the Case for Shaping Culture from the Inside Out

My goal here is not to cover ground that's already been covered by the great voices God has raised up to proclaim the "seven mountains" message. Lance Wallnau, Os Hillman, Johnny Enlow, Loren Cunningham, and Bill Bright have already spoken eloquently on the Seven Mountain mandate and advancing the kingdom of God by impacting culture. They, along with others, are modern-day forerunners and catalysts for finishing the great commission on earth. They are bringing an awareness to the body of Christ globally that I believe will result in the next great church reformation, missions movement, and great harvest. I applaud their efforts and honor their labor of love. I am grateful for their sacrifice and pray for their continued effectiveness.

Bottom Line

Leaders positioned at the gates of culture govern or direct the flow of decisions, laws, and resources. Leaders at the gates of family, government, education, arts and entertainment, business, media, and religion choose what is allowed and disallowed in the sphere of their authority. Their decisions are based on the character of the leader at the gate. Their core thinking and values result in the choices made and determine and shape the culture (the way things are).

An unhealthy culture is the result of unhealthy character in leaders at all of the gates of culture. Unhealthy leaders are the result of generations of unhealthy families and individuals who make decisions at the cultural gates. Unhealthy individuals are incapable of transforming culture for the better before being transformed themselves.

"Of course, that's the problem," you say. You're not the first person to recognize that.

Q: But how specifically?

A: Inside-out transformation.

Here is the challenge we all face together: How do we live it? How do we actually and practically transform as an individual from the inside out? How do we do family in an intentional way that changes things *fast* in a way that *lasts?* How do we move from revelation to results? From knowing and talking to being and doing? How do we equip families in these practices for generations to come? How do we know this truth experientially? Knowing about it won't transform anything. Taking sustained strategic action on what we know will transform everything. How do we live it and equip others to live it?

This is the challenge of the hour and the reason for Cultural Architects, effectively equipping leaders of leaders at the gates of culture. This is the reason for this important book's focus on equipping leaders and families to understand and demonstrate these tools for generations to come.

Whether you are a killer sheep, a change agent, a YWAMer, royalty, or what I call a cultural architect, we are all on the same team. Whether you are in a mega church, a micro church, no church, or a part of a cultural architect cohort, we are all in the same family. Even if you aren't a believer and want your family legacy to matter. We all share the problem and the responsibility for forging a solution. We are in this together … unless we're not.

It's one thing to hear a message or to know a truth and quite another to incarnate that message personally and still another thing to strategically equip others to walk the talk as well. Let's be honest. Most Christians would tell you that we know about healing and divine health, abundance, joy, peace, loving our enemies, and living our dreams, while at the same time we are sick and unhealthy, broke, unhappy, stressed out, at odds with people, and living a nightmare instead of our dreams. That's what's real for so many believers today who have a knowledge and hope of a rich inheritance but an existence of struggle and settling for less or waiting for some day when …

I had a mentor who said, "Randy, the best way to judge anything is by results. They are often harsh but always fair. Faith without works is dead … We live what we truly believe every day. All the rest is just religious talk and jargon."

We can say that we are called and empowered to be transformation agents in culture, and we would be correct. But if we are not being personally transformed with measurable results in ourselves and in our assignments in culture, then we are deceived and just talk. James said it like this: "Don't just listen to the Word; do what it says."

My calling is to move people from theory to practice, from words to action, and from revelation to results. My goal is to equip those who have embraced the Gospel of the kingdom and have been stirred by the seven mountains mandate with a mechanism for personal and cultural transformation. And in this book, to specifically do this through empowering families to do it from the inside out!

Much has been said and written about the why and the what when it comes to transforming ourselves and our culture. I am certain that there will be even more added to this important subject concerning God's original intent for humanity and what it looks like in the here and now.

It is the *how* that I sense God has uniquely prepared me to add to this conversation at this hour. The *how* to do this and get results. The how to take the "why this is God's plan" and "what this plan could look like" into the specific actions that will heal and transform individuals and families and actually shape culture.

But how? How exactly does inside-out transformation work from the individual to the culture?

It is like an apple seed. Entire orchards are contained in a single seed over time. Inside the heart of a person lie the seeds of culture over time as well. "For as he thinks in his heart, so is he" (Proverbs 23:7 NKJV). My choice of what to believe in my heart, or the inside, will determine how I show up and what I create on the outside of me. My inside thinking, values, and choices determine my outside choices, actions, and harvest.

I say it this way: "Our character is the true inventor of our results," or, "Who I am on the inside produces what I have on the outside." The inverse is equally true. What I do outside is produced by who I am inside. Our culture is the outside result of our collective inside identity, values, beliefs, and choices. Our culture outside is disintegrating as a result of the deterioration of our character inside. The same is true for our communities, our churches, our businesses, and our families. The state of our community's outside is the result of the community's inside identity values, beliefs, and choices. The state of our churches, our businesses, and our families is the outside reality of our inside character.

To change the outside (culture), we must change the inside (character):

- one person at a time
- one family at a time
- one generation at a time
- one leader at a time

Once the insides of leaders are transformed, they can begin to govern at the gates of culture with the transformation they embody changing the outside in culture. It is up to us to transform our character if we are to meaningfully shape our culture. The inside transformation must saturate our most enduring and intimate institutions, starting with and expanding from the family.

The intentional process for transformation I use in my work that is biblical, effective, proven, and lasting is what I call the "inducer transformation model." I go into more depth later in the chapter. However, the primary components are as follows:

1. Revelation
2. Personal responsibility
3. Ongoing strategic action

First, we need a revelation. A great big ah-ha! We need to see and know something like we have never seen or known something before. We need to *know* by revelation what the root problems are and what the solutions are. We need a revelation of what we are doing or not doing that is out of alignment with a better way. We need a revelation of how to do family in a way that will shape culture with wisdom. True revelation is like a backbone of conviction that fortifies our will to choose wisely and act confidently in a new course of action.

Revelation is the key to accelerated transformation, to changing things fast. "Where there is no revelation, people cast off restraint;" Proverbs 28:19a (NIV) We will not find the strength of will to govern ourselves and steward our families well until we first see and know certain things the way that God sees and knows them.

Until we have a revelation of our true identity, we will not know who we are and what we are capable of. We must know with confidence who we are, why we are here, and how we are designed to operate. Without a revelation of who God is and His ways of life and prosperity, we will not be aware of how to heal, how to forgive, how to succeed, how to self-govern well, or how to properly steward our families.

Second, we need to each take personal responsibility with these revelations of what both the problem and what the solution is. We must each make new choices in self-governing and in stewarding our families according to that wisdom. Personal action, accountability, and results are the harvest of revelation and personal responsibility.

Third, we need the resolve to persevere in ongoing strategic action and equipping others with these tools for understanding, or what I call Family Legacy Protocols. We must learn them, model them in our families, equip our children to use them, and show how they can equip their children to do the same, generation after generation.

While isolated families following the protocols will transform themselves and their entire family lines, if we are to transform our cultures from the inside out, it will take communities of families, churches of families, and nations of families working the protocols together to truly and measurable transform civilization.

The Family Legacy Model is intentionally designed to equip people to know their true identity, empowering them to properly self-govern, which enables them to generationally steward the family as designed while teaching the next generation to do the same. As a result, the culture will be transformed from the inside out.

The Family Legacy Model

Six protocols for leading your family, living your legacy, and shaping culture in the process:

Family Legacy EQ	EQ = emotional intelligence. Creating an environment of safety, trust, support, forgiveness, love, purpose, and fun.
Family Legacy Identity	Discovering together your family identity and uniqueness: past, present, and future; creating a family coat of arms, family vision values, and purpose, family song, and family painting.
Family Legacy Ritual	The regular family meeting framework: food, fun, story, wisdom, and a supportive coach approach.
Family Legacy Venture	The annual family learning and legacy adventure trip or vacation.
Family Legacy MISSION	The *momentary, intentional, specific, supportive, intervention,* as *one,* in response to a *need.*
Family Legacy Impartation	How to intentionally impart the most important things so your legacy endures. The wisdom, blessing, stuff, unfinished business, and the Family Legacy Generational Covenant.

Inside-Out Transformation

We have what we are willing to tolerate. I have what I am willing to tolerate. We have the life, the family, the business, the community, the culture, and, in fact, the nation that we are willing to tolerate, collectively and individually.

Notice what you are tolerating in your ...

- health
- job

- marriage
- family
- finances
- business
- community
- nation
- faith

Who is responsible for the way things are? Who is responsible for culture? Who is responsible for changing the way things are? Who is responsible for changing culture?

We are! I am! You are!

Let that sink in ...

I have the income, the health, the marriage, the fun, the significance. And certainly, I have the family that I am willing to tolerate, and so do you. We also have the legacy we are willing to tolerate.

- Q: When is enough enough for me?
- A: When I decide it's enough.
- Q: When is enough enough for us?
- A: When we decide it's enough. And we choose to do whatever it takes to change things now!
- Q: Who decides when the time of denial, inaction, analyzing, coping, complaining, and blaming has reached the end of the road inside of us?
- Q: Who determines how things will and will not be for themselves? The family? The business? The community?
- A: I do.
- A: I decide for me when enough is enough and when to take new action to influence change for me, my family, my business, and my community.

You must decide for you.

Those who make the decisions and take action over time will determine the culture.

The Solution

But what decisions? What actions? Not all of them are created equal. Complaining to yourself will not be as effective as holding up a sign when it comes to changing culture. Holding a sign may not yield the same result as choosing where you spend your money or educating a mind, which in turn may not be as effective as brainwashing a generation on social media or overtaking the curriculum in public primary, secondary, and higher education. Which in turn isn't as effective as controlling the media and entertainment content that millions digest over a lifetime or getting elected to serve in government and so forth.

Of all the decisions and actions in play when it comes to shaping culture, what choices are the most important when it comes to transforming individuals, families, businesses, communities, and culture for good?

- A: My choice to live from true identity.
- A: My choice to self-govern well.
- A: My choice to steward my family as designed.
- A: My choice to address and heal generational blind spots in my genetic legacy.
- A: My choice to live and leave a powerful family legacy.
- A: My choice to send healthy generations of leaders into the decision-making centers or gates of culture.
- A: Our collective choice to do the same, as one, for generations to come.

If we are finished with tolerating the way things are and want things to be different, what do we do? What do I do actually, specifically, and practically?

I decided to drill deep into the causes behind what I can no longer tolerate. I studied the roots of the fruit that I refuse to eat any longer, the fruit that will certainly destroy us all from the inside out. What I found was not that the government or education or Hollywood or big corporations or climate change was ruining my life and destroying the way things are, destroying me, my family, and culture.

What I found was that human beings with personal, sphere, positional, and cultural authority wielding decision-making power in these vital gates of culture were shaping reality for the masses. Based upon their own individual set of values, rooted in their ways of thinking, rooted in their genetic legacy, rooted in their ongoing traumatic life experiences that further shape their own DNA. Only then to be passed on through the genetic code to children who receive the preloaded software unknowingly. The cycle then repeats itself.

What I found is rooted deep inside of me, in my core, my DNA. All kinds of toxic and limiting beliefs that hold me hostage as a prisoner to what is possible for me, for my family, for my business, and my community.

Inside of my genetic code and presently impacting my life is the compiled genetic legacy filled with the mind-sets, fears, solutions, values, victories, defeats, joys, and pains of my ancestral family donors, along with my own life contributions to the DNA chain that appear most visibly.

What does this mean?

For human beings to transform the way things are (culture) in any context, that transformation is an inside-out process. Individual transformation at a genetic level is the genesis of profound and lasting change. This transformation happens when all of the parts of me transform. When my spirit, soul, and body all participate. When my spirit gives wise revelation to my mind, my mind triggers my emotions, my will chooses to agree, and my body takes action.

A change in my awareness, a revelation, is the beginning. Then a thought, then a feeling, then a choice, then ongoing action leading to a personal transformation, ultimately resulting in a change in culture. When this happens in an emotionally charged environment, the genes in our DNA light up with readiness to be expressed and locked in agreement with this new way of thinking, and it is captured in the genetic code.

Example:

Fear of failure is suppressed in the gene, while embracing failure as a brilliant teacher is expressed.

Fear of what people think and insecurity are turned off in the gene, while security and confidence are expressed.

That's impossible and *it will never change* is suppressed, and hope with expectation in possibility is expressed.

The inside-out process goes like this: know, be, and do. We experience, then become, then activate. We have a revelation, then take responsibility, then take action.

Somehow people tend to think that if they have a lot of knowledge, it somehow is enough to ensure that they will put the knowledge consistently into practice and turn knowledge into demonstrated wisdom, bringing the results promised from the knowledge. It is not.

Applying the knowledge of the truth over and over and being transformed by it so that our very nature, our being, knows by experience is such a critical part of real and lasting transformation that leads to sustained action or doing what will result in lasting, eternal fruit and results.

Example:

Know that communication is key for healthy and fruitful families.

Knowing by experience, I engage in exercises, practices, and protocols or learning modules with my family so that we actually learn, know by experience, authentically value and practice healthy communication in a sustained way while teaching our children how to teach their children and their children's children ...

I believe that it is one person's transformation at a time from the inside out that is the true solution to the crisis we find ourselves in. It's a character crisis at the core. A crisis in the core thinking and values that predetermine one's behavior and results.

Transformed individuals transform families.

Transformed families transform leaders.

Transformed leaders transform businesses, communities, and culture.

Transformed leaders are the decision makers in the key control centers or gates of culture—family, government, education, business, media, arts and entertainment, and the church. Equipping one another to think and, as important, to act consistently in agreement with biblical truth, together, will transform our nation and halt our decay.

If I don't lead myself powerfully, then how will I lead and empower my children to do so?

If my children aren't equipped to think critically, act morally, lead courageously, and live successfully, then how will my grandchildren do so?

If my grandchildren don't transform culture from the inside out, what will come of this nation and the nations of the world?

How will the divine spark and purposes of the Almighty for the Bixby bloodline be accomplished for the good of humanity and the glory of the Father if I don't step up and do my part while I serve my time on my watch?

You say, "I'm with you, Randy. Theoretically, that sounds like it could work, and God knows we need to do something, but that's the real question for me: what do we do?" Specifically, not only ideologically and theoretically, but practically, what exact action steps do I take that will accomplish this inside-out transformation of me and my family?

> Answer: Practice the Family Legacy Model.
> Q: And when we do practice these protocols for family legacy, what comes next?
> A: The rebuilding of the foundations of our broken family.
> A: The rebuilding of our successful businesses.
> A: The rebuilding of our schools, our churches, our entertainment, and our government.
> A: The transformation of our cities, our nation, and our culture.
> A: The enduring and perpetual transformation from the inside out for generations to come, establishing the divine purposes of my family line—the family legacy.
> Q: How can I be transformed and lead my family in experiencing transformation that will measurably make an impact on my church, business, community, and nation?
> A: By the renewing of your mind. You must think differently than you have been, which then leads to different values, priorities, actions, and outcomes. Then you train and support your family in following the same process you did, which leads to them showing up differently at school, at work, at church, in the neighborhood, at university, and at the gates of culture.

That is what this book delivers. That is a big part of my work over the past twenty-five years, and I am excited to share it with you. This journey is to be experienced! It's not just information or motivation. It is the how-to of living and leaving a powerful legacy that impacts the lives of others in profound and eternal ways.

The protocols are for work on ourselves, then how we treat each other, and then how we treat others and show up at the gates of culture.

Inside, then outside. How to be, then how to do.

The EQ protocols address self-governing and the mastery of what's going on inside of each participant and how that impacts the way family members treat one another and creates an attractive environment for the family to thrive.

The Identity Protocols powerfully address both the individual and the family identity as a whole—past, present, and future. Families will discover their purpose, core values, and characteristics and create a family coat of arms, family song, and family painting.

The remaining protocols—Ritual, Ventures, MISSION, and Impartation Protocols—address both inside and outside focuses.

While the protocols are distinct, they are connected. What happens on the inside of us will drive what happens on the outside of us. It's the thinking from inside the heart that determines the intentional, meaningful action or behavior on the outside of the individual.

When we are on track inside, then we are on track outside. We do the important things intentionally and do them with heart. We experience life from a place of peace, joy, love, kindness, self-control, focus, energy, and priority. We impact others from this place of health. We show up powerfully at home, at work, at church, and in life. And the culture follows suit.

> For as he thinks in his heart, so is he. (Proverbs 27:3 NKJV)

> So above all, guard the affections of your heart, for they affect all that you are. Pay attention to the welfare of your innermost being, for from there flows the wellspring of life. (Proverbs 4:23 TPT)

Stewarding the Family as Designed

An extremely important aspect of the overall solution for individuals, families, and ultimately culture is this insight of design—the stewardship of the family as designed.

Design, as I've used it, is a verb.

Design [dih-zahyn]

verb:

To determine or decide the function of a thing.

To originate, to think up, to create, to conceive.

To produce, to purpose intentionally and deliberately.

There is a Designer behind the design of the family. Who determined or decided the function of the family? Who originated, thought up, created, and conceived of the family? Who produced and gave purpose intentionally and deliberately to the family? Certainly not random cosmic explosions, plus some goo, plus time, plus missing links.

Our heavenly Father did.

The Designer of the family has the highest authority to determine the definition, purpose, function, and framework of the family. After all, it's His design. He conceived of the family. He knows the who, what, when, where, why, and how of the family better than anyone else.

In fact, behind the design of the family is the design of a mother. Behind that is the design of a father. Behind that is the design of a son. Behind that is the design of creation. Behind that is the Designer, who is by very nature a family of three persons, Father, Son, and Holy Spirit.

How does our Designer do family?

He loves.	He cries.
He enlarges the family.	He sacrifices.
He adopts.	He serves.
He teaches.	He provides.
He develops.	He leads.
He disciplines.	He listens.
He saves.	He trusts.
He heals.	He prefers others.
He forgives.	He is one with.
He directs.	He is the head of.
He restores.	He wants relationships.
He nurtures.	He is forever.
He laughs.	He governs.

He models.　　　　　　　　He is just.
He gives us choice.　　　　He is kind.
He gives and shares.　　　He is patient.
He warns.

Wow! I could go on and on.

All in the context of family. He designed family to flow out of Him, and family, by design, is just like Him. This is how we steward the family as designed. We accept the Designer's design of family and do family the way He does, the way He is.

Who wouldn't want to be in a family that's like His family? No one, right? Yet billions knowingly and unknowingly choose not to.

Why?

Deception primarily, along with the reality that very few people have ever experienced family this way. Most of us have experienced wounding, pain, and dysfunction of all kinds when it comes to family. It's hard to believe that family could be that amazing based on our generational/genetic legacy and our own life experience. While that thinking is understandable, it's still built on the deception that God isn't who He says He is. Once we're deceived and choose not to trust His authority, it's easy for us to reject His design for everything, including the family.

But what would it be like if we accepted and embraced His design for family?

For starters, our family would be like He is in all the ways listed above and beyond. Go back to that list. Forgiving, loving, supportive, fun, and safe—to name a few. This is how we would treat one another. This is what the environment of our homes would be like. This is how we would show up for our family. Now that is a healthy family.

In addition, we may want to examine and incorporate the ways God instructed and modeled for us to do family, starting with His chosen family, the family of Abraham and the people of Israel. God set up a framework for doing family, as He did for business, government, church, marriage, education, nutrition, and culture.

Let's take a brief look at some important practices or protocols God put in place as a part of His design for family in His family. Don't underestimate the value of these simple practices and traditions. They have been enough to keep the Jewish culture alive through millennia of persecution, scattering, war, and even the Holocaust.

First, His design made it clear how He wants families to treat one another—the same way He treats us, as listed above. He's given the scriptures, the commandments, the parables, the wisdom, and His own example of how we are to show up in family, including forgiving and healing one another.

Second, His design prioritized the discovery, declaration, and passing on of individual and family identity. He made sure there were intentional practices and traditions to be followed, such as the naming of children and family name significance. He ingrained identity history in the minds of generations by oral tradition and storytelling. He codified His design for the family in the scripture by the meticulous work of scribes. He prioritized the attention given to the genealogy of family lines.

Third, His design included the Sabbath. The Sabbath is for the whole family to intentionally and regularly gather together. He set forward some rituals that make that time together valuable, including the following:

- rest
- fun and laughter
- blessing
- learning wisdom
- story
- reading of scripture
- eating
- worship
- support

Fourth, His design included family trips, cultural events, and learning adventures. Another part of His framework of the family included many festivals, holidays, celebrations, and holy days. The mix of fun, family, and purpose provided for a meaningful emotional implant of family and culture, impacting the genetic code for generations to come.

Fifth, His design included protocols of how the family comes together during times of crisis or in circumstances that were momentary and out of the ordinary. The book of Ruth provides a moving example of how the family is responsible for pulling together in a time of loss, grief, lack, and uncertainty.

And finally, sixth, His design included a thoughtful and intentional impartation of the most important things before the end of life. This included the passing on of the wisdom, the blessing, and the stuff together, making up the inheritance, a final speaking of the truth in love from the maximum life accumulation of wisdom perspective. In addition, this was the time to deal with any unfinished business and to charge the family with the responsibility to continue to pass on the family legacy and the stewardship of the divine purpose for the bloodline.

By His intentional design, the carrying out of these various practices, rituals, and protocols ensured the equipping of the generations to continue these core activities. In so doing, an enduring family legacy was lived and left for generations to come. The practice of these six core protocols has been enough to keep God's chosen family, the children of Israel, along with their culture intact through violent and perilous times.

The Family Legacy Model and protocols reflect these six practices of how God does family. I believe that one of His intentions was to help us know how to do family the way that He designed it. As we steward the family as designed and self-govern well, all from a place of true identity, we will experience transformation that leads to powerful family legacies and ultimately to reshape cultures from the inside out.

Importantly, it's not enough for us to know about these protocols. They must be put into practice consistently over time. They must be lived as a normal rhythm. The Family Legacy Model and protocols are not only a different way to think but a different way to live. They are a framework for how to do family.

You don't have to be Jewish or Christian to reap the benefits of stewarding your family as it was designed to be. These six protocols provide a framework to empower your family to be its very best, a way for you to live and leave a legacy that demonstrates your family purpose and values for generations to come.

The Family Legacy Model and Protocols

The Family Legacy Model is a simple, enduring, transferable framework for doing family. It is a set of six protocols or practices to follow that intentionally build the family as designed, while teaching our children and grandchildren to do the same.

Important Distinctions of the Family Legacy Model

- biblically based and designed
- integrates emotional intelligence into the context of family

- - use of a coach approach in the family
  - transferable process for generational impact
  - experience-based training methodology
  - intentionally designed for maximum legacy benefit
  - more than sixty experiences and tools equip families with the step-by-step how-to
  - provides a meaningful blueprint for cultural transformation from the inside out

The protocols provide a process that families can perform simply that transforms individuals and families from the inside out so the generations downstream can experience healing, growth, and success in life while imparting these practices to their children and grandchildren.

The six effective protocols empower families to do the following:

- treat one another with kindness, love, respect, and forgiveness, creating a family environment that is safe, loving, trusting, fun, supportive, godly (faith filled), and purposeful
- discover the unique (providential) history, true identity, and purpose both as individuals and as an entire family
- establish family rituals that are life-giving and supportive to empower the entire family to succeed
- enjoy family adventures together that are packed with purpose, fun, learning, storytelling, good food, and a deep emotional implantation to establish the family legacy into the family genetic code
- come together as one in times of family crisis to bring clarity, comfort, and shared responsibility
- effectively impart the most important things so the legacy endures: the wisdom, the blessing, the stuff, the unfinished business, and the family legacy generational charge

I believe that practicing these protocols will cut off the power of negative generational influences. Practicing them will preempt the toxic indoctrination of our godless public and university education system. Living the protocols will empower our children to think critically and objectively beyond the smoke and mirrors of the deceptive mainstream media and keep them connected to the God of their faith, working with Him to succeed in a long and prosperous life.

I believe it's not too late to engage in these practices and send our children back into the gates of culture as leaders who are healthy cultural architects who can create a better future for all.

As goes my family, so goes my business, so goes my community, so goes my government, so goes my school, so goes my church, so goes the media, so goes the arts, so goes the world.

Whoever wins the family wins the culture in the long game.

The culture that has the most successful families will have the most successful civilization and will endure.

The most important focus for a healthy world is truly healthy families that are producing healthy children who become healthy leaders at the decision centers of culture while equipping their children to do the same.

This is wisdom. Listen and hear one of the wisest men to ever live weigh in on this:

> Wise people are builders. They build families, businesses, communities. And through intelligence and insight their enterprises are established and endure. Because of their skilled leadership the hearts of people are filled with the treasures of wisdom and the pleasures of spiritual wealth. (Proverbs 24:3–4 TPT)

> Those who find true wisdom obtain tools for understanding the proper way to live, for they will have a fountain of blessing pouring into their lives. (Proverbs 3:13 TPT)

> As wisdom increases, a great treasure is imparted … it is a more valuable commodity than gold and gemstones, for there is nothing you desire that could compare to her … Wisdom extends to you long life in one hand and wealth and promotion in the other. (Proverbs 3:14–16 TPT)

The Family Legacy Protocols are not:

- an end-all be-all silver bullet for the guaranteed success of the family
- an exhaustive guide to marriage, parenting, family finance, or estate planning
- a half-baked form of counseling or therapy

- a bunch of ideas and theories that are not proven and grounded in science and practice
- so complicated that they cannot easily be practiced with skill and efficacy
- a vague information dump of stories that are without clear application steps
- a waste of time, money, and effort

The Family Legacy Protocols are:

- an effective and fun way to measurably improve the quality of your family life and legacy
- a practical set of experiential tools and practices that transform individuals and families
- a healing journey when that is required
- built from a biblical worldview and millennia of proven effectiveness in families and relationships
- a simple, easy-to-follow set of practices that can be modeled, enjoyed, and passed on for generations
- emotional intelligence and a coach approach that will empower you to build your family, business, and community and shape culture
- a meaningful way to transfer the blessing, the wisdom, and the stuff and address the unfinished business in an end-of-life context
- a way to shape culture from the inside out
- worth the effort forever

Family Legacy Model

Six protocols for leading your family, living your legacy, and shaping culture in the process:

Family Legacy EQ	EQ = emotional intelligence. Creating an environment of safety, trust, support, forgiveness, love, purpose, and fun.
Family Legacy Identity	Discovering together your family identity and uniqueness: past, present, and future; family character, values, purpose, and the creation of a family coat of arms.
Family Legacy Rituals	The regular family meeting framework: food, fun, story, wisdom, and supportive coach approach.
Family Legacy Ventures	The annual family learning and legacy adventure trip or vacation.
Family Legacy MISSION	The *momentary, intentional, specific, supportive, intervention,* as *one,* in response to a *need.*
Family Legacy Impartation	How to intentionally impart the most important things so your legacy endures. The wisdom, blessing, stuff, unfinished business, and Family Legacy Generational Covenant

These protocols will empower your family for generations to come to do the following:

- discover individual and generational identity
- shape the character of your children
- clarify your individual and family purpose, values, and mission
- mature in emotional intelligence
- equip and empower your children for success through using a coach approach
- heal wounds and experience forgiveness
- resolve conflicts
- connect deeply with those you love most
- recognize and affirm giftedness

- pass on your most important life lessons and wisdom
- live in freedom from destructive and limiting patterns of thinking and behavior of the past generations
- model healthy family relationships
- have fun and laugh as a family regularly
- create a positive supportive environment for dreaming and risking
- learn to listen and grow in empathy
- learn to give and receive feedback more effectively
- communicate more effectively

I am curious by nature. Perhaps you are too. Since you are reading this book, it's likely that you are curious about what really matters most—family and legacy.

This book addresses some of the most important questions you may have around family and legacy. This book offers solid experiences, processes, and tools for you to discover the answers for yourself with self-guided and (or) professionally facilitated experiences with those you love to address the following:

Family Identity

Who am I?
Who is my family, both as individuals and as a unit?
What character qualities are important to our family?
What is unique about my family—historically, currently, and for generations to come?
What imprint on the world will we leave?

Individual and Family Purpose

Why am I here?
Why is my family here?
What is most important to us in this life (values)?
What is most important that I pass on to my children and the generations to come?
What is my family's role in our community? Church? Nation? Culture?

Intentional Family Rituals

How do I pass on the wisdom I've learned for the good of generations to come?
How do I do life in a powerful, significant, and intentional way that will create and pass on a legacy?
How do I best teach my children healthy values?
How do I connect, listen, understand, and be understood by my spouse and children?
How do I make powerful children?
How do we support one another toward our dreams?

Healing and Handling a Crisis

How do I heal from failures, pain, and dysfunction and heal my family at the same time?
How do I stop destructive patterns in my family line?
How do I become a successful father, mother, spouse, and so on?
How do we move on from loss, divorce, death, failure, addiction, and so on?
How do I show my children the way to joy, peace, and success?
How do I save my family from the pain and dysfunction of mistakes?

Fun and the Emotional Imprint of Legacy

How do I plan a fun and impactful family adventure that is unforgettable?
How do we laugh our legacy into our genetic code?

Impartation of Family Legacy

How do I create and pass on a powerful legacy?
How do we shape culture and live a significant legacy?

This is the tip if the iceberg for sure. The Family Legacy Model and protocols are a powerful framework for doing family. They give families a map to finding solutions. They are a track to run on that leads to a family that is healed, filled with purpose, connected, and significantly impacting the lives of others for the better.

They are a family of cultural architects shaping culture from the inside out.

A Word about Cultural Architects

Cultural Architects, our business/ministry formerly known as Character Genetics 2012-2019, is where we build cultural architects who shape culture from the inside out. We work with leaders of leaders at the gates of culture to build families, businesses, communities, and culture.

We provide a number of training, coaching, consulting, speaking, and resource solutions for our clients. We partner with people to get results, specifically leaders of leaders. People who understand who they are and why they are here and are focused on leading themselves, their families, organizations, ministries, and their businesses into a legacy of kingdom cultural impact. I'm talking about those I call cultural architects, people who understand that *who they are* is shaping the culture from the inside out.

Our solutions are focused on the challenges that leaders face in the gates of culture:

- family
- education
- government
- business
- arts and entertainment
- religion
- media

While I've worked with many leaders from multiple faith orientations, my passion is to address people of faith at the gates of culture. Decision makers and gatekeepers who've been entrusted to direct the flow of what is allowable in culture and what is not. Leaders who open up the flows of the good and healthy and shut off the flows of the destructive and unhealthy. For those who are passionate about making a lasting impact on the world and are willing to do the work on themselves, Cultural Architects is for you.

Kingdom cultural transformation occurs when men and women demonstrate cultural authority in collaboration across spheres through sustained trusting relationships and unified strategic action.

To find out more about cultural architects, formerly Character Genetics, visit us at www.culturalarchitects.org.

Chapter 3
My Story

I was born in Terrell, Texas, (Dallas) in 1966 to humble, loving, hardworking, Christian, sports-loving parents. They raised me as a middle child in a safe, healthy, and happy middle-class home in Waterloo, Iowa, from the age of three. The star athlete turned banker and the beauty queen were married for fifty-two years before my mom received her reward in 2006. They are two of my biggest heroes in life.

Going back generationally on my mom and dad's side, I discovered many of the things that the average family experiences—the good, the bad, and the ugly. There was the solid work ethic, the empathy and care for others, the integrity of character, the generosity and kindness, the love of sport, the health of loving parents, and the examples of healthy marriages. There was also the call to leadership, the commitment to family, and lots of laughter. A powerful example of a living faith in God was one of the best influences on me as a child. And then there were the Norwegian baked sweet bread kringlas and the freshly baked sugar cookies that my mom made regularly.

At the same time, through the generations, my family was touched by alcoholism and early death, mental illness and sexual improprieties, abandonment and divorce, the pressure to look good in front of people, the tendency to find identity and value in performance, the avoidance of conflict, uncomfortable conversations, and shame at nearly all costs.

I grew up attending a small church in a community of about a hundred thousand people and home to John Deere tractors and the University of Northern Iowa. I was told at the time that this little church had sent out more leaders into the ministry field than any other church in the denomination. It was part of my context as a young boy. My grandfather, Carlyle Bixby, committed his life to the Lord at an Aimee Semple McPherson tent revival.

He dug the basement for the church and served in leadership there most of his life. Christianity and following Jesus, on the one hand, looked like passionate prayer meetings, expressive worship, experiencing supernatural signs and wonders, and sending leaders out into the world to make a difference. I knew at the age of twelve that I would give my life to leading leaders and specifically in the work of shaping culture in the context of the great commission.

On the other hand, it looked like thoughtful engagement in various aspects of our community. I watched my parents live their faith practically, not religiously. Whether in the bank, on the ball diamond, in the neighborhood, or at the beauty salon, they were humble, kind, faithful, and trustworthy people who loved to laugh. They helped others, didn't judge people, and contributed to our community. My father played softball into his forties and officiated football for twenty-eight years. I picked up his love for sports and enjoyed playing football and ice hockey for more than a decade. Salt of the earth! Good people!

In many ways, I realize now that I had an innocent and protected upbringing, for which I am grateful. Yet, with all of that good foundation, I was victimized, and I managed to make many poor decisions of my own and suffer tremendous wounds as a result of them.

For many years, I believed that these mistakes and wounds disqualified me from being an effective father, husband, and leader. I chose to cope with the shame instead of getting healed and set free from it. I now see that these experiences and the journey to my own healing have qualified me to help others experience healing from their own mistakes and wounds.

Wounded and Healed

My family of origin has been through the pain and brokenness of early death with the loss of a sister at birth, a brother at age twenty-five, and my mother before her time. My nuclear family has experienced the heartbreak of betrayal and divorce, remarriage and blended family chaos, addiction and recovery. We've faced the challenges of slander and shame, guilt and isolation, the fears of rejection and failure, conflict and abuse, lack and debt, the sleeplessness of anxiety and depression, mental illness and the pursuit of mental health, the heartsickness of hope deferred, uncertainty of job and home moves, disconnection and isolation, purposelessness, insignificance, and more, including abortion and assault.

And we have experienced the gratitude of healing and unconditional love. We have tasted the power and freedom of forgiveness along with the joy of abundance and surplus. We have walked the road of humble confidence in overcoming by the faithfulness and strength of a loving heavenly Father. We have known the wisdom of growth and maturity along with the safety and security of trust. We have enjoyed the sweet and refreshing sleep of peace along with the energy and focus of big dreams and big influence. We are engaged in the success of building our family, building our businesses, and building our communities. We are in process. We remain intentional and committed to one another to overcome together as a family.

In a commitment to love, honor, and respect my family members who may be hurt, embarrassed, or offended by the full and unedited details of the happenings above, I choose to limit my sharing in print. I do take the liberty to share details as appropriate in our private workshops, training, and speaking events.

You and your family are not alone. Our family is there with you. One of our core values and an integral part of our family identity is empathy—walking in another person's shoes with full understanding.

> We have been victimized, but we are not victims.
> We have been abused, but we are not abusers.
> We have fallen and failed, but we have not stayed down or given up.
> We have been broken, but we are being healed.
> We have been wrongly accused and judged, but we have endured and overcome.
> We have been afraid, but we have grown in courage.
> We have been equipped to help you through whatever you have experienced in your family by what we have learned.

I used to believe that all these experiences of wounding and pain had somehow broken me, disqualifying me from being able to offer people help. "Why would they want to listen to someone who has experienced such failure?" I told myself. My feelings told me to just hide, stay silent, and avoid the shame these realities presented.

Until I embraced a different mind-set around my true-life story. I chose to receive the gift of Jesus Christ and His forgiveness. Then I chose to forgive myself and all those who hurt me. And then I chose to believe that God would indeed "work all things together for the good of those who love Him and are called according to His purpose," including me.

I began to see the good that God was doing through our challenges in life that are common to many people and families in the world today. His good work included teaching us the following:

- how to heal from the deep wounds of life
- how to help each other heal and grow
- how to stop the effect of negative generational influences
- how to discover our individual and family identity and purpose
- how to dream again
- how to set goals and provide a supportive environment to help one another win
- how to have fun together and be intentional in building each member of the family
- how to support one another in the pursuit of life dreams, relationships, jobs, and so on
- how to be intentional with our regular family meetings while having fun
- how to do life together, treat one another well, and make a brighter future
- how to transform the genetic legacy for our generations to come
- how to equip my children to carry on the Family Legacy Generational Covenant
- and so much more

We have taken all that we are learning and put it into a set of protocols that we are using in our family. And now we've formalized them into the Family Legacy Model so that we can support other families in a similar way.

I've been developing leaders for thirty years. My calling is to serve leaders of leaders through speaking, writing, coaching, mentoring, and training. So, when it was finally time to turn my focus on developing leaders through the family, I had decades of expertise to draw from. I've pulled from all the years of experience in creating this set of protocols. Believe me, it is not random. Science, wisdom, best practice, and biblical foundation saturate every single protocol. They are proven in our own experience as a family and in the families we have worked with.

For those of you who are curious about how I came to the equipping philosophy that's used in the design of the protocols, the next section is for you. For some, foundations and philosophy matter deeply. For others, they do not. However, I believe everyone wants to know that they *work*. Not only will the protocols work to transform your family and your legacy, the protocols will work to shape our culture from the inside out and create better families, businesses, communities, and nations.

Equipping Philosophy Development

I am wired to see through three primary lenses when it comes to most things in life, including developing leaders, or what those in ministry would call discipleship. The first is the theoretical and ideological lens. I love to know how and why things work the way they do. The second is the biblical lens. I hold a biblical worldview and have a deep respect for the truth in scripture. The third is a practical and experiential lens. Knowledge and information are simply not enough to be transformational and, frankly, even useful.

Experiencing truth, principle, and practice is mandatory for growth and results. Living what you know as a leader is an essential reality to good leadership. Equipping others to live what they know and for them to be able to equip yet others to live what they know, on to generations of yet other leaders, is the key. It is where most leaders, churches, companies, and families fail.

I graduated in 1991 from what is now called New Hope Christian College in Eugene, Oregon. After serving in two churches in Ohio and Los Angeles, I found myself dissatisfied with my level of effectiveness at raising up powerful people and powerful leaders who could lead others in the advancement of the kingdom in ways that impacted families, communities, and nations.

I learned that I had what I was willing to tolerate, and I was finished tolerating pouring my life out for what I saw as meaningful yet limited results. It was not enough for me to just do what had been done, to just go through the motions, expecting more significant measurable outcomes when none came. There had to be more.

My search for solutions led me to resign traditional church ministry, sell nearly everything that we had, and attend a Crossroads Discipleship Training School at YWAM'S University of the Nations in Kona, Hawaii (Youth with a Mission). We raised the money, and I brought my pregnant wife (with Miranda) and my two small children, Garrett (three) and Kara (one), along with a nanny to the big island to find answers.

There are those before-and-after moments in life when the world looks one way before an event and looks totally different after that event, forever—sometimes for the worse and sometimes for the better. That was my experience in the fall of 1996 when I sat in a classroom in Hawaii.

The format of the school was three months of the lecture phase, which included morning times of instruction and afternoon and evening times of application, actually doing what we were learning about, followed by three months of an outreach to the Philippines. The revelation I received from this format alone changed my philosophy around equipping leaders. I saw and experienced firsthand how knowledge without application was not learning at all and sterile. Accelerated, measurable, and sustainable growth happens through experiential learning.

I will never forget one of the first weeks of the school, where ministry founder Loren Cunningham and then chancellor David Boyd taught for a week on the purpose of the church and our mission of discipling nations and how YWAM was attempting to do that through a philosophy of influencing the mind molders of culture. Loren shared about an early 1970's experience that he had with Bill Bright, founder of Campus Crusade for Christ. He told about how he and Bill were talking and noticing how Christians at the time were living an isolation from the world instead of an insulation to the world. They talked about how out of fear, pride, self-righteousness, ignorance, and the perceived need to run church like a business, the focus was on survival instead of being an instrument of God to equip believers to govern as decision makers in places of influence in the nations of the earth. They lamented how leaders structured church so that the mission and philosophy of much of the church was to isolate themselves from the mind molders of culture and build internal programs instead of training and sending workers into these key power centers where decisions are made about the way things will be in a culture or a nation.

The mind molders that they taught about are the same that others refer to as the seven mountains of culture. I have chosen to refer to them as the gates of culture. Loren and David spoke passionately about how their philosophy of training leaders was different from the traditional church in very important ways. They saw the need for people of faith to rise to the top of government, education, arts and entertainment, media, business, the family, and religion to be able to shape culture and disciple nations. They had built large organizations equipping leaders to do with skill and competence whatever their passion wanted in these cultural gates. Instead of withdrawing from places of power and isolating from the world, they built the mission on training leaders to insert themselves into the places of power and lead from their biblical worldview and Christian values, while remaining insulated from the temptations of the world.

That one week of class along with these two revelations changed my life, my ministry, my leadership philosophy, my family, and so much more. It also changed the way I think about the identity and role of the church, the manner and methodology by which we train leaders, and the legacy that I am living to leave. It has influenced my relationships, my calendar, my checkbook, my prayers, and my work and has saturated every part of my consciousness.

It most certainly has affected my construct and framework for my company, Cultural Architects, formerly known as Character Genetics, and for this book. It is why my leadership training workshops and coaching are experiential in design. It is why I have chosen to make the Family Legacy journey experiential in nature. Each of the chapters in this book are a keynote message and a module in training. Each of them includes hands-on experiential exercises, tools, games, and activities that are designed for maximum learning, growth, retention, and sustainable results.

I carried that newfound philosophy into the National Youth Department of my denomination in 1997 in my role as the National Youth Director. For five years, I served there, training youth leaders and young people across the country with an experiential equipping methodology with great fruitfulness.

In 2003, I transitioned out of the national office to a local church in Des Moines, Iowa, where I continued to further develop leaders through experiential training exercises and worship encounter workshops. I continued developing more discipleship constructs for greater effectiveness. I began to see a way of equipping that was effective and could eventually send leaders into the gates of culture as cultural architects.

I had learned that I needed to personally live it to give it, so I began seeking what that would look like. My seeking led me to resign my role at the church and start a nonprofit house of prayer in the Des Moines region, which I directed for six years. In addition, I became the legislative chaplain for the Iowa legislature, stepping into the gate of government, not wanting to ask anyone to do what I was unwilling to do.

In the house of prayer, we prioritized our two-hour worship and prayer sets around seven gates of culture and a couple other mandates that we were passionate about. We began to regularly listen and agree with what God was doing in business, government, education, religion, media, arts and entertainment, and in the family in our region and beyond. We would regularly take what we were sensing (revelation knowledge) and then take action in both prayer and in these decision centers of our community and our culture.

And it clicked! We saw results in legislative reform, in safe passage through the recession of 2008–2009, in new businesses moving or expanding to Des Moines. Changes in our school curriculum, changes in our churches. And in the 2018 *Newsweek* ranking of best states in the union, Iowa was ranked number one over all other states as the overall best state in the country. Don't get me started on this ... just wow!

In 2011, I laid down my guitar in response to a question from the Lord and took a job with a leadership and character-development company that specialized in experiential training in Fortune 100 companies. The founder of the company had a vision to take the work and to contextualize it for the faith community that needed so desperately to find true north again when it came to equipping people and sending them into the gates of culture. I was in full agreement. He and some of his staff mentored me in the ways of facilitation and experiential learning. I was the last one that Brian Klemmer personally mentored, as he died unexpectedly at sixty-one years of age, four days after patting me on the back and saying, "You are ready! Let's get you in the seminar room." I stayed with the company for a year and a half. I learned the skill set, and in late 2012, I launched my own company, Character Genetics.

Character Genetics, now rebranded as Cultural Architects, has been a platform for working with leaders of leaders at the gates of culture. Working with these cultural architects in government, the church, business, and now the family is without a doubt the most fruitful season of ministry in my life. This is convergence for me. While I am excited about this season of convergence, I'm focusing on *legacy* as I look ahead. Thank you for allowing me to be a small part of your life, your family, your ministry, and your legacy. I hope we have the chance to meet.

My Story

So many others along the path influenced me personally and in the development of the equipping philosophy I employ in Cultural Architects, as well as in the Family Legacy Protocols. At the risk of forgetting someone, I want to acknowledge and thank some key people in my journey who have all contributed in some meaningful way to my life and philosophy:

Garry and Jan Bixby

Carlyle Bixby

Lesli Lamb

Mike and Linda Schreurs

Jeff Farmer

Dr. Paul Leavenworth

Doris Hunt

Harold Ady

Curt Arne

Lou Engle

Mike Bickle

Dr. Lance Wallnau

Gordon Pennington III

Dave Olson

Rick Arrowood

Dr. Bobby Clinton

Bill Johnson

Randy Clark

Leif Hetland

Dr. Myles Monroe

Os Hillman

Ric Lumbard

John and Linda Buehler

Jerry and Lilian Wood

There are countless other people who have impacted my life, for whom I am humbly grateful.

I've had the pleasure of working with amazing people in my life. I'm so blessed as a man, a father, a husband, and a son. My continued passion is to create cultural architects by equipping leaders of leaders to show up powerfully at the gates of culture themselves while effectively equipping others to do the same. Through the use of experiential learning, emotional intelligence, and a coach approach together, we will show up at the gates of culture and shape culture from the inside out, from generation to generation.

While most of my work has been in the gates of religion, government, business, and family, my focus for the near future is primarily on the gate of family.

Hope for Your Family and the Genesis of this Book

I'm including this section for one purpose: to give hope to those who don't have hope for their family to be whole and to leave an enduring family legacy.

This is where I was in late 2016. I was at the lowest point of my life. After a recent divorce, I found myself beaten down, exhausted, and out of hope for a strong finish in life, ministry, and family. I had endured a lifetime of challenges, undeterred from wholehearted obedience to the mission I've sensed from age twelve. But this was different. This time, I was cut to the bone and crushed.

My children, all three now adults in their twenties, were wounded and facing their own sets of serious challenges. I considered resigning my all-out passionate lifetime pursuit of God's plan and shifting into neutral for a while. When I expressed that to the Lord, He simply replied, "Randy, just love your family." In the end, I decided to pursue Him and to let go of the expectations I had around what His plan of finishing well would look like. When I found Him, everything changed.

What I found was a loving Father who was for me. What I experienced was a Father who wanted to heal me and to share His heart and thoughts for family with me. What I learned was that He wanted to heal my family and establish a legacy worthy of His purposes. He removed the shame and fear that had gripped my life and began talking with me about my children. I began giving time and attention to my family at a whole new level—thinking about them, empathizing with their journeys of life, and intensely praying for them. Taking

My Story

personal responsibility for my part of their pain while helping them see theirs. I began to see more clearly than ever before the identity, gifts, and value of my children through His eyes. I began to see the good that He was working in all the mess, and as I did, hope flickered back to life.

I began thinking about how I wanted to live my life from that point forward and what would remain long after my time was up. What did they most need to hear, know, and experience to enjoy a long, healthy, and prosperous life? What would I tell each of them that would help them the most in their lives? What healing did they need, and how could I participate in that? What experiences would I want to have enjoyed with them? What stuff, what wisdom, what insights would I want to make sure they received for their good? What do they need to experience as a family so that they can become healthy parents with strong families of their own? What life skills do they need, and how could I help deliver those to them? Where are they heading in their lives, and how can we best be a support to each other? And finally, what is it we could do from where we were at that moment until my time on earth was finished to ensure that they were equipped to live and leave an enduring family legacy?

As I searched for the answers to all these questions, I began to apply the wisdom I've learned over the years in developing leaders and coaching people to growth and success. How would the tools and exercises I use to transform leaders look in the family setting? What would I say to myself if I was one of my own coaching clients? What exercises would I take me through? What would my family need to heal, reconnect, grow, prosper, and thrive as individuals and as leaders in their businesses, communities, and culture?

Hope was fanned from a flicker into a roaring fire!

It was then that I saw the connection between my family experience and the experience of countless other families who have walked a similar path. If my family could turn this around, so could they. If, one by one, families turned around, in a short period of time, so would businesses, communities, and eventually culture.

And it was on!

I have never felt so alive and full of purpose, vision, and hope. I'm filled to the rim and overflowing with love and gratitude. As our family has begun to develop and walk out these protocols, we are experiencing a quality of family that is brand-new, healing, and deeply satisfying.

And to demonstrate just how off-the-charts amazing my heavenly Father is, He brought an angel into my life by way of San Diego. She has brought so much to us and is now one with me in everything, including the development of the Family Legacy work. My family is being restored from the inside out. We are all committed to the process of living and leaving a powerful and enduring family legacy.

Take courage. You are not alone. Your best days are indeed ahead for you and your family. There is real hope available to you. There is a pathway and a map out of the hopelessness. We are honored to have you join us on this journey to restore families and shape culture from the inside out.

Chapter 4
Preparing for Your Journey

Family Legacy—Definition, Purpose, Scope, and Motivation

I have many thoughts as I sit down to define "family legacy."

For many, when asked the question, "What is legacy?" the first thoughts that typically come to mind are as follows:

- what I leave behind
- lists of achievements
- stories of influence
- prominent names of association
- charitable giving and philanthropy
- wealth creation and transfer
- attributes that stand out as noteworthy
- last will and testament
- business or cause notoriety

While legacy may certainly include the items listed above, I see the list as the fruit or results of something more. My personal view is that legacy is deeper, more spiritual, eternal, and essence or character in nature. Simply stated, I believe that legacy is the very character and identity that we pass on to our children. The character and identity that we possess and build in our heirs is our real legacy. The items on the list above are the fruit of identity, the results of who we are.

In the biblical worldview, our triune God (Father, Son, and Holy Spirit) is a family, the first family. The Father's nature or character is the legacy that He passed on to His Son. The Son was made perfect in that nature (character). Jesus said, "All that belongs to the Father is mine. That is why I said the Spirit will receive from me what he will make known to you." John 15:16 (NIV)

God put His character in humanity when He fashioned us in His image in the Garden of Eden. Though humankind fell, His Son restored our connection to the Father and our ability to receive His nature (character) through salvation.

I believe that the ultimate definition of family legacy is the character and nature of God Himself passed down to His Son and through His Spirit to us, generation after generation of those who love Him. Quite literally, He is our inheritance, our legacy.

It is His character qualities that are the most important legacy of all.

His essence of love, peace, joy, humility, courage, hope, wisdom, life, generosity, kindness, power, patience, gentleness, faith, self-control, and so on is the original and eternal legacy. In becoming like Him, we carry this legacy through this temporal life, bearing fruit as we go, and as we steward it well, we guarantee its eternal essence impacts others for eternity as well.

Legacy is the vehicle that carries forward original design from generation to generation.

Simply stated, I pass on the character of God to my family. Family legacy is how I choose to live my life, why, and how those choices influence others in the demonstration of the Father's character.

Eternally stated, family legacy is the offering to our Father and Creator at the end of my time on earth, the end of my family bloodline from our time on earth, and what happens from beginning to end in the lives and from the influence of my family and family line.

On a larger scale, Family legacy is the cumulative sum of generations and their experiences, wounds, healing, wisdom, blessing, lessons, stuff, mind-sets, physical characteristics, spiritual dynamics, influence, impact, and stewardship that are embodied in every individual of a bloodline.

Family legacy is also what gets passed on to me in my genetic legacy and from me as I steward my life in ways that alter, improve, degrade, enhance, or transform that legacy during my watch. It is what is then passed on to my children, along with what they do with it on their watch, and likewise to each new generation.

As each and every individual's life impacts countless other people, families, businesses, and communities while on their watch, their legacy spreads far and wide and, in some measure, lasts for eternity.

To accept this and grasp its significance brings an entirely new level of personal responsibility to do the best job I can do with what I have been given to steward and intentionally live and leave a better family legacy than the one I received.

We are each a catalyst for our family legacy, good or bad.

What will we do with what we've been entrusted to steward?

How will I live the life I am stewarding?

How will I show up to steward my generational flaws, failures, and divine purpose?

What exactly will I choose to do with my life to heal, grow, and transform this legacy for the better?

What can I do to improve, accelerate, and maximize this legacy in my children for their good and the good of others?

How can I equip my children with a set of practices and protocols that will empower them to live and leave a powerful family legacy while ensuring they are committed and equipped to do the same with their children?

How will I connect this legacy work to intentionally shaping culture?

- A: Choose to faithfully partner with God and my family to apply the Family Legacy Protocols regularly.
- A: The same is true for you and your family.

Purpose

The purpose for intentionally living and leaving a powerful family legacy is deep and wide.

This is the foundational scripture for the Family Legacy work. Read this wise proverb thoughtfully, and you will identify much of the purpose of the work, the why:

> Wise people are builders. They build families, businesses, communities. And through intelligence and insight their enterprises are established and endure. Because of their skilled leadership the hearts of people are filled with the treasures of wisdom and the pleasures of spiritual wealth. (Proverbs 24:3–4 TPT)

> Those who find true wisdom obtain tools for understanding the proper way to live, for they will have a fountain of blessing pouring into their lives. (Proverbs 3:13 TPT)

> As wisdom increases, a great treasure is imparted … it is a more valuable commodity than gold and gemstones, for there is nothing you desire that could compare to her … Wisdom extends to you long life in one hand and wealth and promotion in the other. (Proverbs 3:14–16 TPT)

Consider…

1. Because building families, businesses, and communities is wise.
2. Because it takes intelligence and insight for enterprises to be established and endure.
3. Because skilled leadership in building families, businesses, and communities fills the hearts of people with the treasures of wisdom and the pleasures of spiritual wealth.
4. Because to find true wisdom, we must obtain tools for understanding the proper way to live.
5. Because using these tools and living properly results in a fountain of blessing pouring into people's lives.
6. Because a great treasure more valuable than gold and diamonds is imparted to people.
7. Because being wise brings you and others long life.
8. Because being wise brings you and others wealth and promotion.

Pause for a moment and think about the list above.

Why invest yourself into learning and living the Family Legacy Protocols (tools for understanding how to live)?

Because it's worth it.

Because your choice to do so will transform you, your family, your legacy, and everyone else who has the good fortune of being influenced by you and your family legacy. Because lives will be saved and healed. Because businesses and communities will be blessed and prosperous. Because life will be *better* for so many people! Because some of these people will take their places at the gates of culture and share their wisdom by governing well when they are there, shaping culture from the inside out.

Why this Family Legacy Model and set of six disruptive family protocols?

Because they are:

- biblically based (Whether you are a person of faith or not, the principles are from the Bible, they are universally true, and they work.)
- simple to understand and execute (Simple but not always easy, to be fair.)
- distinct from other family resources because of the experiential exercises, the coach approach, and the emotional intelligence practices
- effective (The protocols work—healing, forgiveness, true identity, purpose, and significance for real.)
- reproducible (The tools can be taught to our children and duplicated generationally.)
- fun (While dealing with family can be messy at times, there are a lot of laughs and joy.)
- experiential (So much more than information, the protocols are experiential and transformational.)
- creative and flexible (The framework provides space for personalizing to your family uniqueness.)
- wise (Assuring the benefits mentioned above.)
- eternal (Working these protocols will undeniably affect the past, present, future, and eternity for many.)

Scope

There is a noteworthy distinction of scope between my family using a set of wisdom tools that helps my family be better and the big idea of my family being better and shaping culture as cultural architects.

Inside: focusing on your family and your legacy.

Inside out: focusing on your family legacy *while* connecting your family legacy to the greater purpose of shaping culture from the inside out and expanding the kingdom of God for His glory along with other families.

Both are important.

On the one hand, you may be thinking, *I want to use the protocols to live a long, wise, and prosperous life, doing everything in my power to equip my children and grandchildren to do the same.* Yes! What a wonderful and significant pursuit.

On the other hand, you may be thinking, *Yes, and I want to teach my family to work the protocols with my generation and include a focus on serving others, empowering them to shape culture from the inside out as they lead healthy and purposeful lives in leadership at the gates of culture. Yes!*

The Family Legacy Model and protocols are effective for both inside and inside-out results.

Motivation

When it comes to living and leaving a family legacy, *what* we do profoundly matters. This is why so much time and effort has been invested in creating a simple set of protocols that are effective, enduring, and generational.

However, it may be even more important *why* we are living and leaving a family legacy. Why is it important for me to leave a legacy? Why are you reading this book? Why are you choosing to do with this information and the opportunities we are providing for you whatever it is that you decide to do?

Will you read for knowledge alone? Will you take personal action with the protocols and your family? How dynamically will you engage with them? Will you adapt them as a ritual and habit in the life of your family? Will you take shortcuts? Will you start strong and fade? Will you engage with a Family Legacy coach? Will you take a workshop or host a workshop to equip others in your sphere, community, church, or organization? Will you do whatever it takes to ensure you have done everything within your power to experience these protocols with your family and, in so doing, set these profound practices in motion for generations to come and impact the world?

Or ...

Will you choose to work and spend it all on yourself and nothing more?

Will you choose to work hard, save, write a big check, assign who gets what assets, and stop there?

What will you choose to do regarding your legacy? The answer to this question may be best answered by answering the why question.

Why will you choose to do what you choose to do? Important questions. Important answers.

I am not coming from a place of right and wrong or of judgment here. I am coming from a place of curiosity for *why* you decide to engage with the legacy work. I am simply asking a question that needs to be asked. Like my father always said, "Son, you will get out of it what you put into it."

As I have thought about this, I have come to see a continuum of sorts as it relates to the people who choose to, in fact, intentionally leave a legacy.

Why am I going to the work of living and leaving a powerful family legacy?

The One _____l_____ The Many

On the left extreme is the why that is focused upon the one leaving the legacy:

- how the one individual will be remembered by the masses and the few
- how people will think about the one
- how the one will be revered, appreciated, recognized, and memorialized by others
- how the one will feel about themselves by doing the legacy work (Perhaps they want to feel accepted, generous, admired, kind, justified, good enough, or that they are a good person.)
- how the one is doing what *should* be done or doing the *right* thing

The flow of energy and motivation on the far-left side of the spectrum is toward the individual—for their own reasons, their own feelings, their own ego and outcomes. At the extreme, this motivation is ultimately selfish. There may be wonderful things done for others, but the *why* was rooted in the individual. Perhaps their pain, guilt, shame, insecurity, pride, or unresolved life issues drive the individual to leave a legacy, and in large part, it is for themselves.

The passing on of the most important things along with the equipping of the next generations and the strong sense of personal responsibility for the family to each do their own part for their families, businesses, communities, and culture is largely ignored. The flow of action, thought, and attention is on the one leaving the legacy.

I am not judging this or calling it right or wrong per se. I am making important distinctions that have huge ramifications.

On the right extreme of the spectrum is the why that is focused upon the many receiving the legacy:

- how the many will be empowered to live a successful life
- how the many will live well, love well, lead well, and learn well
- how the many will think about themselves and others for the good of others
- how the many will model for and train up their children in the legacy
- how the many will impact others from the inside out
- how the many will add to the family legacy and ensure it continues
- how the many will shape culture from the good character built inside of them
- how the many (the family line plus their businesses plus their communities plus their life imprint) will be presented to King Jesus someday

The flow of energy and motivation on the far-right side of the spectrum is toward the many—for the good and purpose of the many. At the extreme, this motivation may approach a Messiah complex, an "only and all about others," not anything at all to do with the one or individual.

Since the very DNA of *the one* is present in the many, it seems inauthentic to me to not have some measure of the one present, along with the primary focus on the many.

Here's where I land on this whole thing: Either extreme misses the mark or doesn't result in maximum legacy benefit. I believe falling on this spectrum right of center at approximately middle right of center yields the best outcome of legacy benefit—primarily and strongly for the many, along with a sense of personal responsibility, gratitude, and reward for the one.

I hope indeed that I am remembered lovingly and with a measure of honor and gratitude by my family, friends, and those I've had the privilege to serve and influence over the decades. However, my deepest commitment is to love, to give, and to equip as many as I am entrusted with for their own good and the good of their families, businesses, and communities. Ultimately, I want to be remembered by the Lord and acknowledged by Him that I was a good and faithful steward and pleased Him out of loving obedience.

What is your motivation in living and leaving a meaningful family legacy? Your answer will influence how you engage in this work.

A Word for Blended Families

I have the life experience of a blended family. While every family, no matter the construct, has myriad challenges to overcome, blended families have more. As you blend two families, differences in parenting, discipline, lifestyle, and more can create challenges and become a source of frustration for all. Agreeing on consistent guidelines about rules, chores, discipline, and allowances will show the kids that you and your spouse intend to deal with issues in a similar and fair way.

Other challenges to blended families include the following:

- *Age differences.* In blended families, there may be children with birthdays closer to one another than possible with natural siblings, or the new stepparent may be only a few years older than the eldest child.
- *Parental inexperience.* One stepparent may have never been a parent before and therefore may have no experience of the different stages children go through.
- *Changes in family relationships.* If both parents remarry partners with existing families, it can mean children suddenly find themselves with different roles in two blended families. For example, one child may be the eldest in one stepfamily but the youngest in the other. Blending families may also mean one child loses their uniqueness as the only boy or girl in the family.

- *Difficulty in accepting a new parent.* If children have spent a long time in a one-parent family or still nurture hopes of reconciling their parents, it may be difficult for them to accept a new person.
- *Coping with demands of others.* In blended families, planning family events can get complicated, especially when there are custody considerations to take into account. Children may grow frustrated that vacations, parties, or weekend trips now require complicated arrangements to include their new stepsiblings.
- *Changes in family traditions.* Most families have very different ideas about how annual events such as holidays, birthdays, and family vacations should be spent. Kids may feel resentful if they're forced to go along with someone else's routine. Try to find some common ground or create new traditions for your blended family.
- *Parental insecurities.* A stepparent may be anxious about how they compare to a child's natural parent or may grow resentful if the stepchildren compare them unfavorably to the natural parent.

I acknowledge the challenges in a blended family are many, and they are different in many respects from those of a nonblended family. I am familiar with the wounding, the pain, and the frustration of stumbling through, trying to make things work, minimizing the wreckage, and I have good news!

The Family Legacy Protocols give blended families the tools to address their unique challenges.

All the protocols apply to blended families. There is no need to skip or drastically modify them. In fact, there is the huge benefit of having an objective tool or exercise to do the work for you, helping you stay neutral and supportive.

Here's How

EQ Protocol: With many more layers of challenge, wounding, offense, and misunderstanding in a blended family, the need for high emotional intelligence and its five pillars of self-awareness, personal responsibility, sustained action, trust, and empathy are required even more.

A choice to explore, discover, understand, and support one another is a very important way to experience the Family Legacy journey. It creates an environment of safety, vulnerability, trust, and learning for maximum results.

Criticism, blaming, accusing, and attacking one another is sure to sabotage the Family Legacy journey and limit its effectiveness and value.

The Family Social Covenant Tool alone can transform how you do family. The impact is huge!

Identity Protocol: Addresses the "Who are we?" as a blended family. What's the good, bad, and ugly of us? The result will be a "we are in this together" mind-set requiring kindness, love, forgiveness, gratitude, humility, and more. Empathy will reshape the culture of your home.

You will fashion unified and cohesive family identity, family values, and a family coat of arms in a wonderful and emotional experience that helps you move forward as one.

Ritual Protocol: This regular family meeting works because of the supportive environment and the coach approach. Add to that the fun and laughs, the food, and the art of storytelling, and you have the ingredients for a meaningful family ritual that members *want* to be a part of.

Venture Protocol: This family adventure protocol is an important time of bonding through fun and new learning experiences together for any family. You all will likely laugh and laugh and laugh. Don't underestimate the lasting transformation that can be implanted in our core through fun!

MISSION Protocol: More variables, complex challenges, and problem-solving come along with blended families in times of family need. Having a map or template to navigate these times creates a level of clarity and certainty you all need to get through together.

Impartation Protocol: The transference of the most important things—the wisdom, the blessing, the stuff—addressing the unfinished businesses and the generational charge to the Family Legacy Covenant are going to happen one way or another, or not. Having no plan leaves the door open to deep wounds. Having a plan to do these things mindfully offers the best chance for you to love your family no matter what the construct.

Getting the Most from Your Family Legacy Work by Integrating Emotional Intelligence and the Coach Approach into the Family

Emotional Intelligence

How you show up in this Family Legacy work matters. This can be a difficult experience, or this can be a glorious experience. It is up to you which.

There is no greater opportunity to leave a lasting imprint on your family. How they experience you in this journey sets a lens of how they will remember and experience you in time moving forward. What a huge opportunity for good and bad, healing and wounding, joy and sorrow, acceptance and rejection. There's a lot at stake.

One of the key distinctions of the Family Legacy Model is integrating the practice of emotional intelligence into the family context. Self-governing our emotions and understanding the thinking that is driving them is essential for the success of any relationship. All relationships are improved with the practice of EQ. Whether in business, church, government, family, or school, the benefits of EQ are proven and measurable scientifically.

For some, the overwhelming thought of being with family talking about sensitive areas is what causes them to avoid it. For fear of it, it never gets prioritized. The mess, the pain, the vulnerability, the emotion of it all is a foe many are unable to conquer. Frankly, the fear of things going so poorly is nothing more than a smokescreen of assumptions. I have found that families want to be healed, whole, forgiven, and connected. They are just afraid to go there because they don't know how.

For others, they want to make the most of this opportunity but don't know how to go about it. What do I actually do? When? How? Fear of failing by doing it poorly or doing it wrong stops others.

Yet others live such frenetic and full lives they can't seem to take the time or spend the money for something so consuming when they have so much to do, especially when the family is so disconnected anyway. Hmmm ...

The truth is that you may or may not be able to show up in this legacy work in a productive and effective way. In a moment, I will show you how you need to show up to get the most out of this journey for your family and your legacy. If you begin the work and find you are not able to show up in the way required for success, what will you do?

Quit?

Justify why the protocols aren't for you or how they don't work?

Push ahead anyway, damaging people and outcomes in the process?

How about this? If you find yourself having a difficult time with any of the protocols or with managing yourself in the execution of them, reach out for help. Contact our office. Talk with a Family Legacy coach or facilitator who is there to help you through it.

We have several ways to assist you with your Family Legacy journey. You can attend one of our conferences or workshops that will better equip you to do the work at home. Our facilitators can even be brought into your home either by phone, online, or in person to either coach you through or actually take your family through the protocols.

There are several online e-courses, weekly webinars, video archives, and a monthly membership subscription that give you access to tools and content to further support you in the successful execution of the protocols. One of the best ways to experience the protocols is to do them with a small group or life group in your church.

There is help. Don't quit. Don't procrastinate. Don't make excuses. Just do something … or not.

To do nothing may be the most painful of all for those left behind and generations to come—no priority, no intentionality, no effort, no value, no words, no lessons, no sharing, no wisdom, no blessing, no time, no fun, no food, no help, no attention, no love.

So little passed on for the benefit of our sons and daughters and all of their sons and daughters … and all of their sons and daughters …

What about all those we work with? What about those in our community? Will any of them have a lasting benefit from your life and influence? They won't if you choose to do nothing.

The Family Legacy

To do something may be the best. How well you do it may or may not be as important as the fact that you do in fact do something. As a dear friend of mine says, "Just do something!"

Get out of resistance. Accept what you have in front of you and take the best next step forward.

Here is how you and your family can get the most out of working the protocols on the Family Legacy journey. Talk through this ahead of time and do a self-assessment regularly if you want the most out of this journey.

>   Be kind. Don't be rude.
>   Be humble. Don't be proud.
>   Be empathetic. Don't be selfish.
>   Be teachable (open). Don't be unteachable (closed).
>   Be loving. Don't be hateful.
>   Be vulnerable. Don't be defensive.
>   Be understanding. Don't be harsh.
>   Be intentional. Don't be lazy.
>   Be responsible. Don't be blaming.
>   Be consistent. Don't be inconsistent.
>   Be authentic. Don't be fake.
>   Be forgiving. Don't be bitter.
>   Be supportive. Don't be critical.
>   Be engaged. Don't be detached.
>   Be safe. Don't be unsafe.
>   Be courageous. Don't be fearful.
>   Be truthful. Don't be deceitful.
>   Be fun. Don't be glum.
>   Be a good listener. Don't be all talk.
>   Be present. Don't be distracted.
>   Be aware. Don't be apathetic.

Be aware of the mind-sets that pop up. Don't allow them to sabotage your legacy work.

- It's too hard.
- It's not possible.
- It's never going to be right.
- It's no problem. This will be easy. I've got this.

- It's not important. It will all just work itself out.
- Too bad so sad, is what it is.
- I don't want to do it wrong.
- I don't want to fail.
- It's going to be too painful.
- Nothing is going to change.
- My family won't like this.
- I can't change.
- I don't have time for this.

Be aware of the mind-sets that pop up that will support you and your Family Legacy work.

- We can do this together with love and a plan.
- We can trust others for help and support.
- It will take work, but it's worth it.
- It is possible.
- We have the grit.
- I can choose to show up strong.
- I can change.
- We can change.
- There is help if I need it.
- I'm not sure things will change if I do this, but I'm sure they won't change if I don't.

Your chances for success in every aspect of life increase dramatically if you choose to show up powerfully by practicing emotional intelligence. Just think how your family would thrive if all the family members and participants agree to show up as outlined above. You can do it. You aren't alone. You have help.

The Coach Approach

Another key distinction of the Family Legacy Model is integrating the coach approach into the context of the family. The dynamic of family relationships is transformed when we intentionally partner with family members in a proven practice that supports one another in discovery, growth, and success. Imagine experiencing your family as a primary place of resource in your growth and success. For many, this is beyond their ability to imagine. For others, the concept is familiar, but the step-by-step process in unclear.

Coaching is one of the most empowering and invigorating modalities in creating growth and success offered today. To integrate this into the Family Legacy Model by investing into the personal growth and development of each member is a powerful way to do family. Family coaching is an effective way to build legacy while training our children how to bring coaching into their generations to come.

If you want to ensure the best outcome as you apply the Family Legacy Model, you simply must understand how to facilitate supportive family coaching conversations effectively. Coaching conversations are distinct from conversations where you give advice or where you say, "Let me tell how to do this and what I have done when in your situation." That is more of a mentoring conversation. There is a time and a place for different conversations, no doubt, but the conversation that causes safety, support, growth, and personal responsibility is the coaching conversation.

Good coaching is a dynamic partnership between coach and coachee in a simple and creative process to maximize the coachee's personal and professional potential. It is a growth conversation that can address any aspect of life—from relationships, to career, to health, and spiritual growth. A true coaching conversation is one where the coach asks a few good questions and listens while the coachee finds their own answers to the questions. Once they have their own ah-ha moment, they are supported in taking personal responsibility and choosing what's important, what the learning is, and what they will do next in the pursuit of a clear and meaningful goal.

As you plan for the coaching conversations specifically designed in the protocols, along with having coaching conversations in everyday life informally, you may want to review this section to keep your skills sharp. In addition, I have a digital e-course on the website entitled The Coach Approach to Family that will equip you in a detailed manner in learning a coach approach.

The Basics of a Coach Approach

Goal Setting

Effective coaching conversations are anchored by a clear, measurable, and meaningful goal that a family member is working to achieve. The goal can be focused on any area or topic of their life that they authentically care about improving, changing, or creating new. Any area that they want support in making happen can be made into a specific and measurable goal.

- In the next thirty days, I choose to decide on what career field to go into.
- By the end of the month, I choose to lose five pounds and to eat healthy.
- In the next ninety days, I choose to make a job transition.
- This week, I choose to get an A on my upcoming math test.
- This month, I choose to get all house chores done on time.
- In the next two weeks I will have coaching conversations with my children.
- In the next thirty days, I choose to work and save $300 for a new billiards table for the family.
- This year, I choose to save $5,000 to take the family on a Family Legacy Venture trip to Florida.
- I choose to determine my core values and work on time mastery over the next ninety days.

Here is a list of topics and areas for everyone to consider when choosing a possible goal to work toward with the support of the family.

Potential Coaching Topics

- What am I tolerating that I really want to be different in my life? What exactly does different look like?
- What area of my life do I specifically want to improve over the next thirty days?
  Health, faith, school, job, finances, fun, relationships, energy level, time mastery, serving others?
- Where am I experiencing conflict in my life, and how do I resolve it in the next week?

- What areas of my life (skills, character, career, etc.) do I want to grow in over the next ninety days?
- What challenges am I facing that I want to overcome in the next period of time?
- What projects do I want to complete at home, work, or school in the next thirty days?
- What relationships need to be fixed, healed, stopped, or changed over the next period of time?
- What problems am I facing that need to be solved in the next time period?
- What opportunities are in front of me, and how will I decide what to do?

Each family member decides for themselves what exactly they want to be coached on. Once they have set a clear, measurable, and meaningful goal, it's time for the coaching conversation. The goals may need to be age appropriate for small children.

The Coaching Conversation

Coaching conversations can happen anytime between family members and are a true gift to one another. However, during the regular Family Legacy Model protocols, brief and focused coaching conversations that occur one person at a time for five or ten minutes each, as time permits, are so valuable.

Here are the five simple questions for the coach (leader) to ask:

1. What's important to you today (current goal)?
2. What are the challenges and possible solutions?
3. What are you learning?
4. What will you do before our next conversation?
5. How can we help?

Nearly all the talking that happens in a coaching conversation is done by the person being coached (coachee). The coach only asks the five questions while everyone else listens quietly. Very brief advising may be helpful if the coachee is stuck. As a rule, the coach speaks 20 percent of the time, and the coachee speaks 80 percent of the time.

So much more can be learned about how to be a more effective coach. I enjoy training coaches as much as anything else I get to do. However, keep it simple for best results. Don't overcomplicate things. Don't solve the coachee's problems for them. Help them find solutions for themselves. You will be glad you did when you see them grow before your very eyes.

Additional important guidelines for successful coaching conversations are as follows:

- Be a great listener, not an advisor, teller, or lecturer. Be quick to listen and slow to speak as a coach.
- Don't push your own agenda. Allow the coachee to own their own process, decisions, and actions.
- Be curious and use your limited 20 percent talk time to ask a few good questions. Explore.
- Keep the environment safe. Do not allow criticism, sarcasm, or cutting remarks by anyone.
- Keep it simple. Follow the five coaching questions listed above.
- Make sure there are clear and measurable goals to start with and actions to end with each coaching conversation.
- Stay positive and supportive through the entire coaching conversation.

If you want to focus on learning and implementing just one thing out of this book, integrate these two practices—emotional intelligence and a coach approach—into your family life. You'll be grateful you did.

If you have an interest in growing in your skills as a coach, consider taking The Coach Approach to Family e-course on our website or attending one of our workshops.

Important Tips for Effectively Leading Family Legacy Protocols

Many of the tools and processes contained in the Family Legacy Protocols are easy and straightforward, requiring only the thoughtful attention and consistent use by you and your family. Using the Family Legacy tools we have created for you help make it even easier. You can access all of the tools online by going to www.culturalarchitects.org.

However, there are several protocols that are what I call experiential learning modules. These are planned exercises for the family to experience together and require a leader or a facilitator to properly guide everyone through the experience for maximum insight and benefit. Mom or dad can be the leader, or you can reach out to our office, and we can supply you with support. This is also a good reason to apply the protocols in a small group.

The EQ (Emotional Intelligence) Protocol, the Identity Protocol, the Ritual Protocol, the MISSION Protocol, and the Impartation Protocol all contain exercises that require someone to skillfully facilitate the exercise.

You may be the do-it-yourself type who is eager and ready to dive in and make it happen. Great! Go for it!

Be aware of how you are showing up in the exercises. Are you getting all the value out of it? Are you clear in how to lead the delicate healing modules or the family identity pieces? If you are, wonderful! If you are finding it difficult and get in over your head, remember that we are here to help you. We have created small group leader training to address this need as well.

Reach out to our office and one of our coaches or facilitators. We are here to both equip you and, in some cases, facilitate for you through a number of workshops, coaching services, and even the full-on Family Legacy Encounter Workshop where we take your entire family through the whole process in your home or retreat environment.

If you are the brave one and ready to go, here are the most critically important tips for how you can succeed and effectively facilitate the exercises. If you follow these tips, your likelihood of getting great value from the exercises increases exponentially. If you do not follow these tips, you simply will not get as much value from the exercises. In some cases, you may even create problems that have to be addressed again later.

I'm not trying to scare anyone. But I do want you and your family to get the most out of your Family Legacy journey. Please take these tips seriously and give them the value they deserve. They are all very important or I wouldn't take the time and space to include them.

Facilitator Tips
Neutrality

Being neutral means that you are calm and steady emotionally throughout leading the module. It also means that you are aware of your own personal agenda and where you want to take the conversation or lead the participants, and you choose not to. You allow participants to respond authentically and to follow their own train of thought without overdirecting them to a certain conclusion. If you find yourself being offensive or defensive, it is a clue that you are not neutral.

When a facilitator is not neutral, they insert themselves into the exercise and make themselves and their own opinions an issue. They use their own definitions and language to tell people what they are saying or meaning. As a result, participants shut down, push back, clam up, or give up on sharing their own thoughts and feelings because the facilitator just made it about themselves.

Having a neutral facilitator allows people to own their own thoughts and respond much more authentically. This is one reason to consider having the support of a skilled coach or facilitator. Neutrality makes the environment feel safe and open to participants.

Openness

Great facilitators are open to how things have to look. Openness means that you are willing to follow the flow of conversation and responses as they develop outside of the box.

For example, if a participant begins sharing about a wound or a dream and they get emotional along with others in the exercise, the facilitator would mindfully pause and address what's coming up and allow the process of sharing, forgiveness, or healing to happen instead of insensitively pushing ahead to get the answer to the question that was asked in order to complete the exercise in a particular way.

Don't Personalize

A facilitator cannot be effective when drawn into a confrontation, blame game, justifying past behavior kind of scenario. Don't take the bait. Don't make yourself the issue. Let the issue with each participant be the issue that is in play. Let them own their own feeling and thinking. This is important.

Don't Assume

Don't do it. One of the biggest problems in relationships, communication, and facilitating alike is making assumptions. The truth is we do not know for sure what the thinking in a person's heart is behind what they are feeling, saying, or doing. Neuroscience tells us that individuals aren't even aware of their own thinking underneath their behavior and feelings 85 percent of the time. Do not assume why someone says or does something. Do not ascribe motives to people in life and as a facilitator. Assuming almost always guarantees a misunderstanding, a judgment, a pushback, possibly even hurt feelings and a big mess.

Be Curious

Staying curious is like a gold mine when it comes to facilitating. Coming from the place of "I don't know, but I want to know" is powerful. Curiosity will help you stay neutral and open and keep you from making distracting assumptions. It will assist you in not personalizing comments and being a much better listener. After all, as a facilitator, what you want to deliver is a clean process for participants to become aware of their own thinking and experience authentically.

Be Safe

Do not make people pay a price for sharing vulnerably their thoughts, wounds, experiences, dreams, questions, and more. You will shut everyone down. By paying a price, I mean embarrassing them, minimizing them, being sarcastic, getting angry with them, making fun of them, blaming them, and so on. If it isn't safe to share without fear of punishment, no one will.

Be Vulnerable

Because you are a part of the family and a participant as well as a facilitator, you will be taking your own turn responding to the exercise that you are leading. When you share, be the example to others of how you want everyone to show up in the exercise. Being vulnerable means that you risk and share the really deep things that you are more comfortable keeping hidden. Share your struggles, mistakes, pains, lessons, and feelings. If you do, so will everyone else. This creates great value and lasting bonds of love, empathy, and trust for the entire family.

Listen Carefully

This is a whole chapter or book of its own. The better you listen, the better you will lead the exercise. Don't dominate the airwaves. Let people talk it out to the end of their thought as much as possible. Some of the most important communication happens when you do not fill the silence after a person pauses. They will fill the silence if you don't, and it's usually profound. In addition, expert listening includes paying close attention to the speaker's eye contact, body language, tone of voice, posture, word choice, emotion, and your intuitive sense of their emotions. Good listening helps you form the next question to ask.

Use the online tools and reach out for help. I've included in this book the basics in how to carry out the exercises, tools, planning, and processes. Follow the guidelines laid out for you. If you need more detail or other support, please reach out. We have workbooks, video guides, workshops, coaches, and facilitators to partner with you in your Family Legacy journey.

Bottom Line

If you feel confident to follow the tips and are good, give it a go. You can do this! At the same time, be aware and honest with yourself. If you are having difficulty effectively leading a module, stop.

- Get help. Visit our website or contact our office.
- Look into using the workbook and video guide.
- Talk with a Family Legacy coach who can help you be effective in facilitating the modules.
- Have a Family Legacy coach facilitate the module(s) for you.
- Attend a Family Legacy workshop to learn how to better facilitate the modules yourself.
- Have the Family Legacy team come in and lead your family in a Family Legacy Encounter Weekend where we take care of all the facilitating so you can engage and enjoy the process with your family.

A Word about Age Considerations

For the most part, children can participate in the protocols. Children twelve and older will have little problem participating in the exercises and understanding the material. You may need to help children between five and twelve understand and participate in the exercises. With a little extra work and explanation, they can fully participate. Children under five or those with a short attention span may or may not be able to fully participate. Use your discretion on this. As much as possible, we want every family member, no matter the age, to participate.

Resources and Help in Your Family Legacy Journey

You are not alone in your Family Legacy journey. We have developed a number of resources to support you as you work to understand and implement the protocols. If you are having difficulty of any kind, don't quit. Don't give up. Reach out.

Contact our office, and we will do all we can to help you. A full listing of products, services, workshops, and resources is outlined in chapter 12 and available online:

Family Legacy Membership Subscription

Keynote Messages (Invite Randy to speak at your church or organization.)

Conferences (Invite Randy to come speak or deliver a training track at your denominational, organizational, or church conference.)

Family Legacy Coaching Services

Family Legacy Workshops for leaders, congregations, parents

Family Legacy Small Group Leaders Workshop and Certification

Family Legacy Family Camp Encounter

Family Legacy E-courses, workbooks, and video curriculum

Family Legacy Encounter Weekends

The Coach Approach to Family (e-courses)

The Family Legacy Model and Protocols In-Depth Mastery Training (e-courses)

Family Legacy Coach Certification (e-courses)

Family Legacy Small Group Leaders Training (e-courses)

Strategic Partnership Opportunities

Chapter 5
Family Legacy EQ

The purpose of the Family Legacy EQ (Emotional Intelligence) Protocol is to create a family environment of safety, trust, support, forgiveness, love, purpose, and fun. The work a family does in this space will profoundly impact the family experience and the trajectory of the family line for future generations to come.

Why start here?

Why is the first protocol equipping the family on how they will and will not treat one another in the Family Legacy journey together and in everyday life moving forward?

Because families don't always treat one another well. Getting together with family is more often avoided than you may realize. There are reasons why families haven't done a masterful job at building successful generational legacies. Namely, they don't get along. Unresolved wounding, not knowing how to heal and move forward, and simply not knowing how to do family well top the list. Families must want to gather together, be vulnerable with one another, and experience a safe environment if they are going to be successful at building a family legacy.

People have rarely been taught how to successfully build a family. Even fewer have been shown how to do it, and even fewer have shown their children how to do it and so on. Most of us just go with what we know, hope for the best, and learn a few tips here and there when the wheels come off the tracks. The how-to-do-family school is our own upbringing along with our own trial and error. Wouldn't it be valuable to have some family lessons in order to grow and experience how to build a healthy family as designed?

The Family Legacy EQ Protocols are tools and exercises to show families the following:

- how to listen to one another, understand one another, and honor one another
- how to properly give and receive feedback in a healthy way
- how to be self-aware
- how to take personal responsibility
- how to understand the EQ personality dynamics of the family
- how to not make assumptions and not assign ill motives to others
- how to shape the culture of their home with a Family Social Covenant
- how to mindfully make and keep agreements to build and protect trust
- how to forgive, heal, and restore family relationships
- how to experience healthy conflict
- how to support one another in the pursuit of goals and dreams
- how to effectively steward the environment and create a safe, trusting, supportive, loving, purposeful, and fun family

Q: Why is it uncomfortable for some members of families to be together?

1. Because much of our wounding and deepest pain in life has its genesis in the family, and we hate pain. Unfortunately, most people would rather avoid and cope with the pain instead of doing what it takes to heal. It doesn't have to be that way. Many people are more committed to comfort than they are to what they say they really want (healthy families).
2. Whether it is the family line and genetic fallout from generations past that has prewired us, or the traumatic experiences of our own childhood in our family of origin, or the hurts in our own nuclear family, getting families together in one place at one time to get along and commit to do the Family Legacy work together with a good attitude may be challenging for many.

The truth is that most people have not experienced the way a healthy family treats one another in their day-to-day interactions. We are generally unaware of the boundaries, protocols, and practices required to make family interactions safe, trusting, fun, supportive, loving, and purposeful. That alone can create so much stress and negative expectations in the minds and emotions of family members that they choose to not engage or even show up. They simply refuse to participate by any means available.

In addition, many individuals are still carrying baggage around with them full of unresolved family wounds and pain. It is difficult for many people to have kind, thoughtful, vulnerable, and rational conversations with family members because the noise from the past is so loud and the assumption that it will always be that way is so engrained.

Avoiding the tension and staying comfortable leads to coping with the way it really is. Coping is where the collective effort goes instead of working through obstacles and solving problems so that a new and purposeful family experience and legacy can be lived. And families become experts at avoidance and denial, joking and blaming, yelling and silence, medicating and distracting, all the way to the point of never speaking to each other again.

To leave a meaningful family legacy requires getting uncomfortable, facing challenges, and taking personal responsibility for the way in which each member shows up. And it's worth it. Once a family faces the issues, takes responsibility, and offers forgiveness, the whole environment will shift.

You may say, "Yeah, but it's hard." It may be. However, it doesn't have to be. How hard it is for you is your choice, at least as much as it depends on you. Engage with the protocols with your heart and watch how quickly and dramatically things will change.

Just how hard it is to face this stuff varies for numerous reasons:

- the age of your children
- the dynamic of your family (e.g., divorce, single-parent, blended family, sickness, etc.)
- the degree of pain and wounding generationally and currently
- the degree of shame, guilt, resentment, or bitterness around unresolved issues
- the degree of self-awareness and personal responsibility demonstrated by family members
- how safe each family member feels within the family

- the willingness to put the swords down, stop blaming, and start loving
- the willingness of family members to give and receive forgiveness
- and more

The EQ Protocols have a way of addressing these variables while bringing everyone together and onto the same page with a common set of guidelines, mind-sets, and expectations about how we will do family moving forward.

One thing I've observed is how differently people react to the Family Legacy vision and protocols. Here are a few common reactions that have all happened very recently.

As I shared the vision with an up-and-coming executive, his gaze fell downward and blank, and his eyes began to well up with tears. He shared how this all seemed too good to be true, and to think about what may be possible, how badly he wanted that, and the pain of the realization of what he missed out on with his parents and whether it could still happen. All of this was expressing itself on his face and out of his mouth.

When I shared with a pastor the thought of getting together with his family of origin and what this work was about, he interrupted me and began to say how his skin was crawling and he was shivering at the thought of getting together with them. He also shared how that meant for him that it was exactly what God wanted him to do because staying comfortable was seldom good for him in the long run.

In talking with a friend about recent breakthroughs with my children and the work, he replied, "When is this book going to be finished? Can I get the first copy? Can you show me how to do this with my family?"

Another friend said to me, "I don't think I can stand being around my family long enough to go through this with them. All they will want to do is joke, argue, or blame me for everything."

People have very different responses, expectations, assumptions, and emotions around the thought of doing something new and different with family members.

The truth is, for any inside-out transformation to last and become a meaningful legacy, wounds have to be healed, safety and support have got to be demonstrated, trust and purpose have to be injected, and love has to touch everyone, while being fun.

The way to bring everyone in the family who is willing onto the same page and into the same mind-sets is the Emotional Intelligence Protocols. Your family will learn together, create together, forgive together, heal together, plan together, and connect together while learning life skills that apply to all areas of life.

You are setting a solid foundation for how to create a family environment that is worthy of being passed on as a legacy. If it isn't attractive, meaningful, and rewarding to be around the family, our children won't want to be, and they certainly won't want to pass it on.

EQ Definition, Value, and Framework

> Wise people are builders. They build families, businesses, communities.
> … And through intelligence and insight their enterprises are established and endure. (Proverbs 24:3 TPT)

It takes intelligence and insight to establish a family legacy that will endure. More specifically, it takes emotional intelligence and relational insight to avoid identity drift, to self-govern well, and to steward the family as designed. After all, you may possess the intelligence to send a rocket to the moon or to use chemistry to create a new medicine, but you may not know how to truly resolve a conflict with a spouse or forgive a parent who has deeply hurt you. You may have the insight to make a fortune on Wall Street or run a Fortune 100 company, but you may not know how to create a safe, trusting, and supportive environment in your home. All of the intelligence in the world in your field of expertise doesn't mean you have the emotional intelligence required to do family well, let alone the relational insight it requires to leave an enduring legacy.

Definition

The Family Legacy EQ (Emotional Intelligence) Protocol is a set of exercises that equips families with a process to create an environment of safety, trust, support, forgiveness, love, purpose, and fun for their family. As a family discovers the emotional intelligence and relational insight these exercises deliver, they are empowered to love one another authentically. They are taught to use EQ tools for healthy communication, conflict resolution, self-awareness, personal responsibility, and so much more. The skills learned can be applied to every aspect of life and provide our children with valuable tools for success in life and leadership.

What Is Emotional Intelligence?

According to Daniel Goleman, author of *Emotional Intelligence,* "emotional intelligence (EI/EQ) is the ability to monitor one's own and other people's emotions, to discriminate between different emotions and label them appropriately, and to use emotional information to guide thinking and behavior."

Value

To do family powerfully, we must be able to understand ourselves and our family members deeply and use that intelligence effectively with one another. We need to know how we think and why we think that way, how we feel and why we feel that way, how we make choices and why we make them the way we do.

The greater our understanding of one another, the greater our ability to meet one another's needs, speak one another's language, and create true win/win solutions. The fewer assumptions and judgments we will make toward one another. The more misunderstandings we will avoid. The more we can be supportive in helpful ways. The more we can govern our own expectations and reactions when relating to family members who see things differently than we do. EQ is a big deal when it comes to relating to others.

According to Goleman, the fundamentals of EI /EQ include the following:

- self-awareness
- self-management
- social awareness
- the ability to manage relationships

In spending the last fifteen years in this space, I have come to see the framework of emotional intelligence as these five key practices. Growing in the understanding of these five skills and your mastery of their use in your family, your career, and your relationships will transform your leadership, your results, and your life.

- self-awareness
- personal responsibility
- sustained action
- empathy
- trust

The framework of the EQ Protocol delivers experiences of the five key skills of emotional intelligence within the context of family relationships. The results of learning and practicing these EQ skills instantly and measurably begin to influence every aspect of life, bringing new competencies of self-governing and stewardship.

Self-Awareness

Definition: conscious knowledge of one's own character, thinking, feelings, motives, and desires.

Self-awareness means knowing your values, personality, needs, habits, emotions, strengths, weaknesses, and so on. With a sense of who you are and a vision of the person you want to become, a plan for professional or personal development can be created. Self-awareness is having a clear perception of your personality, including strengths, weaknesses, thoughts, beliefs, motivation, and emotions. Self-awareness allows you to understand other people, how they perceive you, your attitude, and your responses to them in the moment. Being self-aware also enables you to separate what is your part, your perception, your assumptions, or your lens from those of others. Having this understanding empowers you to communicate more effectively, empathize more meaningfully, and govern your expectations with maturity and wisdom.

Personal Responsibility

Definition: conscious awareness, practice and ownership of authority, control, power, leadership, management, influence and duty over one's self (thoughts, actions, behaviors, feelings, perceptions and words).

Personal responsibility is the reality that human beings choose, initiate, or otherwise cause their own actions, and because we do, we can be held morally accountable or legally liable.

It is the acceptance and agreement that life happens *from* me, not *to* me. My experience of my life is up to me. The choices I make knowingly and unknowingly to interpret, respond, and create in response to life is up to me.

Sustained Action

Definition: the ongoing and continued intentional effort applied consistently over time.

In order to receive the benefits of emotional intelligence, we must continue to actively engage in its practices. EQ is powerless if it remains in the realm of knowledge or theory alone. EQ is more than a concept or a teaching. Effective EQ requires the ongoing intentional action and work of its five pillars: self-awareness, personal responsibility, sustained action, empathy, and trust

Action in the form of setting goals and supporting one another with a simple coach approach is a transformational approach to doing family. This is work, friends. Some of the most challenging work you will ever do is work on yourself. And it's worth it. Consistency creates a certainty that becomes a strong foundation to build upon.

Empathy

Definition: understanding; the psychological identification with or vicarious experiencing of the feelings, thoughts, or attitudes of another.

My father taught a class on empathy when I was a boy. He was a banker by trade, not a teacher. It's the only formal class I can remember him leading in my life. He chose to define empathy this way: "walking in another person's shoes with full understanding." He was teaching about a core value and strong Bixby family trait that we all carry in our veins to this day.

What happens when we truly and deeply understand the journey of another human being? In some way, we carry in our DNA the collective generational and volitional life experiences that contain fear and worry, abuse and abandonment, rejection and loneliness, hopes and dreams, victories and accomplishments, and so much more. When we become aware of the wounds, scars, and experiences of another person, along with the thinking they have developed to cope with all that they have been through, something magical happens. We understand and can find mercy and grace in our dealings with them. They make sense to us, along with their words and actions that made no sense before we gained that understanding. Empathy is an EQ super skill.

Trust

Definition: reliance on the integrity, strength, ability, surety, etc., of a person or thing; confidence. The confident expectation of something; hope; to rely or depend on, to believe.

Trust is another EQ super skill. Trust creates an environment of goodwill, peace, and certainty. Trust makes taking the risk of being vulnerable acceptable. Trust allows us to let the walls that protect us down in order to be known authentically. When there is trust in a relationship or in a family, it is okay to show up the way we really are without the fear of exposure, punishment, shame, or greater wounding. When we have the confident belief and hope that others are for us and won't hurt us intentionally, we are able to live vulnerably, transparently, and authentically. We feel safe to open up about our hurts and weaknesses, our hopes, and our dreams. We rest in the certainty that sharing our soul will be respected and kept confidential.

Whether in a family, the workplace, or an individual relationship, having an environment of trust is vital to the productive function of those involved. A high-trust culture addresses the core needs of those in it. When we are in a high-trust family, we are more apt to experience the following:

- acceptance: I (we) belong here
- significance: I (we) matter here
- congruence: I (we) agree here
- excellence: I (we) excel here

Once again, the purpose of the Family Legacy EQ Protocols is to create a family environment of safety, trust, support, forgiveness, love, purpose, and fun.

Don't leave this out of your journey because you are afraid. Fear will rob you of the family and the legacy you want. Engage fully. Ask for support. Go for it! You will be glad you did, and so will your generations ...

Tips for Environment and Execution

As you prepare to take your family through the EQ Protocols, please review the sections in chapter 4. Following the guidelines is essential for getting the most out of the exercises for the benefit of your family. In addition, here are a few additional tips for successful execution.

Environment and Execution

- The EQ protocols are most effective in a low-stress, informal, private setting with only actual family members and participants. No observers, unless they are one of our coaches or facilitators present to assist your family or you are doing this with a small group.
- Everyone should be fed and watered with ample time to complete each exercise without rushing things. You may want to end the time together with some fun, a game and some laughs if appropriate.
- The room should be quiet and free from distractions. Cell phones, digital devices, television sets, and music should all be turned off.
- Secure the proper resources needed for the modules (e.g., blank paper and pens, printed worksheets, workbooks, markers, flip chart, tools, etc.).
- At the most basic level, an experiential learning module has four parts:
    - setup—where a leader talks about the purpose, value, and opportunities of the experience along with the detailed instructions of what to do
    - execution—where members have the experience
    - learning—where participants share what they learned in the experience, about themselves, their thinking, others, the topic, the world, and more
    - application—where participants share how they will apply the learning in specific areas of their lives

- Each EQ exercise in the protocol has a brief description in the next section of this chapter and a tool for executing each exercise online in our Family Legacy Toolbox. www.culturalarchitects.org
- You will find a listing of all the Family Legacy Tools available online in chapter 11 for your use. If you prefer bound paper workbooks containing the tools, you can order those on our website as well. Chapter twelve contains training and resources to further assist you in executing the protocols with your family.
- In preparation, review the entire exercise ahead of time so that you know what to expect.
- Allow enough time for each person to fully answer the questions or perform the exercise.
- Be willing to draw out the thoughts and feelings of participants as they are processing the work and sharing.
- Make sure everyone gets their time to share or be the focus of the family, equally and as needed.
- It is vitally important that you keep the environment safe for everyone. Do not allow criticism, sarcasm, cynical remarks, rude comments, and so on. This is not the time or the place for that. Make sure that no one pays the price for being vulnerable.
- Stay open to how things will play out.
- Deal with things as they come up.
- Reach out for help if you get stuck, don't know what to do, or if things go astray.
- You may decide to join the Family Legacy monthly subscription for additional support, attend a workshop, purchase the video guides, or request coaching and facilitating support.
- Have fun!

EQ Protocols

The core experiential exercises for the Family Legacy EQ Protocol below are transformative. They are designed to produce deep and lasting change to the way we self-govern and steward the family. You may want to review "The Inside-Out Transformation Solution" section in chapter 2 to understand exactly how and the science behind them.

Getting through the exercises is not a race. They take as long as they take. They could be completed in a day or two, as we do within our workshops. They can also be done one at a time over several weeks, as well as anywhere in between. The important thing is to consistently work on them and complete them at the beginning of your Family Legacy journey. You will lay a solid foundation to build on if you do. This protocol is first for that reason.

Remember, we are here to help you if you find leading these exercises to be difficult. Contact our office and talk with one of our coaches, make arrangements for us to lead your family through the exercises, or attend one of our workshops or e-courses. Don't skip the exercises. They are a critical piece to establishing a healthy environment vital to an enduring legacy.

Certain EQ protocols below may be difficult for young children to participate in. Children age twelve or above should be able to engage in the exercises. You may consider going through the protocols as parents, grandparents, and children above twelve years of age. Younger children between five and twelve can participate at age- and maturity-appropriate levels for all six protocols.

I have written a brief description of each of the experiential exercises below. You will understand the purpose and value of the exercises as you read. You will want to go to our website to download the editable PDF Family Legacy Protocol Tools for each exercise to walk you through the execution of each one step-by-step. www.culturalarchitects.org

EQ Protocol Descriptions

EQ Exercise 1—Personal Investigator EQ Exercise

The purpose of the Personal Investigator EQ Exercise is to grow in the knowledge and experience of emotional intelligence practically by learning to use a series of questions, a process, that empowers you to change your results by changing your thinking and agreements. This exercise is an inside-out transformation process.

If there was one tool, one process that I could give you that would increase your emotional intelligence, it would unquestionably be this one. This tool is the starting point of your journey of growth when it comes to emotional intelligence. This process used properly and consistently, will become an engrained practice that becomes a natural part of how you think and self-govern. It will become the way that you choose to show up in the execution of the other protocols, in the everyday of family life or relationships, and the everyday of career and ministry life. When you choose to use it in partnership with the Holy Spirit on an everyday and all-of-the-time basis, you will be walking in the Spirit and self-governing your own soul at a whole new level.

We aren't consciously making our decisions and producing our results most of the time. Our subconscious belief systems are making our decisions for us, and we are for the most part unaware of it.

Neuroscientists tell us that more than 85 percent of the decisions we make are made by our subconscious belief systems, or as the Bible says it, "For as a man thinks in their heart, so is he" (Proverbs 23:7 NKJV). Our heart-level thinking is the autopilot that is running all the time underneath our awareness. These engrained patterns of thinking shape our beliefs and define our sense of reality about the following:

- what is possible and impossible
- what is safe and unsafe
- what is right and wrong
- what is good and bad
- what being a man or a woman means
- how we see God
- how we see ourselves
- how we see others
- how much we care about what others think about us
- how we see money
- how we see work
- our assumptions about cause and effect
- so much more

This is by design and works flawlessly ... until it doesn't. By design, we were created to receive truth from God, and we receive that truth by our choice to agree with it. When truth is programed into our heart or our subconscious, we are equipped to make good decisions that lead to good results and good outcomes.

However, if deception replaces truth at the beginning of this process, we are in trouble. The deception acts like the truth, and our design goes to work to produce the reality of this thinking. Once we receive the deception as truth, with our choice to agree with it, deception is programmed into our heart or our subconscious. Once locked in, we are then equipped to make decisions based on lies that lead to bad results and costly outcomes.

Further complicating this is that we are mostly unaware of the lies and deception that we are unknowingly choosing to agree with. These deceptive belief systems come both from our genetic donors of generations past as well as our own life experiences processed through deception. These belief systems that disagree with truth are cleverly hidden deep within our hearts and continue to produce bad results in our families, our relationships, our businesses, and our communities—until some event, experience, or tool comes along that brings us a revelation of the ingrained thinking and exposes the deception hidden deep in our hearts.

Once we are aware of the thinking and the deception, we can consciously evaluate them and the results they are producing in our lives. With this new awareness, we are then able to make new choices about what we believe moving forward. We decide to disagree with the old and deceptive way of thinking, and we decide to agree with the new, wise, and truthful way of thinking.

Once we choose to agree with a new way of thinking and live that way, we make new decisions and get new results.

This tool is Romans 12:2 (TPT) in practice, "Stop imitating the ideals and opinions of the culture around you but be inwardly transformed by the Holy Spirit through a total reformation of how you think. This will empower you to discern God's will as you live a beautiful life, satisfying and perfect in his eyes."

Imagine a tool that you can choose to use that will transform your life and results from the inside out as your mind is renewed through the process.

The Personal Investigator EQ Tool is available online with step-by-step instructions, but here is the basic framework.

Personal investigators look for clues. This process starts with you discovering your own clues. Pay attention to your behavior and feelings.

What you are doing or not doing (behavior)? What are you feeling? Once you have this awareness, proceed through the following series of questions.

- What is the thinking in my heart causing this behavior or feeling?
- Where else in my life is this thinking showing up?
- What are the costs and benefits of this thinking?
- What is my commitment moving forward (what do I choose to think)?

This is a powerful process of self-governing. It is a tool for inside-out transformation. It is a starting point for greater emotional intelligence that can lead to better choices that can lead to creating a healthier environment in your family. Using this tool will help you to create a loving, safe, fun, trusting, and supportive environment in your family.

Use this tool as you execute all of the other Family Legacy EQ Exercises, all of the Family Legacy Protocols, and indeed in all of the days of your life.

EQ Exercise 2—The Family Legacy Social Covenant EQ Exercise

The purpose of the Family Legacy Social Covenant EQ Exercise is for everyone in the family to create a set of agreements and expectations to govern the family environment in the home. These agreements establish the family culture, with everyone weighing in to ensure their buy-in. This culture-shaping exercise and tool establishes guidelines for how everyone will show up in the day-to-day and for the Family Legacy journey, thus creating certainty, trust, value, personal responsibility, and empathy in your family culture.

The idea and effectiveness of a social contract is not new. Our nation and our culture are established upon a type of social contract. Our Constitution and the laws of our country provide a framework of agreements that in turn shape our culture. The social contract is being used with great effectiveness to improve the culture and performance of public elementary schools, major corporations, churches, and professional sports teams. It works!

Applying this practice to the family will create a culture in the home where everyone has a value and a voice. By its very design, the covenant provides a framework for understanding family identity, self-governing effectively, and stewarding the family as designed. It makes the family an attractive and empowering environment where healthy relationships can thrive.

While the Family Legacy Social Covenant EQ Tool is available free on our website with step-by-step instructions, here are the four questions to ask your family:

- What do you (children) need/want from me (parent(s))?
- What do I (parent(s)) need/want from you (children)?
- What do we need/want from each other?
- How will we handle a broken covenant or agreement?

Do not let the simplicity of this process fool you. This is a potent tool as long as:

- everyone engages authentically
- everyone engages wholeheartedly
- everyone is given a voice for input
- everyone gives their full agreement to abide by the finished covenant
- everyone follows through with agreements
- everyone reviews the covenant regularly for effectiveness and adaptation

This process can be used in marriage, in friendship, in business, and in any organization or leadership structure. It is an effective culture-shaping tool to have in your toolbox.

EQ Exercise 3—The Healthy Communication Empathetic Listening EQ Exercise

The purposes of the Healthy Communication Empathetic Listening EQ Exercise are to equip the family with the important communication skill of empathetic listening; to equip the family to listen for understanding beyond listening to respond; to set an expectation in the family that it is safe to speak, that everyone has a voice that needs to be heard, and that everyone matters; to eliminate misunderstandings, assumptions, and judgments; all for the purpose of more deeply connecting with family members in an environment of honor, safety, and love.

I believe that one of the most important qualities we can possess is empathy. If I were asked to pick one competency that I believe would make the biggest immediate difference in my relationships, my faith, or my business, I would say empathetic listening.

Perhaps a good way to understand what empathetic listening is, is to first look at what it is not. Dr. Melvyn Toomey published a paper where he identified what he called "Six ways of Automatic Listening." He described them as default ways that human beings most often listen to others and process the information that's coming in. According to Toomey, these listening styles are automatic or default because we don't consciously choose to listen these ways; we just do.

In brief, here are the six ways of automatic listening Toomey describes. They describe what empathetic listening is *not*:

1. Agree/disagree—unending assessment
2. Personalizing—taking everything personally
3. Already know it / not clean slate
4. Safety—looking good at all costs
5. Accurate/inaccurate describing or labeling
6. Resignation—won't matter any way

All the above listening styles have one thing in common. The energy and conversation that is happening in the mind of the listener is focused on themselves, not the one who is speaking. They are allowing in just enough information from the speaker to empower their own thoughts and conversation with themselves about what they think about what is being said.

This is the core distinction between automatic listening and empathetic listening. Empathetic listening is quiet. It starts with a clean slate in the heart and mind of the listener. The listener takes in what the speaker is saying in order to fully understand what they are communicating period.

My father, Garry Bixby, defined empathy as "walking in another person's shoes with full understanding."

It is listening to fully understand the who, what, when, where, why, and how of the speaker. Empathetic listening starts here and then adds to this the emotions, facial expressions, body language, and tone of voice of the speaker.

All of this is done with a focus of energy on the speaker, not on the listener, for the purpose of fully understanding the experience of another human being.

When we are listened to this way, we feel honored, understood, and validated, and we experience the safety of being vulnerable and transparent, which only leads to deeper trust *every time*.

The Healthy Communication Empathetic Listening EQ Tool online will walk your family through a process, helping you recognize your automatic listening styles and how to grow in the skill of empathetic listening. www.culturalarchitects.org

EQ Exercise 4—The Healthy Communication Speaking the Truth in Love EQ Exercise

The purposes of the Healthy Communication Speaking the Truth in Love EQ Exercise are to equip the family with how to give and receive feedback in a healthy way; to avoid making assumptions about motives; to avoid misunderstandings and judgments; to ensure that family members receive the benefits of truth spoken in love instead of blame, accusation, sarcasm, or criticism; and to show the family how to take personal responsibility in both giving and receiving feedback. All of this keeps the family environment a safe and supportive one where family members help one another learn and grow.

Not getting accurate feedback is like a pilot flying a plane in the clouds with faulty instrument readings. He may be a gifted pilot, but if he has instruments that aren't giving him accurate readings, he will fly that plane right into the ground.

The same is true in marriage, family, friendships, business, and ministry. We must be able to give and receive good information in such a way that we can take productive action once it's received and understood.

However, it's complicated. What is said is one thing, how it is said is another, and how it is received is a whole other matter. Giving and receiving feedback is critical to the success of any relationship or endeavor. It will fail, and people will get hurt if this isn't managed properly.

Here is the challenge with all of this: "Life happens from you, not to you," according to Proverbs 4:23 (NASB) "Watch over your heart with all diligence, for from it *flow* the springs of life."

What does this mean in the context of feedback? It means that I am responsible for what I experience when I am giving and receiving feedback. I am not responsible for what is or is not said by others. However, I am responsible for choosing how to interpret what they say, and I am responsible for how I feel in response to what is said. I define and create my own feelings and behavior in response to feedback, and I can control that. I have the power to self-govern my thinking, my feelings, and my behaviors, so my experience of life flows from me, not to me.

Here are some important questions to ask yourself while giving and receiving feedback:

- What do I hear when others give me feedback?
- Do I speak openly and honestly when giving others feedback or do I hold back?
- What feelings or behavior come up for me when I give or receive feedback?
- What is the thinking in my heart creating these feelings or behavior?
- How can I self-govern effectively so that I experience good when giving or receiving feedback?

Our lenses (belief systems) create our experience of life.

The Healthy Communication Speaking the Truth in Love EQ Tool online walks your family through an exercise to grow in this very important skill. www.culturalarchitects.com

EQ Exercise 5—The OOOH NO! EQ Exercise

The purpose of the OOOH NO! EQ Exercise is to equip the family with a way to let go of resentment and bitterness in order to avoid self-destruction and to grow in love, forgiveness, conflict resolution, and problem-solving within the family context. Unresolved conflict is a deadly blow to any relationship, especially in the family. This exercise will create a pathway for resolving offenses in order to create a loving, supportive, and safe environment at home.

This exercise addresses one of the most self-destructive belief systems or mind-sets that keeps families disconnected and isolated from one another. When you are in this mind-set, you pay a price. This thinking is the chief cause of divorce, child abuse, crime, drug and alcohol abuse, and even war.

What's more, you've likely been in this mind-set in the last twenty-four hours! So, if this thinking is so self-destructive, why do you do it? Because it's a subconscious belief system in the heart that we are unaware of.

Below are the three parts to this mind-set that runs so quickly while cloaked and almost invisible to our awareness.

- offense—any negative emotional response to something you think was said or done
- opposition—putting up a wall or breaking off communication
- onslaught—the attempt to get even

If you are scratching your head trying to figure this one out, try answering these questions:

- Do you ever have a negative emotional response to a family member?
- Do you ever put up a wall, stop communicating with, or avoid a family member when you have that negative emotional response?
- Do you ever attempt to get even?

If you are a human being who is alive and breathing, your answer to all three of these questions is yes, and so it is in most of the human race. What's important to notice after acknowledging that you find yourself in this mind-set from time to time is that you are the one being harmed most when you are in it. It is self-destructive.

Bitterness and resentment are like taking poison and hoping that somebody else dies. It poisons the soul of the one who drinks of it, which is particularly troublesome given the way that so many people in our PC culture are offended so easily today. If the offense isn't addressed immediately in one of the three ways, opposition and onslaught follow closely on its heels, and it gets ugly fast.

When this happens in the family, people avoid one another, don't share openly and vulnerably with one another, and get in resistance to healthy flows of interaction with one another. They "forget" to clean up after themselves in the kitchen. They "forget" and leave the toilet seat up. They "forget" to be home on time for curfew. They choose to avoid conflict, cope with the distance, and begin a tit-for-tat response to wrongdoing. Perhaps an even more serious outcome of this expressed resistance is that now those you acted out upon find themselves locked into the same OOOH NO! mind-set, and round and round it goes.

When this happens, there is a deep breakdown of the kind of healthy environment in the home required for healthy family interaction and the creation of a powerful family legacy.

The remedy to this self-destructive belief system is to do the following:

1. Engage in open, honest, responsible communication.
2. Give a gift.
3. Forgive and let go.

We walk you through these solutions in the OOOH NO! EQ Tool found on our website. www.culturalarchitects.org

EQ Exercise 6—The Fact/Story EQ Exercise

The purpose of the Fact/Story EQ Exercise is to equip the family with a process to self-govern their healthy choice of responses to whatever life has to throw at them. This elite EQ process will empower the family to find the good in any situation—past, present, or future—and ensure the most valuable outcomes. This EQ exercise and tool will bring freedom to families from the lies that could ensnare them for decades. By self-governing their thinking, they can redefine their past, present, and future through active agreement with a good God and His wisdom. Romans 8:28 (NIV) in action: "And we know that in all things God works for the good of those who love him, who have been called according to his purpose."

We live in several realms at the same time as human beings. I want to address two of those realms in this exercise, the realm of fact and the realm of story or meaning. They are, in fact, two separate realms. However, difficulty occurs when we start to combine these two as if they are the same.

How would you define a fact? A fact is something that is definable, observable, and even measurable. It is objectively true. Whatever the date of this day is, it is a fact. It has a name and a measurement. Its beginning and end are definable and observable.

How would you define a story? A story is the interpretation or perception of what a fact means. It is the meaning assigned to a fact by a person's choice.

The first day of January each year can be measured and is a fact. This fact could have countless stories or meanings assigned to it by different people. One story for person A is that January 1 is a wonderful day for a fresh start. Person B has a different story, that January 1 is the worst day of the year because a loved one was killed on that day. Person C has yet another story for January 1 because, for them, it represents the best day of their lives due to the birth of their first child on that date. For person D, January 1 is another meaningless day among 364 other meaningless days in the year.

It is profoundly important to recognize that facts and stories are separate and not one in the same. They only become one in the same when a person chooses to connect a story to a fact. We each have been given the ability to choose what story or meaning we want to assign to any given fact.

Why is this important? Because healthy self-governing means that we are actively engaged in determining which story we will assign to life's facts that come our way. Actively choosing to agree with God and His meanings of a fact will bring life, freedom, peace, joy, and fruitfulness.

Poor self-governing means that we passively or unknowingly allow untruthful stories to be assigned to life's facts coming our way. Passively choosing to agree with a lie or with any other story that disagrees with God's version of a fact will bring death, bondage, frustration, anger, and deception.

The choice of which story to agree with around a fact is up to each individual.

Let me give an example: divorce

The fact of divorce is that two individuals who were previously legally married are no longer in a legal marriage relationship.

The stories around divorce are multiple and varied:

- Men are pigs.
- Women are controlling.
- Pain and suffering.
- Freedom and a new beginning.
- Financial devastation.
- Financial windfall.
- Children irreparably harmed.
- Children getting a taste of reality.

- All the child's fault.
- Not at all the child's fault.
- Rejection and betrayal.
- Act of personal integrity.
- Never love again.
- Finally, can love again.
- It's all my fault.
- It's not any of my fault.

I could go on all day with this. The meanings and stories that can be given to the dissolution of a marriage covenant are almost endless. So which story is true?

This is important. The one you choose to agree with is the one that will become what you experience. Life flows from you, not to you.

Once we choose to agree with a story, we connect it to a fact, and the mind-set around that fact is set. What happens next is that we go back out into life and start experiencing life as if that story is true, and we look to find confirmation of it by choosing to assign the same story to other facts in our lives.

For example, if I choose to agree with the story around a divorce that I am rejected, not enough, not valuable, and not ever going to find love again, then if I ever go out on dates again, I will read into every action of my date as confirming the story I've chosen to assign to me.

All of that to say this: we are not victims. We are responsible for self-governing our choices of agreement, and those choices will empower an ingrained pattern of thinking in our lives. Choose wisely. Choose to agree with God on His version of the facts.

This is one of the most powerful truths and EQ skills there are. Your choices of agreement will determine how you experience life. In addition, your choices will impact your family in profound ways both genetically and real-time experientially.

When we choose stories that agree with lies and deception, we are in trouble. Until we have a revelation and choose to agree with God's version of the facts, we are doomed to fail and to suffer. When we agree with God, we can turn all things into good for us, our families, and our generations.

The Fact Story EQ Tool on our website will walk your family through this step-by-step. Get ready to be empowered to self-govern like never before! www.culturalarchitects.org

EQ Exercise 7—The Love Without Hooks EQ Exercise

The purpose of the Love Without Hooks EQ Exercise is to equip the family with a process for experiencing the restoring power of forgiveness and unconditional love while setting themselves free from the torment of unforgiveness and unmet expectations. There are few things that shut us off from one another faster and divide us more deeply than unforgiveness. To maintain an environment of safety, trust, support, forgiveness, love, purpose, and fun in the family, forgiveness and properly managing our expectations is mandatory.

One of the obstacles that has come up for people as I have talked with them about applying the Family Legacy EQ Protocols is a concern of being vulnerable with their families in the protocols due to the presence of unresolved pain, unhealed wounds, and the discomfort of unforgiveness when the family is together.

I was in a place like this in a business relationship a few years ago. Someone had promised some important things and then not followed through on them as I understood them to have committed to. They had not met my expectations as we had agreed.

I was tormented by the injustice, the cost, the rejection, and the loss of an unfulfilled debt, and I reached out to a mentor for help. His advice to me was to choose to "love without hooks." He said to let it go. That sounds so easy now, but at the time, it was beyond me.

I canceled all my appointments the next day and got alone with God to get to the bottom of it. He led me through a process of questions, and as I answered them, I made some life-changing discoveries.

We will walk you through this entire process of questions in the Love Without Hooks EQ Tool, available free on our website, but here is the genesis of the tool.

Matthew 18:21–35 contains the parable of the unmerciful servant. It is the story about a man who was forgiven a great debt and set free, only then to go and demand that someone who owed him a small debt be thrown into jail for not paying it. He was then thrown back into jail to be tormented because he would not release the debt of what someone owed him.

Many aspects of this story struck me and are worth noting here:

- The man was forgiven five thousand lifetimes of wages, a huge debt.
- He chose not to forgive a debt of ninety days' wages owed to him.
- As a result of his unwillingness to forgive, he was delivered to the tormentors to be tormented in prison until the debt was paid, or forever.
- Jesus said, "So shall my heavenly Father do to you if you do not forgive from the heart the debts of others."

Bottom Line

If we hold debts and keep demands of what other people owe us, God will deliver us to be tormented based on our choice to not forgive the debt.

1. Ouch! But truth.
2. I took the time to answer the questions and let my demand for debt settlement go. I let go of my expectations around the promises, however legitimate, and I found healing. As a result, I was set free and restored to relationship and peace with those on my list almost immediately.
3. I've included this very list of questions in the Love Without Hooks EQ Tool.
4. Take the time to prayerfully answer them. Take your entire family through the exercise. You will be set free from the torment that you are imposing upon yourself.
5. Freedom is wonderful! Intimacy happens in the context of freedom. Change the environment of your home and your heart from one of prison and torment to one of freedom and unconditional love without hooks with forgiveness. It's worth it.

EQ Exercise 8—The Powerful/Powerless EQ Exercise

The purposes of the Powerful/Powerless EQ Exercise are to equip the family with a process and a tool to live a powerful and impactful life from a place of personal responsibility; to choose to experience life through a powerful lens of dreams, growth, happiness, and possibility instead of choosing to experience life through a powerless lens of excuses, blame, hopelessness, and settling for less. Your family legacy is dramatically impacted by your choice between the powerful and powerless mind-sets.

We are fearfully and wonderfully made as human beings in our design. In this design, our emotions play a critical role in the process of implanting mind-sets deep into our subconscious (hearts), both for good and bad. In times of trauma or a heightened emotional state, the genes in our DNA begin flashing and become open for expression orders. You may have heard it said that "What fires together wires together." Whatever thinking is present during the fire of trauma and high emotion wires into the genetic programing, and an ingrained pattern of thinking is established. It is in these instances that we are extremely vulnerable to negative and harmful mind-sets being programmed into our hearts, especially when we are children.

Have you ever been a victim? Have you ever found yourself in a set of circumstances that you didn't deserve to be in, that were out of your control? Have you ever experienced undeserved betrayal, rejection, or abuse? Have you ever been the victim of theft, false accusation, a no-fault car accident, or a violent crime? Most of us have vivid recollections of these kinds of victim experiences where we feel powerless.

Victim experiences tend to produce powerless mind-sets that reinforce the deceptive belief that life happens to me, not from me, and that I am just along for the ride. These deeply implanted lenses cause individuals to see the world with the shades of the following:

- I'm not in control.
- I'm not safe.
- It's hopeless.
- I can't recover.
- I am powerless to change my circumstances.
- It doesn't matter what I do; things won't change.
- That's just the way the world is.
- That's just the way men or women are.
- Other people can have life good but not me.
- I'm entitled to help and special treatment because I was wronged.
- Why dream and set goals when everything is out of my control?
- Why set high expectations only to have them smashed to pieces?
- I'm stuck in life and don't have what it takes to get going.
- I have to lower the bar and just settle for less than I want.

The powerless mind-set is a dream killer, a thief of energy and innovation, an enemy of joy and peace, a deception of our true identity, and a mortal wound to a meaningful family legacy.

And importantly, *it is a choice.*

Bad things happen to good people. In this world, we will all be victimized at some point and in some way, some worse than others. However, these experiences and the choice to agree with powerless mind-sets do not have to ruin our lives and undermine our legacies.

Those who choose to live life from powerless mind-sets tend to be angry, frustrated, depressed, critical people who complain and blame others for their circumstances. In many cases, these individuals choose self-destructive ways to cope with the negative emotional results of their choice to experience life as a powerless victim. We were made for more than this.

We have been given the power to make a different choice. We can choose to see these experiences through a different lens, a powerful lens. If I choose to believe that life happens from me, instead of to me, then I realize I can choose to look through a powerful lens at my life experiences and see my life through shades of the following:

- I'm am in control and personally responsible.
- I'm as safe as I choose to be.
- I'm hopeful.
- I can recover.
- I am powerful to change my circumstances.
- It matters what I do, and I can change things.
- This is how my world is.
- Every man and woman is responsible for how they are.
- I and everyone else can have a good life.
- I am responsible for my life and results.
- I have dreams and set goals to reach them because I can reach them.
- I am the only limit to what I can create with God and others.
- I'm growing and can overcome every obstacle put in my way.
- I don't have to settle for things.

Those who choose to live life from powerful mind-sets tend to be happy, focused, energetic, growing, problem-solving, get-stuff-done kind of people who take personal responsibility for their circumstances. They tend to make lemonade out of life's lemons and influence others to do the same. Powerful mind-sets lead to powerful lives, healthy families, growing businesses, thriving communities, and impactful legacies.

In the Powerful / Powerless EQ Tool online, we provide you with step-by-step instructions to discover where you may knowingly or unknowingly be choosing to experience life through a powerless victim lens. We will also show you your opportunity to choose a different way to experience life through a powerful, responsible lens. Your life and your legacy will transform before your eyes when you make the choice to live responsibly from your divine design.

EQ Exercise 9—The Personality Profile Comparison EQ Exercise*

The purposes of the Personality Profile EQ Exercise are to equip the family with a process and a tool to better know themselves and one another through the use of a leading EQ analytical tool; to grow in the insights of self-awareness and empathy as a family; to learn to speak one another's language; and to avoid assumptions, misunderstandings, and poor communication. The use of this tool will result in a more supportive, safe, and personally responsible environment in the family. Insights applied consistently from this tool can help ensure a lasting legacy.

The foundational scripture of this book is Proverbs 24:3–4. Contained in this text is this very important truth, "through intelligence and insight, their enterprises are established and endure" (TPT). Proverbs 4:7 (ESV) encourages us this way, "The beginning of wisdom is this: Get wisdom, and whatever you get, get insight."

The Family Legacy EQ Protocols are, by design, mechanisms for getting wisdom and, more specifically, for getting emotional intelligence and insight. They are more than motivation and conceptual theory. The exercises and tools are intentional and practical; they must be experienced to gain the wisdom they carry.

For nearly thirty years, I have chosen to invest my professional life into building leaders. Through various ministry and business endeavors, I have trained, mentored, counseled, and coached leaders in a myriad of circumstances, organizations, and challenges.

All of that to say that one of the most important and impactful insights I wish I had known starting out is that having robust insight into a person's personality style unlocks their individualized blueprint for growth and maturity. The understanding and insight of the following increases empathy, one of the EQ super skills:

- how a person thinks
- what a person values
- how a person makes decisions
- what a person prefers to do and not do
- a person's priorities, motivations, fears, and limitations
- a person's natural strengths and weaknesses

When we understand ourselves and others, especially in our own family, we have insight that empowers us to navigate life's challenges with wisdom and intentionality.

The EQ insights gained through this top-tier analytic personality tool, when put to use, will result in better communication, conflict resolution, problem-solving, and healthier, more connected family relationships overall. This exercise will create one-on-one personality comparisons within and between pairings of all family members, with insights and recommendations for improving each relationship.

I have found that these insights will only help *every time* they are used!

The Personality Profile Comparison EQ Tool will guide you through a personality-assessment exercise. Additional tools are available through our office.

★This particular tool and one-on-one comparison reports are available for a small fee through our office.

Once again, go to our website to download the editable PDF Family Legacy Protocol Tools for each exercise to walk you through the execution of each one step-by-step. www.culturalarchitects.org

Chapter 6
Family Legacy Identity

The purpose of the Family Legacy Identity Protocol is to discover together your family identity and uniqueness—past, present, and future—while growing in the understanding of each individual's unique personality. Together, you will establish the family character, core values, and purpose, which determine legacy, and create a family coat of arms. Engaging everyone in this process will equip the next generation to do the same.

I've said that the only legacy I leave is the one I live, and I believe it's true. However, it is an even deeper truth to say that the only legacy I live is the one that "I am." This is an important distinction. If the ultimate legacy is the character and nature of our Designer (who He is), passed on to His Son and then built inside of every other child of His over a lifetime, then my legacy is who I am expressed through the life I live. My identity expressed is my legacy.

This is another example of the inside-out reality. Who we are will determine what we do. What we do will determine the life we live and, in turn, the legacy we leave. Our legacy is an inside-out journey. Who I am will ultimately determine the legacy I live and leave. Who you are will ultimately determine the legacy you live and leave as well. Identity determines legacy.

If what I'm suggesting is true, then to intentionally create a legacy, each of us must answer the question, "Who am I?" In my thirty years of experience as a minister, speaker, trainer, and coach, answering this question is one of the most important things you can do in life. It's also one of the most avoided, procrastinated, and laughed-off inquiries. Many people never adequately answer this question for themselves, and their life and legacy show it.

My son-in-law posed this question on his social media recently, "Who are you?" We were talking over dinner a few days later, reflecting on the answers people were sharing. There was one serious answer to his question; it happened to be mine. The other answers were jokes, lighthearted funnies, jobs and roles of what people did for a living, and pushback for even asking such a question. How would you answer his question? Who are you?

If we don't know who we are and who we want to be, it's nearly impossible to intentionally work a plan to become that person. Personal growth and development, along with maturity and self-governing, are all vital to the good stewardship of my identity, my life, and therefore my legacy.

Where does a person find the answer to the question "Who am I?" How does one know their true identity? Philosophers, teachers, and rabbis alike have written extensively in response to these important questions over thousands of years, and still, people lack the clarity and conviction of their own true identity. The guesswork of answering these questions results in a legacy that is built on the same unstable guesswork. If you don't know who you are, you don't know the legacy you're leaving.

In the end, it takes what it takes! I suggest it takes four key experiences for any individual to discover and know their true identity. This is true for myself and the thousands of people I've worked with over three decades. When a family has these experiences together, the family knows their true identity as well. The framework for the Identity Protocols is designed with these experiences in mind:

1. An authentic search
2. A revelation
3. A choice to believe
4. An unwavering commitment to inside-out action

What I have come to believe is when you know who you are, you know. There is no doubt or wavering. There is a peace and a quietness in your soul that is satisfied and sure of who you are. And you are able to articulate it from that place of experiential knowing. Sure, we all continue to grow, learn, and mature in the fullness and expression of our true identity, but when you know, you know. This knowing becomes true north for making decisions, a compass that guides how you self-govern and steward all you've been entrusted with.

Connecting the Dots

Let me give you an example and connect the dots from above.

If identity determines legacy, then …

- Our Designer's identity and character are the ultimate legacy.
- His legacy is one of love, wisdom, truth, honor, humility, loyalty, justice, faithfulness, courage, peace, joy, power, patience, gentleness, kindness, self-control, and integrity, to name a few.
- He passed this identity, this character, His legacy, on to His Son, Jesus, the only begotten, fully God and fully man, firstborn Son of God.
- This was the first family legacy impartation.
- The Holy Spirit now makes the character/legacy of Jesus live and grow in those who choose to be children of God.
- With this character/legacy alive and growing in His children, they are empowered to live life in agreement with it and demonstrate the fruit of His nature—acts of love, honor, integrity, justice, and so on.
- A life lived demonstrating this character/legacy impacts the children, families, businesses, communities, cultures, and nations they touch.
- At the end of this life, what is left that will continue on is not only the results of the impact of the life lived but the character/legacy of the person, if they have passed this character/legacy on intentionally.
- And they must know what it is, live it, and intentionally build it into others so that nature can continue to impact families, businesses, communities, cultures, and nations.
- This is the inside-out family legacy that was designed from before time began. It is also the family legacy that, by design, will remain forever after time is swallowed up in eternity.
- Identity determines legacy.
- Make sure you know who you are. Your character/legacy will impact others whether you know your identity or not, by design. Don't leave it to chance. There's too much at stake for you and your children and the generations that follow.
- Wow!

- Now, how exactly are we going to simply and practically live this in our families?

Well, for starters, we have designed the Family Legacy Identity Protocols to give you the experiences mentioned above that lead to knowing your personal and family identity. These experiences will help you find the answers to the questions "Who am I?" and "Who are we as a family?"

Not only that, you will come away with the clarity and confidence needed to know that you know! And you will have gone through an experience of creating a family coat of arms together that will forever symbolize and memorialize your agreed-upon family identity, character, values, and purpose. All of these will be expressed in an image that can be passed on from generation to generation with the stories and explanations of each and every legacy quality represented in it.

If that isn't enough, you will have also engaged in this process with the participation of your children and perhaps grandchildren. You will be instructing them in the family legacy while teaching them how to do this for themselves in their own families in perpetuity.

This excites me to no end! When we can get this kind of transformation of character and identity from the inside out in motion, it's only a matter of time before our children take their place of leadership in the gates of culture. Once there, they will have the character it takes to turn our families, our businesses, our communities, our churches, our government, our arts and entertainment, and our education system around!

Inside-out transformation into His character from the individual to the culture is the Family Legacy journey.

Identity Definition, Value, and Framework

Definition

The Family Legacy Identity Protocol is a set of exercises that equip the family with a process to discover together the family identity and uniqueness—past, present, and future—while growing in the understanding of each individual's unique personality. Together, you will establish the family character, core values, and purpose, which determine legacy, and create a family coat of arms. Once the family identity is clear, intentionally living the legacy and passing it on to the generations becomes possible.

Value

The experiential nature and intentional design of the exercises in the Family Legacy Identity Protocol create the perfect conditions for participants to authentically search for the life-changing revelations or big ah-has that provide answers to some of life's most important questions.

- Who am I?
- What is my purpose?
- What is the purpose of my family?
- What is my part?
- How do I gain clarity and confidence in my identity?
- How do I support other family members in this process?
- How do I pass this on to my children?

Identity determines legacy. Once equipped with the answers to these questions in an experiential delivery system that includes an emotional implant, the choice to believe deeply in your identity and to live your legacy from the inside out becomes your new normal.

In addition, the journey of discovery as a family together through the identity protocol exercises result in a deep connection between family members. As a common history is shared, a sense of gratitude for generations past is met with a common present experience of the family from a new perspective. The experiences in the identity protocol inspire and guide future actions to powerfully steward the family legacy. The outcomes of the exercises include the following:

- affirmation of the identity and legacy of both individuals and family as a whole
- awakening to the personal responsibility of stewarding these well
- commitment to invest into other family members' growth and success
- inner healing of identity wounds and self-deception
- reconciliation of broken relationships and a fresh start

- common identity language and symbolism that can be passed on
- understanding of the genetic and generational flows and legacy of your family
- more

The Family Legacy Identity Protocol framework flows out of the four key experiences required to know your true identity that I mentioned in the last section.

1. An authentic search with an open heart and mind where I examine who I am in light of:
    - true identity from the Creator as designed (the design)
    - family history (the context for my existence)
    - genetic history (the facts and science)
    - generational history (the flows)
    - inner healing (healing identity wounds)
    - DISC Profiles, personality types, and styles (the analytics)
    - family characteristics, core values, and purpose (the why)
    - affirmations and the creation of a family coat of arms
2. A revelation
    - an eye-opener to see and know something never seen or known before (an ah-ha!)
    - an uncovering of understanding of true identity that's been hidden
3. A choice to believe (to agree, faith)
    - in my identity (as I think in my heart, so am I)
    - in my purpose
    - in the purpose of my family line—past, present, and future
    - in my personal responsibility to steward my life and legacy
4. An unwavering commitment to inside-out action with a coach approach
    - the coach approach to stewarding your identity and your legacy

1. An Authentic Search

"Seek and you will find" is a wise and eternal promise from the one who designed you. The one who "knows the plans He has for you, plans to prosper you and not to harm you, plans to give you hope and a future." Jeremiah 29:11 (NIV) From a biblical worldview, an eternal Father knew you before you were conceived in the womb. He knew the outcome of your days before you ever lived one. From before the foundations of the world, before time began, the Bible states that God knew you and had a good plan for you.

He put those plans into His design. He knows all about who you are and what your purpose is in life. He designed the family line that would eventually produce *you*. He knows everything about your design you don't. He has hidden it from you as a part of that design. But you can find it. Why would He hide it? I believe it is so that He can reveal Himself and His design plans for you through a relationship with Him that includes the wisdom and delight of a divine game of hide-and-seek. He honors those who cultivate a hunger to know Him and His good plan. The authentic search to discover them demonstrates that hunger. "He rewards those who earnestly seek Him." Hebrews 11:6 (NIV)

Even if you don't have a biblical worldview, you understand the value of hidden treasure and how we tend to place a much greater value on things that require effort and cost to obtain. When we put the effort in, the value goes up. This is true in a family company when the generation that establishes and builds a successful enterprise at great cost is determining a succession plan and wealth transfer. How will the children or grandchildren steward the treasure that was given to them if they haven't done the hard work or taken the big risks? If they have not participated in the treasure hunt and experienced the work of learning (searching out) the deeper purposes and plans of the founders, they typically won't fully value what they are being entrusted with.

All of that to say who we become through engaging in an authentic search to know our identity and purpose is so important that an all-knowing and good Father designed it so that when we seek, we find. The reward is who we become in the seeking and in what we find in the search.

In light of this design, the Family Legacy Identity Protocol exercises and tools provide processes and support to conduct an authentic search with an open heart and mind, where the family examines "who I am" in light of the following:

True Identity from the Creator as Designed (the Design)

We start the search by providing a process for each family member to do some healthy introspection to observe various aspects of their own individual design. We want to create a starting point. What are you currently aware of when it comes to answering for your own identity? Don't let this scare you. If you don't have the clarity and confidence to answer these questions, it's okay. What you have then is a road map for next steps in your authentic search journey.

Family History (the Context for My Existence)

Believe it or not, the world did not start with you, the world is not all about you, and the world won't end with you. I like to say it this way: "It is about you; it's just not all about you." The same is true for all of us. We are a single member in a long line of family members who have come before us and a long line of family members who will come after us. We are deeply connected to our family past, present, and future. Whether we like it or not, understand it or not, or accept it or not, the facts are the facts. And we each have the ability to influence that family line when it is our time on the clock. It's not all about you, but it is about you.

We carry in our being the physical, emotional, intellectual, and spiritual genetic legacy of those in our family line. There is good, bad, and ugly in all of our family histories for sure. It is important to authentically search this out in order to understand identity and answer the question, "Who am I?" We cannot fully understand our identity outside of the context of family, past, present, and future. By design, we are set in our family. He has a purpose for each family line, each family unit, and each family member.

There are three different perspectives that we will examine in the family history portion of the Identity Protocol. All of them have exercises and tools to guide your family through them. The sharing of this history with one another is profound and emotional. Most of the heavy lifting will be done by the parent(s). You choose how deep and detailed of a search you want to do.

- Family history—the general research of your ancestors to current day; the stories of generations past that have been passed down; the thoughtful observations around certain skills, gifts, passions, roles, character qualities, challenges and failures, achievements and honors, and so on

- Genetic history—the facts and science, geographic roots, medical history, predispositions to addiction, physical features, adoptions, blended families, and so on
- Generational history—the intellectual, emotional, and especially spiritual flows that have influenced family generations past, including flows of lust and early death, addiction and criminal behavior, deceptions and violence, justice and leadership, wealth and poverty, mental illness and barrenness, innovation and creativity, faith and philanthropy, and so on

Inner Healing (Healing Identity Wounds)

The deepest and most devastating wounds are the wounds to our identity, and frankly, most of these wounds come in our childhood and from our family experiences. Identity wounds are soul wounds that are targeted at our identity, aimed at what we believe about ourselves. Wounds to our mind, will, and emotions are soul wounds. When soul wounds target our identity, they tear away at the truth of who we believe we are. These wounds come in all shapes and sizes and come from all different kinds of experiences. At the core of soul wounds are painful experiences that bring us to choices we make knowingly or unknowingly to agree with the following:

- lies that assault our identity, value, design, and purpose
- deceptions that diminish our dreams and our effectiveness
- false accusations of who we are and who we are not
- limits to what we believe is possible

The choices we make in times of wounding when we are vulnerable, especially as children, limit our faith, erode our confidence in what is possible, deceive us into believing lies, and enslave us to living life far below our design capacity.

And the good news is that if we identify these wounds along with the lies we chose to agree with as a result, we can then change our thinking and choose to believe something else. This change of mind will produce a change of emotion and a change of will that will literally change how we experience life moving forward. It is what we think about ourselves on the inside that creates our experience of life on the outside. The Family Inner Healing Tool will give you a process to heal these wounds.

DISC Profiles, Personality Types, and Implications (the Analytics)

One of the major distinctions of the Family Legacy Model and design of the protocols is the inclusion of emotional intelligence principles and practices into family dynamics. A deeper understanding of ourselves and family members that leads to clearer communication, greater trust, safety, and insight into supporting one another in self-governing and stewarding responsibility more effectively is extremely valuable.

While a lot of EQ practice is experiential and intuitive in nature, using a top-shelf suite of EQ analytics and tools helps the left-brained people who prefer a more scientific-based approach to understand and implement EQ. With personality profiles, reports, and specific assessments, a wealth of insight about one another, with clear and objective recommendations for a personal-development plan, is established. These plans may include one-on-one reports and recommendations for every possible pairing of family members to improve interactions and ultimately improve relationships.

While most of the EQ analytic tools must be purchased in consultation with our office staff, the online tools are inexpensive and easy to use. In addition, we have provided a free EQ tool as a part of the online Family Legacy Tool Kit you can access anytime. Our free tool will get you started down the road to growing your personality-based emotional intelligence.

Family Character, Values, and Purpose (CVP)

Any authentic search for family identity that determines family legacy must include a look at the obvious yet sometimes hidden family characteristics, core values, and purpose. I believe that a revealing of these three vital aspects of family identity will uncover a lot about the who, the why, and the how the family will live their legacy practically and intentionally.

I say that these are obvious and sometimes hidden because they are easy to be seen, if you know where to look. With even a little intentional focus on asking questions and observing the answers together as a family, in a short period of time, you can gain clarity and insight into your family identity and your family legacy.

This exercise and tool will guide you through a few important questions as a family. Once you gather the family's observations and prioritize them, you will know the following:

- the primary family character qualities
- the eight to ten most important family core values
- the purpose for your family

This simple and effective process will bring a profound sense of agreement in your family identity while teaching everyone present how to do this with their own family one day.

Affirmations and the Creation of a Family Coat of Arms

I have to say, of all the Family Legacy Protocol exercises, this one consistently comes back as a crowd favorite. There is something about the positive energy that is created when we begin to affirm the identity and character of each person, one at a time, as a family. The family always ends up jumping up and down, chanting the name of each member after having lavished affirmations of the good in them. After they jump and shout and clap and hug, then the tears of love, acceptance, and destiny begin to flow. This is just a straight-up *awesome* experience!

Once everyone has written the affirmations from their family members onto their own big flip chart paper with markers, a leader has everyone identify the eight to ten most common character traits that appear on everyone's paper. And then the magic starts to happen.

This exercise and tool will guide you through this amazing process to take all the information from the entire Family Legacy Identity Protocol family history exercises and bring them down into a work of art, a family coat of arms. We will guide you through identifying and articulating your family identity. Then you will craft this raw gold into a uniquely fashioned masterpiece of imagery, symbols, and sayings that all declare your family identity in an image that can guide your generations in your family legacy.

2. A Revelation

It is essential to have an experience of revelation if we are truly going to know our true identity and have the will to live it out intentionally over a lifetime. Revelation knowledge isn't talked about widely because it is misunderstood and intentionally undervalued. *Common knowledge* or *knowledge of the mind* is powerful no doubt but not as powerful as *soul knowledge,* a knowing of the mind, will, and emotion. And in turn, soul knowledge isn't as powerful as *revelation knowledge,* a knowing in your spirit, mind, will, emotion, and body that is transcendent in nature.

Without getting too mystical here, let me try to explain. You may know you need to lose weight to be healthier.

Common knowledge says, "You are thirty pounds over the scientifically identified ideal weight and being overweight has the following ten consequences to your health. You can exercise sixty minutes a day at this heart rate and burn 250 calories when you do. If you eat this diet and follow this program, you will lose the weight in a specified amount of time."

Soul knowledge says the same as common knowledge plus, "I feel the strong emotions of fear, shame, determination, and desire to change my ways and change these feelings. I have a strong sense of personal responsibility to use my will to better steward my body, my health, and my energy, so I choose to do whatever it takes to responsibly self-govern my choices."

Revelation knowledge says all of the above plus, "Because my choices and feelings and thoughts are all given to me by a Designer to help me live this temporal life in such a way that I fulfill my purpose for the good of myself and others, my family, my neighbors, and the world, I will do whatever it takes to be healthy. In so doing, I will demonstrate and reveal the design of my Creator and honor Him in this temporal life, and that will make a difference eternally for me and others. Revelation knowledge receives downloads of very specific strategies for my success and on and on and on. All the dots are connected in an instant, not studied, thought out, taught, or learned.

There is actually a "Spirit of wisdom and revelation" in the scriptures. This is the Holy Spirit, who the Bible says searches the deep things in the heart of God Himself and makes what He finds there known to those who love Him. Wow!

Revelation knowledge is a transcendent understanding and wisdom that is uncovered or unveiled to those who seek it. It is an epiphany, a disclosure, and a deep knowledge that is opened up to the seeker.

All of that to say this. I believe that the most powerful way to live from true identity, where we self-govern well and steward our families as designed, is by having a revelation experience of my identity, purpose, and legacy. This process and exercise will provide you with an opportunity to receive this revelation experience.

"Where there is no revelation (vision), the people cast off restraint (self-discipline)" (Prov. 29:18 NKJV).

What does this mean? Simply, it means if we don't have revelation, we won't have the self-governing strength to do whatever it takes to live the legacy we were designed for.

In the Identity Protocol revelation exercise, you will simply prepare yourself and then ask for a revelation of your identity and purpose both as an individual and as a family. You will write down what you receive, and that's it.

3. A Choice to Believe

Once you have completed an authentic search and asked for a revelation, the next big step is the simplest of all … unless it's not. You make a choice to believe. That is it. You choose to agree with what you have seen, heard, experienced, and sensed. And you begin living differently because of your new belief.

I often say, "The wisdom of God is cloaked in simplicity." And it is. Choosing to trust and live differently is not very complicated, unless it is. It is complicated when we don't actually trust and live differently. If we choose to doubt, choose to keep analyzing, choose to not believe, choose to make excuses, then we complicate the process by our own choices. It can be this simple: choose to believe that what we sense is the real thing and embrace the change with action.

The beauty of my fifty-three years in relationship with my Designer is that I trust Him. It's easy. His ways work. His ways are good, and they lead to life. I believe it. And I experience it. Simple. It's just taken these many years to prove this simplicity to myself. Our choices are powerful. Choose wisely.

This exercise is the most basic exercise of all. It's an invitation to choose to believe:

- in my identity
- in my purpose
- in the purpose of my family line—past, present, and future
- in my personal responsibility to steward my life and legacy

4. An Unwavering Commitment to Inside-Out Action with a Coach Approach

Another key distinction in the Family Legacy Model is the intentional integration of a coach approach into the various protocols and exercises. Coming alongside of one another with an intentional process to cultivate and nurture identity, purpose, and legacy is a valuable and effective partnership. The coach approach to stewarding your family identity and your legacy works!

Using a coach approach to family is one of the wisest and most effective decisions that you will ever make regarding stewarding your family as designed. The basic coaching conversation tools that we are teaching you in the Family Legacy Model can be used for the following:

- to improve your marriage
- to parent your children more effectively and with far less stress
- to instill your family identity, values, and purpose
- to increase the emotional intelligence of every family member who engages in them
- to improve communication
- to increase personal responsibility and results
- to teach family members how to have coaching conversations with others
- to improve family life, work life, church life, and indeed every area of life
- to set and reach an infinite number of goals (e.g., health, business, character, and relationships)

The coach approach to family is not the coach telling everyone what to do as the coach. The coach approach is a partnership in a creative process between family members to produce the desired results. Those results can be anything from better health to growth in stewardship, from growing in faith to starting a business, from choosing good friends to choosing a date or future mate. The genius is in bringing the coach approach into the family and using the coaching conversation as a mechanism for discipling and maturing the family.

Honestly, there are so many valuable processes and practices in this book for you to take your family and your legacy to the next level, and the next, and the next. Learning to use the coach approach as a mechanism for effectively stewarding your family is a total game changer, a complete life changer, and a lasting legacy changer. If you have ears to hear, hear what I'm saying. Do it! Your generations will be grateful you did.

Tips for Environment and Execution

As you prepare to take your family through the Family Legacy Identity Protocols, please review the sections in chapter 4. Following the guidelines is essential for getting the most out of the exercises for the benefit of your family. In addition, here are a few additional tips for successful execution.

Environment and Execution

- The identity exercises are most effective in a low-stress, informal, private setting with only actual family members and participants. No observers, unless they are one of our coaches or facilitators present to assist your family.
- Other than the research elements of the family history exercises, the entire family is encouraged to complete the exercises and tools together for best results.
- Everyone should be fed and watered with ample time to complete each exercise without rushing things. You may want to end the time together with some fun, a game and some laughs if appropriate.
- The room should be quiet and free from distractions. Cell phones, digital devices, television sets, and music should all be turned off.
- Secure the proper resources needed for the modules (e.g., blank paper and pens, printed worksheets, workbooks, markers, flip chart, tools, etc.).

- Each identity exercise in the protocol has a brief description in the next section of this chapter and a tool for executing each exercise online in our Family Legacy Toolbox. www.culturalarchitects.org
- You will find a listing of the Family Legacy Tools available online in chapter 11 for your use. If you prefer bound paper workbooks of the tools, you can order those on our website as well.
- In preparation, review the entire exercise ahead of time so that you know what to expect.
- Allow enough time for each person to fully answer the questions or perform the exercise.
- Be willing to draw out the thoughts and feelings of participants as they are processing the work and sharing.
- Make sure everyone gets their time to share or be the focus of the family, equally and as needed.
- It is vitally important that you keep the environment safe for everyone. Do not allow criticism, sarcasm, cynical remarks, rude comments, and so on. This is not the time or the place for that. Make sure that no one pays the price for being vulnerable.
- Stay open to how things will play out.
- Deal with things as they come up.
- The Inner Healing Exercise may require some additional sensitivity for members, depending on the circumstances. Reach out to our office for help if you get stuck, don't know what to do, or if things go astray.
- You may decide to join the Family Legacy monthly subscription for additional support, attend a workshop, purchase the video guides, or request coaching and facilitating support.
- Have fun!

Identity Protocols

The experiential exercises for the Family Legacy Identity Protocol below are insightful, unifying, and empowering. They are designed to create deep connection between family members—past, present, and future—by identifying the family identity, character, core values, and purpose, which are the real legacy of the family line.

While the exercises can be completed one at a time on different days, there is a momentum and synergy that come when completing them together over a short period of a day or two. First, sharing the family history, then building up to the family characteristics, values, and purpose, then building up to individual affirmations, and reaching the summit by creating a family work of art in the coat of arms for the big finish. This creates a larger family context and connects all the pieces with an emotional bond that lasts.

Remember, we are here to help you if you find leading these exercises to be difficult. Contact our office and talk with one of our coaches, make arrangements for us to lead your family through the exercises, or attend one of our workshops or e-courses. Don't skip the exercises. They are included for a reason.

I have written a brief description of each of the experiential exercises below. You will understand the purpose and value of the exercises as you read. You will want to go to our website to download the editable PDF Family Legacy Protocol Tools for each exercise to walk you through the execution of each one step-by-step. www.culturalarchitects.org

Identity Protocol Descriptions

Identity Exercise 1—True Identity from the Creator as Designed (the Design)

The purpose of this exercise is to get a picture of the current understanding family members have when it comes to a sense of their own identity. A simple set of questions contained in our True Identity Tool will probe each family member's thinking around their identity. Who are they? What has the Designer said about them? What character qualities do they possess? What are their natural, learned, and spiritual skills or competencies? What are they passionate about? What is their current understanding of their purpose or design?

This exercise will open up an awareness of the characteristics, values, talents, and purpose for family members and for the family as a whole. You may need to modify as needed for young children, but include them. The formation of identity and a growing sense of positive self-awareness is important for us no matter our age.

Family History

In the family history portion of the identity protocol, we have created simple and effective tools that guide you through searching and sharing important aspects of your specific family context. The research, observations, and reporting of your family history will empower family members to decide how each will choose to govern the good, bad, and ugly while on their watch, as much as it depends on them.

There are three exercises that guide you through the exploration of the family history and include the sharing of what you discover. You choose how deep and detailed of a search you want to do. Parents, most of this work falls to you.

Identity Exercise 2—Family History

The purpose of this exercise is to give context to identity by exploring the general history of your family by researching your ancestors up to current day, by gathering the stories of generations past that have been passed down, along with the thoughtful observations around certain of the following:

- skills
- gifts
- passions and interests
- roles and careers
- character qualities
- challenges and failures
- achievements and honors
- sense of humor and funny stories
- stories of value (risk, character, values)

Hidden is plain sight and on display in the telling of the family stories are the clues to identity, purpose, and legacy.

If you are fortunate enough to have ancestors who took it upon themselves to gather, document, and pass down any family history, this is the perfect time to pull it out, dust it off, and share it with all. If not, go to work online, interviewing older family members still alive, and so on. The online Family History Tool will guide you through an exploration that will deliver the important information.

Identity Exercise 3—Genetic History

The purpose of this exercise is giving context to identity by relaying the important details around what you know to be true about your family line when it comes to the following:

- facts
- science
- geographic roots and tradition
- medical history
- predispositions to addiction
- physical features
- adoptions
- blended family details
- and so on

While these may appear to be dry facts, they are important for the good stewardship of the family from generation to generation. The online Family Genetic History Tool will guide you through this important exercise.

Identity Exercise 4—Generational History

The purpose of this exercise is to give context to identity by conveying the intellectual, emotional, and especially spiritual flows that have influenced your family from generations past up to today. Many of the problems that we are working to resolve in our own lives today are rooted in generational choices and patterns of behavior from family past. These generational flows influence us through our genetic link to the past. These influences may be good or bad and include flows of the following:

- lust
- early death
- addiction
- criminal behavior
- vulnerability to deceptions
- violence
- justice
- leadership
- wealth
- poverty
- mental illness
- barrenness
- innovation
- creativity
- faith
- philanthropy
- more

The truth is we are ultimately personally responsible for the choices we make that drive the results in each of our lives. And it is also true that there are flows of both good and bad generational influences that do affect our daily lives to varying degrees. Identifying these influences is the first step to stopping the unhealthy flows and embracing the healthy flows as we resolve and steward these influences while we are on our watch for a better tomorrow for our generations downstream. We have a responsibility to clean up the litter in the generational stream before it continues to our children. The online Family Generational History Tool walks you through this process.

Identity Exercise 5—Inner Healing

The purpose of this exercise is to provide the family with a process for the inner healing of identity soul wounds that are undermining the abundant life and legacy that you were designed for. There are multiple inner-healing models delivered through a variety of healing modalities, far too many to dive into here. However, most all the models have a very basic framework for healing that nearly anyone can implement.

This simple inner-healing framework is a process for discovering wounds, lies, and truth in an environment of love that leads to a choice to disagree with the lies (old way of thinking) and to agree with the truth (new way of thinking). Once we choose (will) to change our thinking (mind), our feelings (emotions) amplify the new choice and thinking, and a soul wound is healed.

The online Inner Healing Tool will guide you through this four-part inner-healing model.

- reveal—identifying the lie, deception, and false accusation from the wound
- repent—choosing to disagree with the lie and agree with the truth
- renew—receiving grace and setting your mind, will, and emotions on a new path
- restate—speaking out loud from the heart your new choices of thinking, believing, and actions moving forward

Please reach out to us if you recognize the need for support in healing these deep wounds.

Identity Exercise 6—DISC Profiles, Personality Types, and Implications

The purpose of this exercise is to engage with a scientific tool for the purpose of understanding each family member's unique personality type and the implications that come along with it. These tools help us explore our unique design along with others in our family unit. With this expanded knowledge and the recommendations contained in the tools, we can better understand, relate, communicate, and empathize with family members.

Your personality is a part of the answer to the question, "Who am I?" The DISC tools will help us understand personality preferences such as whether you are more:

- task driven or relationship driven
- face or slow paced
- extroverted or introverted energy
- methodical or spontaneous
- precise or innovative
- challenging or accepting
- decisive or analytical
- expressive or contemplative
- and more

The analysis will show you where your predispositions and assumptions are, your blind spots, along with those of other family members. The benefit is that we can then choose to know and respect the design of every individual and use this information to improve our family relationships.

Many of the assessments are available for a nominal fee and provide a wealth of information and recommendations for better interactions with one another. The Family Personality Profile Tool is a free tool we have created for you and is available for download with the other Family Legacy Protocol Tools. www.culturalarchitects.org

Identity Exercise 7—Family Character, Values, and Purpose (CVP)

The purpose of this exercise is to provide a process for gaining clarity and insight into your family identity and your family legacy. Through a fun and simple look into all the data generated in the first six exercises of the Identity Protocol, we will distill it down to the following:

- the primary family character qualities
- the eight to ten most important family core values
- the purpose for your family

The Family Identity CVP Tool (Characteristics, Values, Purpose) will guide your family through a series of questions. Once you've answered and prioritized the results, you will have panned out the gold nuggets and found the family treasure of family *identity*.

This experience leaves most families with the following:

- an emotional moment together
- clarity of identity and purpose
- a gratitude for the gifts they carry
- a sense of responsibility to steward this identity
- a desire to live up to the identity and legacy they've received
- an appreciation for one another
- a desire to support the family in living this identity
- a commitment to pass on this legacy

Treat this exercise and this moment with your family with the sincerity and honor it deserves, together.

Identity Exercise 8—Affirmations and the Creation of a Family Coat of Arms

The purpose of this exercise is to deeply connect the family emotionally to one another and to their family identity while creating a one-of-a-kind work of art together in the form of a family coat of arms.

The Family Coat of Arms Tool will guide the family through a powerful experience of affirming the identity and character of each and every family member, one at a time. The entire family will declare characteristics they experience of each family member as they write what they hear on a flip chart paper. When they are complete and the paper is filled, the entire family will celebrate every member one at a time. It's glorious!

Once everyone has had their turn, a new creative process begins. We will guide you through a process of taking all the information from all eight identity exercises and fashion them into a work of art for the ages—your very own family coat of arms.

We realize that you may or may not be a family with creatives and artists to bring this piece of art across the finish line. If you have the skill set in your family to produce a finished piece, have at it! If, on the other hand, you want some help with design through to final production, we are here to help. Contact our office, and we will put you in touch with our preferred vendors who can work with you to produce a family coat of arms that is meaningful and enduring. Their information can be found on our website with the free tools as well.

Once you have this finished identity art piece, it becomes a priceless tool for the following:

- communicating the family identity, character, values, and purpose to generation after generation
- stories and conversations around the table and in the practice of the other Family Legacy Protocols
- coaching conversations and personal-development plans
- true identity gear—the creation of unique products and services using your family coat of arms
- passing on your family legacy effectively, powerfully, and visually

If a picture is worth a thousand words, your family coat of arms and its ten to fifteen images is declaring a narrative about your family identity and legacy of more than ten thousand words at a glance.

Identity Exercise 9—Revelation and Rule 51

The purpose of this exercise is to equip the family with a process to receive a revelation around your individual and family identity, purpose, and legacy. It is important to note that the tool I'm going to share with you will work to bring you revelation on any matter you seek deeper wisdom, knowledge, and understanding on.

I call this exercise and tool "Rule 51." I developed the process while leading a house of prayer. After launching the ministry and praying night and day for six months, I found myself praying the same prayers over and over and needed a breakthrough. When I asked the Lord for help, I heard an instant and direct reply in my spirit. "Randy, when are you going to stop telling the One who knows everything what you think He ought to do and start asking the One who knows everything what He is doing?" I replied, "Right now!" In an instant, I had a revelation, a download of knowledge that has changed my life and the lives of so many others as we put Rule 51 into practice.

I named it Rule 51 for this reason. It serves as a reminder to me to spend the majority of my personal prayer and meditation time listening instead of talking. It is my commitment to listen 51 percent or more of my time in prayer, most of my time spent. That's it. I've learned to ask a few good questions and then to cultivate my own "ears to hear" what God is thinking, saying, or doing in relation to my question. It is this ability to listen or to hear that is the secret to experiencing a revelation.

The Rule 51 Tool will walk you through three questions that you can ask of the Lord every day. As you write in a journaling style what you sense and hear Him saying in response to your questions, you will receive revelation wisdom, knowledge, and instruction. It is the skill of learning to have "ears to hear what the Spirit of God is saying" that is the skill of receiving revelation.

This is a very simple process. So simple that you may be tempted to dismiss its power to deliver life-changing epiphanies and revelation. The choice is yours; it always is. I would encourage you to use the tool for thirty days and then judge for yourself the value you are receiving from its use. If you don't experience deeper revelation knowledge in the matter of your inquiry, something is amiss. I have only seen this tool work 100 percent of the time when used as directed. Reach out to our office or website for help using this and other tools.

Identity Exercise 10—Choice to Believe

The purpose of this exercise is to provide the family with an opportunity to live their legacy to the full by starting with a fresh choice to believe. The choice to agree with the true identity that the identity exercises have uncovered, along with the choice to agree with the revelation that they received in Rule 51, will shift things profoundly. "For as he thinks in his heart, so is he" (Proverbs 23:7 NKJV). In other words, we create the life experiences that we agree with from the heart. Belief or faith is a key to living life in agreement with your identity and your legacy.

The Choice to Believe Identity Tool will guide you and your family through a simple invitation to believe all you have uncovered around the family identity and legacy. Do not overcomplicate this and do not underestimate the power of belief. You will create what you choose to believe. Choose wisely.

Identity Exercise 11—Coach Approach

The purpose of this exercise is to equip the family with a coaching conversation process that will empower family members to live from a place of true identity and family legacy. The coach approach will empower the family to self-govern well and steward the family as designed.

In this exercise, we will equip the family with a simple coach approach conversation tool that can be used to support family members in consistently demonstrating their identity, purpose, and legacy. It will serve as a guide for specific and measurable actions that bring growth and maturity to how members show up in day-to-day life. Over time and with consistent practice, the coach approach will produce meaningful results.

For example, if a family has creativity, leadership, and loyalty as three of their core characteristics, the coach approach would support each member in determining the following:

- the short- and long-term goals they set to live in alignment with these characteristics
- the specific actions to take in the next thirty days to show up as a loyal and creative leader at work, at home, and in life
- the lessons they are learning and how they have grown in creativity, leadership, and loyalty over the past thirty days
- how to make decisions in life through the lenses of loyalty, creativity, and leadership

As in the other protocols, the coach approach is an intentional process of:

- goal setting
- measurable action
- curiosity and exploration
- asking good questions
- empathetic listening
- a partnership in problem-solving
- learning
- support

The Family Legacy Coach Approach Tool will guide you through a simple coaching conversation model that you can use with your family in multiple contexts and for a variety of outcomes. It is indispensable as a mechanism for growth and stewardship.

A frequency of even one coaching conversation per month with each family member will change the trajectory of the family legacy. Furthermore, it will teach our children how to embody the family identity and steward the family legacy for generations to come. This is an inside-out process that will transform our families, businesses, communities, and culture.

Once again, go to our website www.culturalarchitects.org to download the editable PDF Family Legacy Protocol Tools for each exercise to walk you through the execution of each one step-by-step.

Chapter 7
Family Legacy Ritual

The purpose of the Family Legacy Ritual Protocol is to equip the family to engage in a regular, intentional family meeting that makes doing family together life-giving, supportive, purposeful, and fun while empowering the entire family to succeed. It is an intentional and loosely structured gathering where families build memories, learn lessons, share life, and honor God as appropriate to each unique family dynamic.

The family ritual is the meat and potatoes of the week-to-week journey of living a lasting legacy. The protocol is somewhat reflective of the Shabbat practice of the Israelis. The consistent rhythm of gathering together as a family to enjoy rituals in a framework of delicious food and sharing stories, listening and learning, laughing and crying, while having fun and supporting one another in life's journey with a basic coach approach, is a profoundly impactful practice. This protocol works with adult children on a less frequent basis as well.

According to the research, simply eating family meals together brings measurable physical, mental, and emotional benefits to family members. Some of the specific benefits of family dinners are as follows:

- better academic performance
- higher self-esteem
- greater sense of resilience
- lower risk of substance abuse
- lower risk of teen pregnancy
- lower risk of depression
- lower likelihood of developing eating disorders
- lower rates of obesity

It is noteworthy that the number of families having dinner together continues to decline. In addition, the content and quality of the time spent together continues to degrade significantly. The invasion of technology into the home and mealtime has introduced new distractions and brought a deeper disconnect among family members who do eat together. Couple this with the growing number of two-income homes, single-parent families, and the frenetic pace of extracurricular student activities, and families are having less and less quality and quantity of time together around meals. Merely spending time together in the same place is no guarantee of connection, learning, intimacy, or growth. Have you ever been in the same space with your family, only to be distracted with your cell phone and not have meaningful interaction?

That said, the Family Legacy Ritual Protocol addresses much more than the loss of important benefits to family time together around meals at home described above. The rituals are an intentional, purposeful, and transferable set of practices that bring focus, clarity, collaboration, and quality to the family that directly impact the family legacy for generations downstream.

I've often said that the wisdom of God is cloaked in simplicity. My experience has been consistent with the scripture where it states, "He hides things from the wise and learned and reveals them to babes" (the simple). How many times in our journeys of faith do we overcomplicate things and miss all together the ease, wisdom, and effectiveness of simplicity? Simple obedience to prescribed protocols that sustain a legacy for generations through the testing, trials, and travesties the Jews have endured should be all the proof we need to grasp the magnitude of this protocol.

A weekly, or at least a regular, family gathering where there is a simple set of practices that build the family in a myriad of vitally important ways is brilliant! Only a master Designer could accomplish so much with so little.

It is so simple to do … and so simple not to do.

Why?

Simple to do because:

- The rituals are not complex, costly, or difficult to execute.
- Who doesn't like their favorite foods?
- Who doesn't like to hear the real-life stories of people they love?
- Having fun together, praying together, and learning together are amazing times for the family.

- Who doesn't like their voice to be heard and to be truly understood?
- Who doesn't want to give and receive support in chasing after the dreams and purposes that we have been given life to fulfill?
- The repetition of the framework embeds the practice in our children and grandchildren.

Finally, it is simple because there is a framework to follow and tools to support you each step of the way. With a little planning and simply using the Family Legacy Ritual Tools to take action, you will intentionally live a legacy that matters and leave a legacy that endures.

At the same time, it is simple not to do because _____. (Fill in the blank, any excuse will do.)

- Life is too busy.
- My family won't disconnect from technology long enough.
- It might get a little uncomfortable to speak openly and be vulnerable.
- I'm tired, stressed out, have somewhere to go, somewhere to be.
- I don't believe it can be that easy; there must be more to it.
- I'm not good leading other people.
- I don't know what to do.
- My children are too young with short attention spans.
- My children are too old, and it's just too late to change things.
- My family is too broken.
- I am too broken.
- I've got time; my children will be around for years.
- More …

It is like changing the oil in the engine of your vehicle. Simple to do and simple not to do. However, the consequences couldn't be any farther apart. Change the oil, and your vehicle will likely keep right on going, getting you where you and your family want to go in life. Don't change the oil, and your vehicle will likely break down and no longer carry your family where you want to go in life.

It's about what you value most. It's about priorities. It's about choice.

If you value your family and your legacy, then you will prioritize them above competing priorities. If your family and your legacy is a priority, then you will choose to do whatever it takes to build your family from the inside out. If you choose to carry out the simple Family Legacy Protocols, then you and your family will succeed in living and leaving a family legacy that makes a difference for generations to come. This protocol works with adult children as well.

Choose and move!

Ritual Definition, Value, and Framework

Right up there in the top ten priorities of God from Exodus 20:8 is the command to "Remember the Sabbath (seventh) day to keep it holy (set apart, dedicated to God)" (AMP). And remember, "Man was not made for the Sabbath, but the Sabbath was made for man."

The Designer, in His wisdom, purposed a regular weekly family meeting where there was a stoppage from work and a set of rituals for the good and blessing of the family.

> Those who find true wisdom obtain tools for understanding the proper way to live, for they will have a fountain of blessing pouring into their lives.
> (Proverbs 3:13 TPT)

The Family Legacy Protocols are tools for understanding the proper way to live, and using them will lead to blessing pouring into your family's lives. They will extend to you "long life in one hand and wealth and promotion in the other."

Don't miss it because of its simplicity.

What is the Family Legacy Ritual Protocol?

The Family Legacy Ritual Protocol is the weekly/regular family meeting that empowers your family to succeed by intentionally engaging one another over delicious food, great fun, interesting stories, timeless wisdom, and a supportive coach approach.

A ritual is any practice or pattern of behavior regularly practiced in a set manner. What do I mean by *regular*? The biblical idea of regular in this context seems to suggest once a week and would certainly produce a lot of fruit at that frequency. If not weekly, then how often should the rituals be practiced ensuring a full blessing?

That's up to each family to decide, based on their own set of circumstances and the outcomes they are committed to. Every other week is a good frequency and will produce solid results. At a minimum, once a month is necessary to gain the full benefit of the protocol. In cases of adult children and infrequent ability to gather together, practice the ritual whenever you can.

Value

The value of stewarding your family as designed in this protocol is immense and generational. Doing family regularly with the ritual framework below is like water is to a seed. No harvest will grow from the seed without the life-giving water breaking through the hard surface to nourish the tender plant inside. In fact, no plant can survive without the regular practice of soaking up water and delivering its elixir to every cell of the plant. If the plant grows and bears fruit, then there is a harvest now and plenty of seed for future harvests, as long as every generation of seed continues to have the regular experience of water, soil, and sun.

The intentional engagement of your family through this practice will result in deep and profound growth of character, intimacy between family members, the development of next-generation leaders and culture shapers, the creating and transfer of the family legacy, and your children being equipped to repeat this protocol for generations to come.

If you are committed to the ongoing generational harvest of an enduring family legacy, then you must water the seed regularly over and over again. The Family Legacy Ritual Protocol is the water, and you and your children are the seed.

The Family Legacy Ritual Protocol framework is a simple yet profound set of practices that never grow old. There are endless combinations of foods to eat, games to play, cat videos to watch, life stories to tell, subjects to cover, questions to ask, goals to go after, and prayers to pray.

The Family Legacy Ritual Protocol Framework

- planning
- focus
- food
- story
- coaching
- wisdom
- fun
- clean up

Planning

When it's time to begin your family rituals, you are wise to spend a little time intentionally planning for the next three months so you know what you are doing on purpose. There can always be flexibility to go with the flow if the circumstances warrant. On your own or by using the Ritual Idea Tool, you can fill out the Ritual Planning Tool, which will guide you through the big-picture planning process where you will determine things like schedule, responsibilities, menu preferences, topics of story, fun and games, prayer or scripture focus, and so on. A little planning goes a long way.

Each family ritual will have its own Ritual Agenda Tool, which is the individual meeting agenda and specifics for that ritual, start to finish. You may pull from your Ritual Planning Tool to select individual meeting details and then follow it as an agenda.

Focus

While having fun and enjoying one another's company is a must, it is important to remember the why behind the what that you are targeting for the ritual. The purpose is to equip the family to engage in a regular, intentional family meeting that makes doing family together life-giving, supportive, purposeful, and fun while empowering the entire family to succeed. It is a loosely structured gathering where families build memories, learn lessons, share life, and honor God as appropriate to each unique family dynamic. Strike a balance between the precision technician and the anything goes facilitator as you lead the family ritual for best results.

Food

Sharing a meal together as a family has almost unlimited variety and potential to be experienced, enjoyed, and celebrated while connecting with those closest to us. This casual yet fun, sensory experience can easily lower the walls of protection that are erected between family members, if it is a safe place to be open and outstanding conflict between members is addressed and not brought into the ritual. If fun is brought into shared menu selection, preparation, and cleanup, it's even better! Add to that the desire to share stories and receive support around a meal, and you have created an event that your family looks forward to attending because of the value and connection they experience.

It is best to have the meal at a home and not at a public restaurant or eatery. There are far too many distractions, interruptions, and a lack of privacy that will diminish the value and opportunity for all to participate meaningfully. In addition, for best results, avoid consumption of alcohol all together or limit it to a single beverage for the ritual. It is important to remain fully present and to demonstrate strong self-control of the words that roll off the tongue when family members are risking vulnerability. Careless words can destroy the environment in a hurry and cause members to be offended, shut down, or even blow up.

Story

Who doesn't love a good story? An important part of the Family Ritual Protocol is everyone sharing a brief story with the family on the selected topic for each ritual. The benefits around this simple practice are wide-ranging and include the following:

- giving everyone a voice in the family ritual
- giving opportunity for members to grow in self-awareness
- growing in communication skills through the practice of speaking, listening, and responding
- learning social etiquette
- sharing life with family as a way to know and be known
- gut-busting laughter and howling
- improves memory and packages wisdom and experience in a manner that can be retold

- experience the enduring power of passing on legacy through oral tradition and storytelling
- understanding one another and growing in empathy
- implanting shared memories with emotion for lasting connection
- more

Everyone is notified ahead of time to come prepared to share a personal story from your life addressing a selected topic or answering a specific question. Shares can be humorous, serious, thought-provoking, or deeply personal in nature. You decide. Keep in mind that the purpose of the ritual is to address the most important things that are legacy worthy and helpful for the growth of all. Stories are limited in time to three or four minutes, depending on the number of participants, allowing time for the other parts of the family ritual. Contextualize the shares for younger children as appropriate. Finally, it's important for everyone to listen without constant interruption while each member is sharing and then offer brief comments after the share is complete.

Don't overcomplicate story selection. I've provided a list of story and question ideas in the Ritual Idea Tool for you if you need ideas. Here are just a few ideas to get you thinking:

- Victory or defeat and the lesson(s) learned as a result.
- Success or failure and the lesson(s) learned as a result.
- Thoughts on family character qualities (e.g., kindness, integrity, authenticity, courage, passion, love).
- What is the most important aspect of family to you? Why?
- What would you change about our family, city, country if you could? Why?
- What's the best memory you have of school?
- See the Ritual Idea Tool for more ideas—and keep it simple.

Coaching

This is one of the most innovative and effective exercises in the Family Ritual Protocol. More than that, it is one of the most important distinctives in the entire Family Legacy Model. How attractive it is to be able to create a safe place in your family where members can openly share their dreams, goals, challenges, and possible solutions and receive the benefit of accountability, support, and encouragement from one another. This exercise provides a platform for growth and success for family members that is refreshing.

Unfortunately, the experience of having a safe and supportive family when it comes to going after your dreams is not a common one for most people. I've heard so many stories of how families have torn down the hopes and dreams of members with negative words, sarcasm, accusation, and even slander toward one of their own. If, by chance, the family doesn't tear them down, few are equipped with a simple series of questions that can breathe life into the hopes and goals of family members, leaving a lasting sense of "one for all and all for one."

While I give more detail in the Ritual Coaching Tool, here are the simple questions to include in the life coaching exercise of the family ritual.

Coaching Conversation

One at a time, each person shares for five to ten minutes (as time permits) on five questions:

- What's important to you (current goal)?
- What are the challenges and possible solutions?
- What are you learning?
- What will you do before our next ritual?
- How can we help?

Having the meaningful support of our family in the pursuit of our dreams is like wind in our sails!

Wisdom

"Wise people build families" (Proverbs 24:3a TPT). In order to build a family and a legacy that will endure and make a difference, wisdom is required. Where does wisdom come from? How do we teach, practice, and instill wisdom into our family members exactly? By intentionally engaging with wisdom, reading together, praying together, and having exploratory conversations around wisdom that lead to understanding and application in our lives.

Wisdom can be found in any number of places and shared with the family. In my life journey as a man of faith, I have found wisdom in the scriptures of the Holy Bible, primarily in the book of Proverbs. Reading a short passage of scripture and having a brief conversation around what it means and how to apply it in our daily lives is life changing.

Praying together as a family is also another important practice and model for our children of how to live life from a place of wisdom. There is no need for a soapbox, a sermon, or a song, unless that is the dynamic of your unique family context. Just an intentional and thoughtful consideration around how to think and live in a better way.

Fun

Do not underestimate the value of fun in your home. If family isn't fun, then members will seek fun outside the family. Strong emotional bonds are formed by the experience of fun, laughter, pleasure, and excitement. By design, human beings seek out the enjoyment of fun with others. Creating opportunities for fun in the family are like a magnet drawing us back together to play another game, take another trip, tell another joke.

In the design of the Family Legacy Ritual Protocol, there is an intentional purpose underneath having fun after connecting deeply with one another in the previous exercises of the protocol. Fun will create a strong and lasting emotional implantation of the experiences, lessons, stories, and coaching exercises. This is another mechanism for the effective passing on of an enduring family legacy. So ... have fun already!

If you find yourself fresh out of ideas for fun, just ask your family for a list of things they find fun and work them into your family rituals. The Ritual Idea Tool also contains a list of fun activities. If all else fails, Google it. A world of fun ideas is waiting for your family there.

Clean Up

And the part that everyone loves after a family gathering: cleaning up! It goes without saying that many hands make light work. Keep the family ritual from becoming a burden on anyone by lending a hand in the cleanup of the family activities. Enough said.

This simple framework is a powerful tool in your family legacy toolbox. However, it is powerless if it is not used. We must put these protocols into practice to reap the benefit the offer.

Just do it.

Tips for Environment and Execution

As you prepare to take your family through the Family Ritual Protocol, please review the sections in chapter 4. Following the guidelines is essential for getting the most out of the exercises for the benefit of your family. In addition, here are a few additional tips for successful execution.

Environment and Execution

- The ritual exercises are most effective in a low-stress, informal, private setting with only actual family members and participants. No observers, unless they are one of our coaches or facilitators present to assist your family. If necessary, have participants join by phone or digital app.
- Remember to apply the lessons from the EQ tools from chapter 5. Empathetic listening, speaking the truth in love, fact/story, the Family Social Covenant, and so on. Governing yourself well is vital to stewarding the family during this protocol.
- Everyone should have a role to play in this protocol, with ample time to complete each exercise without rushing things.
- The room should be quiet and free from distractions. Cell phones, digital devices, television sets, and music should all be turned off.
- Secure the proper resources needed (e.g., food, the completed Ritual Agenda Tool, game supplies, scripture reading, Ritual Coaching Tool).
- You will also find the Family Legacy Tools for the exercises listed in chapter 11. Download the tools from our website www.culturalarchitects.org.
- In preparation, complete and review the Ritual Agenda Tool and the entire exercise ahead of time so that you know what to expect.
- Allow enough time for each person to fully answer the questions or perform the exercise.

- Be willing to draw out the thoughts and feelings of participants as they are processing the work and sharing.
- Make sure everyone gets their time to share or be the focus of the family, equally and as needed.
- It is vitally important that you keep the environment safe for everyone. Do not allow criticism, sarcasm, cynical remarks, rude comments, and so on. This is not the time or the place for that. Make sure that no one pays the price for being vulnerable.
- Stay open to how things will play out.
- Deal with things as they come up.
- Remember to announce the date, time, story topic, and menu for the next Family Ritual meeting.
- Reach out for help if you get stuck, don't know what to do, or if things go astray.
- You may decide to join the Family Legacy monthly subscription for additional support, attend a workshop, purchase the video guides, or request coaching and facilitating support.

Ritual Protocols

The experiential exercises for the Family Legacy Ritual Protocol are practical, fun, and effective. This weekly (regular) family meeting empowers your family to succeed by intentionally engaging one another over delicious food, great fun, interesting stories, and a supportive coach approach ritual. Using the stories and coach approach to make a connection to your family legacy is wise.

I have written a brief description of each of the exercises below. You will understand the purpose and value of the exercises as you read. You will want to go to our website to download the editable PDF Family Legacy Protocol Tools for each exercise to walk you through the execution of each one step-by-step. www.culturalarchitects.org

Ritual Exercise 1—Family Ritual Launch Gathering

The purpose of this exercise is to equip the family to engage in a regular, intentional family meeting that makes doing family together life-giving, supportive, purposeful, and fun while empowering the entire family to succeed. It is an intentional and loosely structured gathering where families build memories, learn lessons, share life, and honor God as appropriate to each unique family dynamic.

When it is time to introduce the family to your decision to begin having regular family ritual meetings, gather everyone together for a Ritual Launch Gathering. In this gathering, you will introduce the purpose and framework of the of the Family Ritual Protocol. You will complete the Family Ritual Launch Tool together to build the interest and commitment of family members by including them in the planning process. You may have heard it said that without weigh-in there is no buy-in. From the beginning of this protocol, it's important to involve everyone in the process of formulating your unique family ritual.

The leader explains that the Launch Gathering is to get everyone's help and input for the rituals. In addition, everyone will have ritual responsibilities of some kind, including food prep, talking, listening, playing games, and cleaning up. The Family Ritual Meetings are not a spectator event; everyone gets to engage.

With a flip chart up on the wall and a marker, the leader begins to gather everyone's input.

The leader proposes a time, place, and frequency of upcoming ritual meetings and gets agreement. Then they write up on the flip chart the details of the agreement. As a family, you will plan out the various aspects of your ritual, including the following:

- food
- story
- coaching
- wisdom
- fun
- cleanup

The Family Ritual Launch Tool will guide you through the planning process step-by-step so that your family is offering input and excited about upcoming family rituals.

Ritual Exercise 2—Family Ritual Advance Planning

The purpose of this exercise is to reengage family members and breathe fresh air into your family ritual meetings by going through a Family Ritual Advance Planning Exercise every three months. It is essentially the same process as the launch gathering without some of the foundational introductory remarks. Family members can make new menu suggestions, select new story topics, plan new fun activities, set new goals, and identify new wisdom topics.

Get out the flip chart and markers and go through the process again. It may be fun to invite a different family member to lead the exercise and perhaps even the next three-month segment of meetings. This will engage people in a new way, equipping them with new leadership skills and mentoring them in how to do this with their own families one day.

Another valuable part of this exercise is the simple evaluation by the family of how they think the rituals have been going. By asking a few simple questions, your family can make your ritual even more meaningful moving forward. The review questions include:

- What worked?
- What didn't work?
- What did we learn?
- What next?

The Family Ritual Advance Planning Tool will guide you through every step of the exercise.

Ritual Exercise 3—Family Ritual Agenda Exercise

The purpose of this exercise to maximize the focus and intentionality of each family ritual meeting by providing an agenda to follow. It is important for the family ritual meeting to strike a balance between planning and free flow in order to address the topics that will build a healthy family legacy. If you want to end up at a specific location, you need a map. At the same time, occasionally, you can do a little exploring along the way.

Planning out the details make it much more likely that each meeting will be executed effectively for the good of everyone and for the family legacy. I've provided a simple Family Ritual Agenda Tool to plan and distribute to everyone prior to each family ritual meeting so everyone is prepared for their assignments and their contributions. Intentionality is the name of the game here.

When family members have had time to think about what to share on the story topic of loyalty or leadership, the quality of their story and the impact on others are increased. The same logic applies to every aspect of the ritual.

By using this tool, you can both plan intentionally and communicate the plan to family members. You will also have a record of your meetings to keep so you can see what you've covered and what is left to cover that is important to your family legacy. In addition, you are leaving a codified record of how you did family that you can pass on to generations to come to reinforce the importance of the family ritual meeting.

Ritual Tools

I'm including here two valuable resources that I encourage you to download from our website and use in several of the protocols. They are especially effective here in the Family Legacy Ritual Protocol.

Ritual Coaching Tool

The purpose of this tool is to help you understand how to facilitate supportive family ritual coaching conversations effectively. Coaching conversations are distinct from conversations where you give advice or where you say, "Let me tell how to do this and what I have done when in your situation." That is more of a mentoring conversation.

Coaching is one of the most empowering and invigorating modalities in creating growth and success offered today. To bring this into the family ritual and to invest in the personal growth and development of each member is a powerful way to do family. Family coaching is an effective way to build legacy while training our children how to bring coaching into their generations to come.

This tool will guide you through the following:

- coaching definitions
- goal setting

- potential coaching topics
- the coaching conversation template
- guidelines for successful coaching conversations

Integrating the coach approach into the family is wise.

Ritual Idea Tool

The purpose of this tool is to provide you with some solid ideas to choose from when planning out your regular family ritual meetings. The ideas below are a starting place. The only limits to your options are your own creativity and family preferences. You may also want to consider factors such as the age of participants, nutritional restrictions, time constraints, and physical limitations. If you have additional ideas that you are willing to share with other families, go to the Family Legacy social media pages and post your ideas.

As you plan for your family ritual meetings, periodically review chapter 4.

Food Ideas

- Family Favorites. Have everyone submit a favorite meal request and put them on the menu.
- Tour of Nations. Mexican, Italian, Thai, Chinese, American, Vegetarian—more than two hundred to choose from.
- Chef's Choice. Assign a different chef for each ritual and empower them to see it all the way through from start to finish. Menu selection, shopping, preparation, cleanup. (With help of course.)
- Family Traditions. List the family traditional favorites passed down from ages past and teach family members how to prepare them at each ritual.
- Sandwich Shop. Gather ingredients and let everyone prepare their own sandwich and sides.
- Pizza Factory. Gather ingredients and allow everyone to make their own personal pizza with sides.
- Takeout. Let's not forget about the ease and convenience of ordering takeout or delivery from a favorite family establishment.

Story Ideas

- What family character quality or core value from your family coat of arms?
- What is your favorite memory as a child? Teenager? Adult?
- What was the most rewarding part of the last week (month, year)?
- What was the most challenging part of the last week (month, year)?
- What is one thing that you are excited about in your life right now?
- What is one of your biggest or most important life achievements? Why?
- What do you want your family to know about you more than anything else right now?
- What is one of the things you love about the person to your right?
- What are you grateful for in your life right now?
- What are you looking forward to in your future? Why?
- What is the worst job you've ever had? Why? (Best job?)
- What is a big life dream for you?
- If you could change anything in the world, what would you change and why?
- If you could solve any problem in the world, what would it be and why?
- What is stopping you from doing something you really want to do but haven't done yet?
- What are you best and (or) worst memories from your school days?
- What do you like best about our family and why?
- What would you like to change about our family and why?
- Answer this question in three minutes or less. Who am I?
- Share an experience from your life where you felt like a success or a victor.
- Share an experience from your life where you failed and what you learned from that.
- Share an experience from your life where you really needed help from others.
- Share an experience from your life where you overcame a difficult challenge.
- What characteristics best define our family? (Give examples.)
- What does it take to be a good friend?

- How do you want to be remembered at the end of your life and what will it take to do that?
- What makes a great family?
- What makes a great marriage?
- What makes a great parent?
- What make a great legacy?
- What would make an epic family vacation or family experience?

Coaching Ideas

See the Ritual Coaching Tool for tips, topics, and tools in using a coach approach in the family ritual.

Wisdom Ideas

- Read one verse or chapter in Proverbs per family ritual meeting and have open discussion exploring the meaning, real-life personal application, and implications of choosing to follow or not follow wisdom in real-life examples.
- Invite everyone to submit a wise saying, quote, or thought and have each one share one thought per ritual with discussion following.
- Have everyone answer the question, "What piece of wisdom have you experienced in your life recently and how so exactly?"
- Invite every member to share a prayer request and pray together for the requests.
- Select a book, have everyone read a portion/chapter, and then discuss for learning.
- Watch an educational, spiritual, or informative video and discuss for learning.
- Pick a topic and invite everyone to share their best piece of wisdom regarding the topic (love, relationships, dating, faith, prayer, hearing God, career).
- Discuss a recent teaching, sermon, or lecture that was particularly meaningful.

Fun Ideas

- Board games—age appropriate and time appropriate. A three-hour game of the Settlers of Catan may not work at every ritual, but it is a current favorite in our house. Monopoly, Life, there are thousands of games to choose from. Ask Google.
- Card games—Go Fish, Uno, Blackjack.
- Dominoes, Sequence, Connect Four.
- Speak Out—this one is hilarious.
- Jam time! If you happen to have musicians in the house, this can be a blast.
- Jokes around the bonfire or fireplace.
- Watch crazy cat videos or other YouTube favorites.
- Homemade malts or dessert bar can be a nice add-on.
- Outdoor games, yard games such as yard darts, paintball, cornhole, whiffle ball, bocce ball, croquet.
- Round-robin tournaments in basketball horse, air hockey, billiards, or foosball.
- Watch a family-appropriate comedy movie together with popcorn.
- Go swimming or take a dip in the hot tub.
- Go for a hike together.
- Service projects—helping a neighbor, helping at a feeding kitchen or downtown mission.
- Take suggestions from all family members for fun ideas and work through the list.

Family Legacy Rituals are the habits of healthy families who choose to leave an enduring legacy.

Chapter 8
Family Legacy Venture

The purpose of the Family Legacy Venture Protocol is to intentionally create a fun, memorable, learning adventure (experience) for the whole family to enjoy annually, while anchoring the moments and milestones of family legacy deep into their hearts and DNA for generations to come.

Research shows Americans work more than anyone in the industrialized world. They also take less vacation, work longer days, and retire later than their global peers. We arguably have the hardest-working labor force in the world. And that grand distinction comes at a steep price.

- We pay with heart disease and chronic insomnia.
- We pay with burnout and blowout.
- We pay with tired and underperforming brains.
- We pay with tolerating distant and disconnected relationships.
- We pay by forgetting how to play, explore, and connect emotionally with our family.
- We pay by not filling our memory banks and DNA with laughter, adventure, discovery, and fun.
- We pay by ensuring that our children and grandchildren will follow our example.
- We pay by bankrupting our legacy from deep and eternal purpose, love, and influence.

There is a different way to do life. There is another choice besides all work and no play.

In fact, there are measurable and research-proven benefits to taking a regular vacation away from work, including the following:

- improved physical health—*NYT*
- improved mental health—*US News and World Report*
- greater well-being—Gallup
- increased mental power—UC Irvine (Hickock)
- improved family relationships—Susan Whitbourne, PhD decreased burnout—about.com
- more productivity—*NYT*
- new perspectives—CNN

Add to these benefits the effective emotional implanting of positive family experiences and memories, and you have the recipe for powerful family legacy creation.

Here's a question for you. What positive memories do you have from your childhood as you think back for a moment?

When I think about my childhood and access the archived memories, it's interesting to note what memories come up for me.

Walking to school, family, birthdays, church, church camp, sports, Kringla, school, safety, fun, laughter …

And interestingly, for me, I have expansive, vivid, detailed, and tender memories of many family trips and vacations. They are some of my favorite memories to enjoy.

I remember family vacations to all sorts of fun and interesting destinations:

- Arkansas where we caught catfish and visited family
- Ames, Iowa, for fun with the Larsons, my mother's side of the family
- Hollywood, Universal Studious, the Pacific Ocean
- Disneyland, Magic Kingdom
- Colorado and its breathtaking natural beauty
- Orlando, the fun center of the world that it is
- Epcot Center
- St. Louis with Cardinal baseball and the Arch
- Chicago with Sears Tower and Wrigley Field
- Minnesota fishing trips in the Land of 10,000 Lakes
- Canada and weeklong fishing expeditions

Family Legacy Venture

I remember the countdown calendar.

I remember the powerful feeling of anticipation as a young boy trying to fall asleep the night before our family was leaving early in the morning on a family adventure.

I recall getting dressed in day clothes to go to bed so that I could literally hit the ground running.

I remember taking my pillow to the car.

I remember the cooler, the snack bag, and the coffee can.

I hear the thundering exhaust of race cars.

I feel the warm California sun.

I hear the Pacific's waves.

I smell the Arkansas catfish.

I remember the sights and experiences …

- Wrigley Field
- Sears Tower
- The St. Louis Gateway Arch
- Bush Stadium
- Pike's Peak
- Grand Canyon
- Pacific and Atlantic Oceans
- Disneyland
- Royal Gorge
- Las Vegas Strip lights
- beauty of Ogden, Utah

I remember the soundtrack of those trips …

- Dad's radio blasting sporting events and country music
- voices from the CB radio asking if people with weird names had their ears on
- questions from all of us kids asking if we were there yet
- family planning conversations about what we were going to be doing

- knock-knock jokes
- storytelling
- car travel games
- the road rumble when approaching a stop sign on a country road

But above all, the most memorable sound was laughter …

Lots and lots of gut-busting, can't-breathe, stop-you're-making-me-pee laughing and laughing and laughing.

I'm grateful for those opportunities. That was living! Thanks, Mom and Dad.

As a boy, I traveled across the Midwest, playing hockey and football, loving it every mile.

As an adult, my love for travel and exploration mixed with my choice of work and learning are a part of my everyday mindfulness and experience. To travel with family and experience life together, doing interesting things in interesting places, for me is a wonderful pleasure.

All of that to say that based on results, some of my most enjoyable, meaningful, and lasting memories include my family adventures as a kid.

What I now know as an adult professional is this: The most fertile soil to plant legacy into is an emotional experience like a family vacation. When the good stuff (seed) is imparted into this vacation kind of soil, it is a powerful genetic DNA implant that will be transformative and go on from generation to generation in the DNA.

In addition, family vacations can act as happiness anchors. According to 2015 research conducted by the Family Holiday Association out of Britain, the happiest memory of 49 percent of those surveyed was on vacation with family. A third of the respondents said they can still vividly remember their childhood family vacations, and a quarter of them reported using such memories to get them through tough times.

"Reflecting on our happiest memories of joyful time spent together as a family can be extremely powerful in bringing relief and respite when faced with the darker times that life can bring," John McDonald, director of the Family Holiday Association, told the *Huffington Post*. "By using these memories as an anchor to take us back to more cheerful moments, we're often able to approach problems with a fresh sense of perspective."

Happy memories need to be created before they can be remembered.

Some friends I know have purchased a time-share for their families to enjoy regular vacations together in places they love. What a great idea, especially when you add to the trip a time of regular family fun and adventure, along with some of the other important protocols like family stories, a learning adventure, great food, bonding, book discussions, setting goals together, and laughing till it hurts.

All the while, you are intentionally passing on the family legacy.

And this is the big payoff. The literal legacy is the accumulation of all of the real-life memories of time together, fun together, learning together, eating, and telling stories together … And because it is wrapped up inside of an experience, it is embedded deep into the DNA and imprinted in an irrevocable way that screams to be repeated in the future, and it will be.

Venture Definition, Value, and Framework

Definition

The Family Legacy Venture Protocol is an annual learning adventure (experience) for the whole family to enjoy that is fun, memorable, and intentional. This protocol combines a family vacation with fun, food, stories, learning adventures, book talks, service projects, and coaching conversations to effectively live and leave an enduring family legacy. The experiential nature of the protocol equips future generations to continue this rich practice for generations to come.

Why connect a fun trip or family vacation with a Family Legacy Protocol? Because you get a huge return on your investment of time and money when you do. Because it works.

Why does it work?

It is fun and feel good that lasts. The emotional implant that accompanies a fun and feel-good experience causes gene expression and lasting change.

It empowers the family to grow. Experiential learning causes deep, accelerated, and lasting growth by design.

It is multigenerational. The richness of wisdom that is shared and passed on in an environment of honor, respect, and love invigorates legacy.

It is reproducible. The framework can be easily learned and done for generations yet contains an infinite variety of possibilities.

It is a multisensory memory that sticks. This protocol includes fun, rest, food, learning, joy, story, imagination, activity, play, and love. It contains gratitude, honor, and vulnerability that build trust and goodwill.

It creates a deep bond in the family. One of most important parts of the family legacy is the connectedness and bond that must be present if it is ever going to be passed on.

It is intentional. The Venture Protocols work if you work them. Simple to do and simple not to do. The protocols provide a template for creating an amazing Family Legacy Venture.

Value

In addition to the eight major benefits of vacationing mentioned in the last section, let this sink in.

Quality time with our children as a family when all are rested, in good spirits, having fun, and making memories replenishes and builds the whole person. This protocol will refresh body, soul, and spirit of participants, engaging their physical, mental, emotional, psychological, and spiritual well-being and development.

Here are some sobering statistics and conclusions from an article in the *Telegraph* by Dr. Margot Sunderland, "The science behind how Holidays make your child happier and smarter":

- Two-thirds of conversations between parent and child are about daily routine (Elizabeth Buie, TES).
- Sixty-five per cent of parents say they only play occasionally with their children.
- One in six fathers say they do not know how to play with their child and a third say they simply don't have the time to play (Parent-Play survey, Playmobil UK).
- Only a quarter of children say they talk to parents more than once a week about something that matters (Child of Our Time).

Sunderland continues, "As adults, we countdown to our summer holidays to recharge our batteries. But they can also be a profoundly beneficial time for children. Parents are focused not on work, but on play, thereby giving their children the prized gift of time."

Dad or mom, building sandcastles, playing badminton on the beach, jumping over waves. It seems like fun, but it's also attachment play, and it's vital for bonding. Attachment play also enhances self-esteem, sending a child the psychological message, "You have my full attention. I delight in you. I delight in being with you."

Family holidays take on an even greater importance if you compare them with what goes on at home. So many families have stress-filled lives.

> We worry about our physical health, but we need to pay just as much attention to relationship health within the family. And, of course, research shows that relationship health is vital for physical health. (Holt-Lunstad et al. 2015)

Brain Development

What is less widely known is that holidays can also advance brain development in children. This is because on a family holiday, you are exercising two genetically ingrained systems deep in the brain's limbic area, which can all too easily be "unexercised" in the home. These are the play system and the seeking system (Panksepp 2016).

The brain's play system is exercised every time you bury your child's feet in the sand, tickle them on the pool lounger, or take them for a ride on your back. The brain's seeking system is exercised each time you go exploring together: the forest, the beach, a hidden gem of a village.

These brain systems were discovered by Professor Jaak Panksepp, a world-leading neuroscientist at Washington State University. Once your family holiday experiences activate these systems in your brain and your children's brains, they trigger well-being neurochemicals, including opioids, oxytocin, and dopamine. Panksepp calls them "nature's gift to us." They reduce stress and activate warm, generous feelings toward one another and a lovely sense that all is well in the world. With all the anti-stress aspects of these systems firing, family members get to emotionally refuel.

"We can choose activities and pursuits that release the oxytocin stored in our own inner medical cabinet … We have this wonderful healing substance inside us and need only to learn the many ways we can draw upon it," Panksepp explains.

The amazing thing is that these systems are like muscles: the more you use them, the more they become part of your personality. Or, as the neuroscientist Bruce Perry puts it: "Emotional states become personality traits" (Kerstin Uvnas-Moberg, neuroscientist).

So, when you take your child on a holiday or vacation adventure, you are supporting their explorative urge (seeking system), a vital resource for living life well, and their capacity to play (play system). In adulthood, this translates into the ability to play with ideas, essential, for example, to the successful entrepreneur.

Really using the brain's play and seeking systems well, as often happens on a family holiday, brings about brain growth and maturation in the frontal lobes, the very part of the brain involved in cognitive functioning, social intelligence and well-focused, goal-directed behaviors that may last a lifetime (Panksepp 2015; Burgdorf et al. 2010).

Building Concentration Skills

But what about being outside, a key aspect of many family ventures? Research has revealed improvements in a child's attention and concentration levels after being in nature for only twenty minutes. Green-play settings were found to be as good as, or better than, medication for children with ADHD.

There is also evidence that a walk together in green space calms the body, lowering blood pressure and stress hormone levels and even cholesterol—so parents and grandparents stand to benefit too (Roe et al. 2013).

The Relationship between Ventures and IQ

An enriched environment offers new experiences that are strong in combined social, physical, cognitive, and sensory interaction (Hannan 2014). Think: family together in the pool; walking together through the forest; touching long, tall grasses waving in the wind; toasting marshmallows on campfire;

hanging out together under warm sun, feeling sand between the toes. As Nietzsche put it: "All good things have something lazy about them and lie like cows in the meadow."

Enriched environments turn on the genetic expression of key "brain fertilizers" in the frontal lobes, enhancing executive functions such as stress regulation, attention, concentration, good planning, and ability to learn, also improving physical and mental health. The brain fertilizers triggered in enriched environments are also associated with higher IQ in children (Gunnell 2005). So, spend time exploring together in a new space, and you're making your child smarter.

Dr. Margo Sutherland, a child psychotherapist, is director of education and training at the Centre for Child Mental Health.

The Family Legacy Venture Protocol framework is another simple, intentional, and powerful set of practices with nearly endless possibilities. There are so many combinations of places to see, trips to take, foods to eat, stories to tell, subjects to cover, books to read, activities to enjoy, and questions to ask.

The Family Legacy Venture Framework

Pre-Venture Preparation

- venture selection
- joint planning
- naming the venture
- shared responsibilities
- logistics
- paying for the trip
- schedule
- buildup
- book discussion
- guidelines and agreements

Venture Execution

- experiential module(s)
- service project
- mealtime

- food
- fun
- use of story
- coaching conversations
- legacy connection

Post-Venture Learning

- Debrief

Framework Detail

Venture Selection

Without weigh-in, there is no buy-in. It is important for every family member to have a voice in the Family Legacy Venture process and decision-making. That includes receiving input from everyone in the venture selection for each year. Doing so shows honor to everyone involved, increases engagement, and models how families make decisions together.

Ask each person to bring at least one solid legacy venture proposal to the family at a designated time such as a year-end family gathering or as a final part of the current legacy venture.

The proposals should be shared and then written on a large flip chart for everyone to see and include the basics:

- where—location, destination, and (or) attractions
- when—date and time of year for planning purposes
- who—who is invited and who is not invited
- what—ideas about what to include: food, fun, experiences, and so on
- why—the greater why or purpose behind individual proposals

Joint Planning

As much as possible, include everyone in the planning process. This increases ownership and involvement in the legacy venture while training members how to do it. Avoid striking out on the menu or spending time and money on attractions that really aren't a priority for family members by getting suggestions and feedback from everyone.

Naming the Venture

Naming each venture gives it a distinct identity and allows the family to discuss the purpose or focus of the trip, which further embeds the entire experience into their memory banks and DNA.

This allows your family to create T-shirts, key chains, or journal covers that are distinct for each of their family ventures. Since we have creative types in our family, names and images for the trips communicate deeper and allow for the giftedness of family members to be expressed and enjoyed.

Some of our past Family Legacy Venture names include Launch, Kaleidoscope, Familia, and Family University.

Shared Responsibilities

By design, everyone shares responsibility in the legacy venture by using their unique giftedness to bless other family members. Doing what you love and are good at isn't a burden and doesn't drain your energy. Everyone doing their part in this way also shares the workload and ups the quality of experience while affirming the gifts in each member.

First, take note of who is good at what. Take the ages of family members into account as well. Second, assign responsibilities with this in mind, after giving necessary guidelines important for their success. Third, check in to help if needed.

For example, Lesli oversees food because she loves to cook for people and is great at it. Kara has a heart and gift for service, so she plans our service projects. Joel is a gifted musician and will bring the acoustic guitar soundtrack to the family. Garrett oversees fun because he is Mr. Fun. Miranda has a gift of administration and attention to detail, so she helps handle logistics. As for me, I handle the experiential exercises, facilitate discussions, and do as much as I can to pay for trip expenses. We all have a help where needed attitude, so no one is overwhelmed.

Logistics

If you have someone in your family who enjoys the detailed work of logistics and is gifted at that kind of work, assign the venture logistics to them. There is a lot to plan to include: travel, schedule, menu, activity or attractions, shopping, cooking and cleanup, pre-venture communication, and so much more.

It is important to have them help facilitate and execute the process with input from others, not to control and run all aspects of the process alone.

Paying for the Trip

However you decide to handle the financial piece of the venture is ultimately up to you. Having said that, there are at least three important principles to address as you make your decisions.

- ✓ It will always be wise to be a good steward of all the resources God has entrusted to us. Don't go into debt, overspend, or do things beyond your capacity as a good and faithful steward for anything, including a family venture. Keep things simple. Maximize relationship and interaction.
- ✓ Everyone shows up better when they have skin in the game. Meaning, everyone should do what they can, and the trip should be planned within that capacity. It also means that "where your treasure is, there your heart will be also." Our money is an extension of our lives. We invest our time, energy, and strength into work, in exchange for money. Here is the logic: when we spend our money, we spend our lives. We spend our lives on what we value. We tend to bring our best to the things we value. So, we bring our best to the Family Legacy Venture when we invest our money in the experience. Each according to their capacity with no one left out.
- ✓ Affordable for everyone so that no one is left out due to money. It's far better to take the entire family to a local state park for the day than to take only three members of the family on a venture to New Zealand. Include everyone, have everyone contribute something, and plan the experience in budget accordingly. For example, if mom and dad have 1 percent of their annual income available for a family venture, then what if everyone put in 1 percent as well. If that made-up number totaled $3,000, then that is the budget for the family venture, and we plan a venture that would work within that budget.

Schedule

A detailed schedule of daily activities is a must for the Family Legacy Venture. Intentionality is the name of the game when it comes to creating value. The reason we all get so much value out of the venture is because we choose to make the most of every opportunity. Sure, there is time and a plan for rest and fun and spontaneity, along with a time for structure, purpose, framework, and process for getting the most out of the time. Assign someone who delights in this kind of work to the project. You'll be grateful you did.

Buildup

"Research shows the biggest boost in happiness comes from planning the vacation. A person can feel the effects up to eight weeks before the trip!" (Shannon Torberg, PsyD, LP).

As a child, I loved the anticipation and buildup of a trip. I still do. I send countdown texts to the kids leading up to a venture. I talk about the trip at our regular family ritual meetings. I plant the reminders of the fun we will have, the food we will eat, and the lessons we will learn for weeks leading up to go time.

Do it!

Book Discussion (Optional)

Reading a book in the days leading up to the venture together and making a time during the trip to discuss it may or may not be valuable to every family. My family is a family of learners and readers committed to growth. Therefore, we have decided to include the book discussion as a part of our ventures.

Here are some things to ponder when considering adding the book discussion to your family venture.

- ✓ Vocabulary and subject matter can vary widely, so that makes the age of members something to factor into your book selection.
- ✓ Content can be controversial, and not all families can handle controversy well. If your family is unable to stay neutral, curious, and open while discussing certain content, it is wise to not select that hot topic for discussion.

- ✓ Select a book that will inspire, educate, or equip your family to be more effective in life.
- ✓ An open discussion where each person has a chance to share what stood out to them, or what they learned, or how the book applies to their lives is a simple format that works well.

Guidelines and Agreements

Most families have certain boundaries that they know not to cross with one another. Hot topics that are hot buttons should be avoided. Politics, religion, and past relationships top the list of possible subjects that are off limits when there are strong or emotional "points to prove" by family members. Going there creates division, focuses on disagreement, and prevents intimacy.

While sometimes these hot topics make for passionate conversations, they may undermine the sense of safety necessary for trust to be created. Setting guidelines and making agreements about how things will go so that everyone feels safe and can show up authentically and vulnerably without fear of paying a price is vitally important. Let everyone know what topics are off limits and then respect those boundaries. We want to fill the venture experience with good memories and meaningful moments with our families.

It has been my experience that once a safe, vulnerable, and open environment has been created in the family, where all members views can be heard and understood without the need for proving right and wrong, or demanding that everyone come to the same viewpoint, healthy and constructive conversations on nearly any topic are within reach.

Experiential Module(s)

By design, the Family Legacy Venture is an experiential module in its own right. However, I agree with the science that including at least one focused learning experience during the course of the venture produces long-lasting benefits.

At the most basic level, an experiential learning module has four parts:

- setup—where a leader talks about the purpose, value, and opportunities of the experience along with the detailed instructions of what to do

- execution—where members have the experience
- learning—where participants share what they learned in the experience, about themselves, their thinking, others, the topic, the world, and so on
- application—where participants share how they will apply the learning in specific areas of their lives

Example:

For one of our recent Family Legacy Ventures, we included a visit to the Kennedy Space Center in Cape Canaveral.

Setup: I set up the experience in the context of inspiring my family to explore their dreams in life.

Execution: We enjoyed the day together touring the facility, reading the stories, and watching the videos about how the dream of human space travel and walking on the moon grew from a dream into a reality and what it took to realize this amazing achievement.

Learning: That evening, and many times since then, we discussed what stood out to each of us and what lessons we learned from the experience.

Application: Each member then had the chance to share one or more of their own life dreams and their thoughts around what it would take for them to make it a reality. We offered support to one another in bringing the dream to life. Practical action steps were developed and embarked upon.

And we all have an experience we can go back to whenever we need inspiration while pursuing our life dreams. Powerful!

Service Project (Optional)

Your family may or may not choose to include some type of service project as a part of their venture. Because empathy and service of others are a part of our family true identity, we value service and have decided to include it in some way as a part of our ventures.

We have served in both formal and informal ways. We visited a men's rehabilitation ranch in Mexico one year. This year we are focused on serving one another and my dad.

We follow the project with an open discussion on what we did, what we learned, and how we will apply it to our lives in the future.

Mealtime

In every millennium and in every culture, the family mealtime is a valuable time of connecting, socializing, learning, and, let's not forget, eating! You may be thinking, *I'm on vacation. I don't want to cook and clean up. Let's just eat out!*

I understand where you are coming from. I do. However, preparing and enjoying meals together in a controlled environment provides many benefits and opportunities beyond the convenience of eating out:

- saves money
- addresses nutrition restrictions
- allows for input on menu and family favorites
- opportunity to serve one another
- allows everyone to contribute
- quiet enough to hear everyone
- provides privacy out of public ear
- avoids interruptions of servers
- allows unrestricted time to talk

The mealtime provides a simple structure to share family stories, dreams, goals, and struggles. It's a time to listen to one another, to support one another, to connect, to laugh, and to pass on legacy. Many of the most meaningful conversations we have had as a family have happened at mealtime.

Food

What's not to like about food? Enjoy it together. It's always better to talk about important things on a full and satisfied stomach than when people are "hangry." Gather input from everyone on the menu and make sure to include family favorites and legacy offerings. Yum!

Fun

Fun is a choice—just like being grumpy, skeptical, isolated, or bored is a choice. When you finally gather the family on a legacy venture, make sure that you all choose to have fun together! Play games, swim, ski, watch funny videos, tell fun stories, give fun gifts, see fun attractions, live it up a little, and *laugh!*

Fun is a powerful emotional implant that anchors the lessons and experiences of the family venture deep into the soul for generations.

If you don't know, ask. If it has been a while and you are out of touch with what fun looks like for your family, simply ask everyone for ideas. It's always fun to share the funniest stories from childhood. Whatever it looks like for you and your family, just do it! Have fun!

Use of Story

I encourage you to review the use of story in the previous chapter around the family ritual protocol. The same insights apply here in the Family Venture Protocol.

I will add this important and distinct recommendation for the family venture when it comes to story: intentionally tell stories that address legacy topics. Legacy topics are the areas of life experiences and wisdom that are most important for building your family identity and legacy for generations to come. I've listed several examples for you in the Venture Protocols section.

Coaching Conversations

Family coaching conversations are one of the distinctive practices that set this entire Family Legacy Model apart from any other. The coach approach in the Family Venture Protocol brings safety, support, discovery, personal responsibility, and practical application together into a five-question conversation that builds families, businesses, and communities.

> What did you experience and observe today?
> What did you learn?
> How does your learning specifically apply to your life?
> What will you do as a result?
> How can we help?

Lasting legacy is advanced as we build our families from the inside out. A coach approach in the family equips our children to grow into kind people of good character, strong and skilled leaders who show up with courage and humility as they make earth a little more like heaven.

And they teach their children to do the same.

Legacy Connection

As I stated earlier, the soil of a Family Legacy Venture is one of the most fertile opportunities to pass on legacy there is. The secret to making the most of this amazing opportunity is to be intentional and to keep it simple. Simply following the protocols as designed will equip you and your children to pass on the most important things when it comes to your family legacy. Choose to trust the process.

Being intentional means to do things on purpose and by the design of the protocol. For example:

- Include everyone in the planning and preparation process.
- Choose a book and have a discussion on the learning (age appropriate).
- Share stories that are character, wisdom, and legacy focused.
- Have the basic coaching conversations.
- Have a family experience and debrief on the learning from it.
- Have fun together!

Keeping it simple means to choose not to get overwhelmed and to let go of the expectations you have of how it has to look.

- The protocols seem overwhelming because you are learning them as brand-new.
- They become natural and simple once you learn them.
- Choose to be open to how members respond, what they learn, and how they apply it.
- Choose to trust that the process will work if you do it.
- Choose to trust that modeling these things for your family will influence your legacy.
- Do what you can in partnership with God and trust that He will do His part as well.

For those of you with young families and others who have families that have been devastated and are barely holding it together, who are reading this and thinking, *I can't possibly find the time, energy, and resources to do this*, I get it. I understand your feeling and thinking here. And I would say this in love:

whatever is keeping you from making this happen at some level with your family regularly is keeping you from some of the very most important things that make family worth having and life worth living.

Even if you do the Family Legacy Protocols and do them poorly, you are doing the best you can with what you have at this moment for the healing, enrichment, and equipping of your family legacy. What more can you do? Having said that, you alone know if postponing a start for a season is in the best interest of all. Trust your heart.

Post-Venture Learning

Debrief

The intentional asking of a few important questions can make all the difference in the world when it comes to the venture and experiences being a "been there, done that, next" and an experience of learning, growth, and transformation that can be put into practice in every life to further advance the family to its legacy.

At the very end of the Family Legacy Venture or just after you have completed the venture, gather the family together and ask everyone the following questions. Include everyone in the discussion.

1. What was the most important learning for you on this venture?
2. How does this learning connect to our family legacy?
3. How will you specifically apply this learning to your life moving forward?

That's it.

Keep it simple.

A follow-up inquiry as to how it is going for each member during family rituals or at the next venture is another effective way to further implant the new behavior.

Tips for Environment and Execution

As you prepare to take your family through the Family Venture Protocol, please review the sections in chapter 4. Following the guidelines is essential for getting the most out of the exercises for the benefit of your family. In addition, here are a few additional tips for successful execution.

Environment and Execution

- The venture exercises are most effective in a low-stress, vacation-like, informal, private setting with only actual family members and participants. No observers, unless they are one of our coaches or facilitators present to assist your family.
- Remember to apply the lessons from the EQ tools from chapter 5. Empathetic listening, speaking the truth in love, fact/story, the Family Social Covenant, and so on. Governing yourself well is vital to stewarding the family during this protocol.
- Everyone should have a role to play in this protocol with ample time to complete each exercise without rushing things.
- The room should be quiet and free from distractions as much as possible. Cell phones, digital devices, television sets, and music should all be turned off or used very sparingly during free time in the schedule.
- Secure the proper resources needed (e.g., food, the completed Venture Agenda Tool, game supplies, attraction resources, etc.).
- You will also find the list of Family Legacy Tools for the exercises in chapter 11. Download the tools at www.culturalarchitects.org. In addition, you may want to order workbooks for everyone to keep everyone's collective work in one place for easy use and reference.
- Allow enough time for each person to fully answer the questions or perform the exercise.
- Be willing to draw out the thoughts and feelings of participants as they are processing the work and sharing.
- Make sure everyone gets their time to share or be the focus of the family, equally and as needed.
- It is vitally important that you keep the environment safe for everyone. Do not allow criticism, sarcasm, cynical remarks, rude comments, and so on. This is not the time or the place for that. Make sure that no one pays the price for being vulnerable.

- Stay open to how things will play out.
- Deal with things as they come up.
- Reach out for help if you get stuck, don't know what to do, or if things go astray.
- You may decide to join the Family Legacy monthly subscription for additional support, attend a workshop, take an e-course, or request coaching and facilitating support.

Other environment considerations:

- *Music.* Make a soundtrack for your family venture. Music is a powerful reminder and bridge to our emotions and to memories. Have fun with it.
- *Movies.* Select a movie or two for the family that is funny or inspiring as a part of the fun.

Venture Protocols

The experiential exercises for the Family Legacy Venture Protocol below are practical, intentional, educational, and empowering. They are designed to create fun experiences, learning opportunities, lasting memories, and legacy implantation. By including everyone, engagement is high, and the experiences train the generations to come.

I have written a brief description of each of the experiential exercises below. You will understand the purpose and value of the exercises as you read. You will want to go to our website www.culturalarchitects.org to download the editable PDF Family Legacy Protocol Tools for each exercise to walk you through the execution of each one step-by-step.

Venture Protocol Descriptions

Venture Exercise 1—Family Venture Launch Gathering

The purpose of this exercise is to inform the family of your decision to begin having Family Legacy Ventures by gathering everyone together for a venture launch gathering. In this gathering, you will introduce the purpose and framework of the of the Family Venture Protocol. You will complete the

Family Venture Launch Tool together to build the interest and commitment of family members by including them in the planning process.

I recommend that you hold the venture launch gathering at one of three ideal times.

1. At one of your regularly scheduled family ritual meetings—just eat and then implement launch gathering.
2. At a special year-end family gathering during the holidays in planning for the upcoming year.
3. During the regular time in your schedule when you are planning the next family vacation.

In preparation for the launch gathering, you will need to determine the following:

- Who is going to facilitate or lead your family venture launch gathering?
- What are the gathering details? (Date, time, location, etc.)
- Who is invited? Send invites.
- Take the age and maturity of family members into consideration as you execute the launch.
- Gather resources needed for the venture launch gathering.
- Snacks.
- Flip chart and markers or worksheets printed out.
- Review the venture purpose, definition, framework, and tips.
- Pray and prepare for the launch.

In the family venture launch gathering, you will share the following aspects of the venture:

- purpose
- definition
- framework

The leader explains that the launch gathering is to introduce the family to the venture concepts and to get everyone's help and input for the first official Family Legacy Venture. In addition, everyone will have venture responsibilities of some kind, including destination selection, menu and food prep, logistics and planning, facilitating the experience module(s), leading the fun, planning and leading the service project, book selection and discussion, and cleaning up. The family venture is not a spectator event; everyone gets to engage.

With a flip chart and a marker, the leader begins to gather everyone's input. The process for planning the various parts of the venture framework at the launch gathering is the same. The leader writes a word or short phrase from below at the top of the flip chart, while members can use a copy of the tool worksheet and write their responses. The leader facilitates discussion and a selection process that produces the top agreed-upon responses from the family, which become the components of the first Family Legacy Venture.

When you've gathered all the input and the paper is all over the walls, let everyone know how fun and exciting this is going to be! This is a great time to share your heart around family and legacy. It is also a great time to pray and ask for God's guidance and blessing on your family venture plans.

You now have a great deal of input from the family, and it should be easy to plan out the finer details of the Family Legacy Venture. By doing it this way, you have also engaged everyone in the process and gotten greater buy-in from members to show up. You have also modeled for everyone how to do this with their own families for generations to come.

The Family Venture Launch Tool will guide you through the gathering in detail.

Venture Exercise 2-Family Venture Advance Planning

The purpose of this exercise is to plan for the next big family adventure by completing the Family Venture Advance Planning Exercise together. It is essentially the same process as the launch meeting without some of the foundational introductory remarks. Family members can make new location and activity suggestions. You can make new menu requests, identify different story topics, recommend new service projects, and make new book selections. It's time for new fun activities along with new learning adventures. This exercise also adds an element of learning and opportunity for improvement by inviting feedback from the previous venture.

Your family will get out the flip chart and markers and go through the process again. It may be fun to invite a different family member to lead the exercise. This will engage people in a new way, equipping them with new leadership skills and mentoring them in how to do this with their own families one day.

Another valuable part of this exercise is the simple evaluation by the family of how they think the last family venture went. By asking a few simple questions, your family can make your next venture even more meaningful moving forward. The review questions include the following:

- What worked?
- What didn't work?
- What did we learn?
- What next?

The Family Venture Advance Planning Tool will guide you step-by-step in planning the next Family Legacy Venture, including the following:

- location
- activities
- food
- fun
- learning adventure
- books
- service projects
- assignment of responsibilities
- trip costs
- story topics
- naming the venture
- more

Venture Exercise 3—Family Venture Agenda

The purpose of this exercise is to maximize the focus and intentionality of the Family Legacy Venture by creating an agenda or schedule to follow. It is important for the family venture to strike a balance between planning and free flow in order to address the topics that will build a healthy family legacy and make room for learning.

Planning out the details make it much more likely that each venture will be executed effectively for the good of everyone and for the family legacy. I've provided a simple tool to plan and distribute to everyone prior to each family venture so everyone is prepared for their assignments and their contributions. At first, it may seem overwhelming to think about including all these new practices into a vacation. However, once you are familiar with them, it is fairly easy and very much a natural flow of conversation. The difference is that you are doing things intentionally in order to connect and impact the family.

By using Venture Agenda Tool, you can both plan intentionally and communicate the plan to family members. You will also have a record of your ventures to keep so you can see what you've covered and what is left to cover that is important to your family legacy. In addition, you are leaving a wonderful codified record of how you did family that you can pass on to generations to come, which will reinforce the practice of the Family Legacy Venture.

Venture Exercise 4—Family Venture Service Project (Optional)

Serving others together as a family leaves a powerful and lasting imprint on everyone involved. As you decide whether to include a service project in your family venture, consider the following benefits in doing so:

- blesses other people
- blesses your own family
- demonstrates empathy and service to others
- provides a growth experience for members
- can double as one of your experience modules

The service project can be large or small. It can take up several days or just a few hours. From building a home in Mexico for a poor family to visiting the elderly in a care facility, or from sprucing up the lawn to painting a relative or neighbor's home, there are endless possibilities to serve others. You will model social responsibility and a compassion for people to your family with long-term and even eternal impact.

Remember, the service project can be formal or informal in nature. Serving an organization works great! Serving one another in the family or a particular person in the family intentionally can work great as well.

The Venture Service Project Tool will help you plan the details for a service project as a part of your Family Legacy Venture and is available online with our other Family Legacy Tools.

Venture Exercise 5—Family Venture Book Discussion (Optional)

Including a book discussion may or may not be something you choose to add to the Family Legacy Venture. Vocabulary and age appropriateness, along with subject matter and comprehension are all important considerations in making a book selection should you choose to include it.

Here are some compelling reasons to include a book discussion as a part of your family venture:

- Third-party expertise allows the family to discover ideas together from an expert instead of hearing something again from mom and dad.
- A book is lasting and can be referred to in the future.
- Leaders are readers. It's always a good idea to foster reading, comprehension, and discussion for growth.
- Modeling a value for learning in your family has long-reaching effects.
- Prayerful selection can bring a spiritual growth opportunity as well.
- Discussion creates an opportunity to listen and share with one another for deeper connection.
- Discussion then leads to application of concepts into real life with supportive accountability.
- Book selection can address Family Legacy values, characteristic, and practices to further equip members to live the legacy.

The Venture Book Discussion Tool will guide you the experience step-by-step as you:

- make a book selection
- facilitate a book discussion
- facilitate a coaching conversation around applying the learning

Make sure to have someone take notes or even record a video of the discussion in order to capture the insights, learning, and commitments to action for the family moving forward.

Venture Exercise 6—Family Venture Mealtime

The purpose of this exercise is to deeply connect with family over food, fun, story, wisdom, and a supportive coaching conversation focused on a legacy connection. A legacy connection is simply the intentional focus on family core values, character qualities, or the family purpose during the share times in story, wisdom, and coaching conversations.

The way to think about mealtime during a Family Legacy Venture is like you are having a week of Family Ritual Meetings (protocol 3) with some minor adjustments.

These areas of mealtime remain the same as the family ritual meeting:

- menu selection
- food preparation and cleanup
- fun

The adjustments are simple and bring a focus to the legacy connection within the context of a family venture. Adjustments are recommended in the following areas for the family venture:

- wisdom focused on legacy connection
- coaching conversation focused on venture learning from book, service project, experience module, legacy
- story focused on legacy connection

The flow of mealtime during a family venture is the same as the family ritual:

- ritual meeting
- food
- story
- coaching
- wisdom
- fun
- cleanup

The difference is that the story, coaching, and wisdom pieces are all focused on making the legacy connection.

Story topics should focus on family legacy characteristics and real-life examples (e.g., empathy, faith, trust, love, etc.). Choosing topics for story from the family crest and family identity reinforce the practice and importance of who we are as a family. This bolsters our sense of true identity and purpose as a family while deeply connecting with one another.

Coaching conversations are slightly adjusted as well for the family venture mealtime. The adjusted coaching conversation is listed in the next section. Use this set of questions during the venture.

The wisdom portion of mealtime is also adjusted to share content that is focused on the legacy connection. This is the time to share family scriptures, life verses, and promises from the Lord. It's the time to connect the dots of God's wisdom to our family agreement and practice of that wisdom.

Venture Exercise 7—Family Venture Coaching Conversation

The purpose of this exercise is to take advantage of the emotional implant opportunity that is deepened within the dynamics of a learning adventure by integrating a coaching conversation addressing legacy with a family venture, resulting in a big return on investment.

As you plan for the coaching conversations during the family venture, review the sections in chapter 4. Family coaching conversations are one of the distinctive practices that set this entire Family Legacy Model apart from any other. The coach approach in the Family Venture Protocol brings safety, support, discovery, personal responsibility, and practical application together into a five-question conversation that builds families, businesses, and communities. During the Venture Protocol, a special legacy connection is added to the coaching conversation.

Coaching is one of the most empowering and invigorating modalities in creating growth and success offered today. To bring this into the family venture and to invest in the personal growth and development of each family member is a powerful way to do family. Family coaching is an effective way to build legacy while training our children how to bring coaching into their generations to come.

Here is the five-question coaching conversation model for use during mealtime in the Family Venture Protocol. It is important to bring the context of family legacy into these conversations.

- What did you experience and observe today (book, service project, stories, meals, experience modules)?
- What did you learn?
- How does your learning specifically apply to your life and our family legacy?
- What will you do specifically moving forward?
- How can we help?

The Venture Coaching Tool will guide you through step-by-step in these important coaching conversations and is available online with the other Family Legacy Model tools.

Venture Exercise 8—Family Venture Experience Module(s)

The purpose of this exercise is to include at least one focused learning experience during the course of the venture in order to produce life-changing and long-lasting benefits. Experiential learning is effective on its own. When integrated with an intentional legacy connection, the most important aspects of legacy can be caught and taught in a manner that will last.

What do you want to teach your family?

- How to dream?
- How to hear God?
- How to be successful in marriage, parenting, or on the job?
- How to heal?
- How to bring healing to others?
- How to be good stewards of their health, finances, and talents?
- How to be grateful, generous, and loving?
- How to make good decisions?
- How to grow in leadership, integrity, or courage?
- How to keep their word and follow through on their agreements?

There is a nearly endless list of things to teach our families to help them succeed in life and legacy. Choosing to teach them by intentionally giving them an experience is wise. Giving them an experience equips them to give similar experiences to their children and grandchildren.

Do not underestimate the eternal transformative power and results to your family legacy from a simple and intentional experience.

At the most basic level, an experiential learning module has four parts:

- setup—where a leader talks about the purpose, value, and opportunities of the experience along with the detailed instructions of what to do
- execution—where members have the experience
- learning—where participants share what they learned in the experience about themselves, their thinking, others, the topic, the world, their faith, and so on
- application—where participants share how they will apply the learning in specific areas of their lives

I've created a Venture Experience Module Tool that will help you successfully plan and execute an experience learning module as a part of your Family Legacy Venture. Available online. www.culturalarchitects.org

Venture Exercise 9—Family Venture Legacy Connection

The purpose of this exercise is to support the family in intentionally connecting the various pieces of the Venture Protocol to the family legacy. The big idea here is to simply connect the stories, experiences, and coaching conversations you select in your family venture to the heart and essence of your family values, purpose, and character. Through intentionality and the skilled use of powerful questions in a time of debrief, you can connect the doing and the learning to the being and the becoming.

Believe it or not, every single aspect of the family venture is directly connected to your family legacy, as are all the Family Legacy Protocols. The choice you make to do family life the way you do is living the legacy that you will leave. Choosing to intentionally give your family emotionally implanted experiences connected to important family values, identity, purpose, and practice will impact the trajectory of your family. Your choices will determine your family legacy.

It is important to have the legacy connection in mind as you are planning the various parts of the family venture. When selecting and planning the destination, book, service project, story topics, experience modules, and so forth, think family legacy values, identity, purpose, and practice.

As you are planning, ask yourself these questions:

- How can I reinforce our family true identity?
- What does our family need in this season to more fully step into our family values, purpose, and mission?
- What is the best and most practical book out there on healing, trust, honor, courage, leadership, or any other family core characteristic?
- What kind of service project will cause the family to grow in a specific character quality we want to build in our family?
- What story topics will address and reinforce our family true identity, values, and purpose?

Your answers to these questions will connect the parts of the family venture to family legacy in an effective way.

Don't overcomplicate it here. If integrity is a family value, then share stories on examples from your life of integrity. If leadership is an aspect of your family mission, choose a book on leadership for discussion. If your family has been devastated by divorce, then choose an experience around healing and forgiveness or divorce recovery and talk about what you are learning.

Keep it simple.

The Venture Legacy Tool will guide you through this process to ensure a strong legacy connection.

Once again, go to our website to download the editable PDF Family Legacy Protocol Tools for each exercise to walk you through the execution of each one step-by-step. www.culturalarchitects.org

Chapter 9
Family Legacy MISSION

The purpose of the Family Legacy MISSION Protocol is to equip and empower your family to stay connected and meaningfully engaged in challenging times of need. The protocols provide you with an intentional and effective way to steward your family with wisdom during a time of great vulnerability when mind-sets are fashioned that have both real-time and generational consequences.

Whether the need is an opportunity or crisis for one or more members of the family, the MISSION is a momentary, intentional, specific, and supportive intervention as one in response to a need.

Why?

It is often during a traumatic family event where we are most vulnerable to soul wounds that bring lasting pain, skewed perspectives, and broken relationships in families. These wounds are perhaps the biggest and most dangerous threats to successfully living a powerful family legacy. Many of the mind-sets that we struggle with today originated in our genetic donors in times of crisis generations ago. The same will be true of your children and theirs.

Because of the high emotion in these traumatic family life events, the perceptions that we arrive at through those experiences lock into our DNA, and we begin expressing deep genetic and outward responses to these perceptions. A mind-set is formed and followed, sometimes for generations, resulting in ongoing consequences of fear, distrust, identity drift, performance-based value, and the list goes on and on. These mind-sets then begin producing their fruit in the lives of those we love. Stewarding these experiences well and governing our thinking in the very moments when so many lasting mind-sets are being developed and implanted is wise.

Likewise, positive and productive mind-sets can be formed and followed from these traumatic experiences as well. We have been designed with the power to choose what mind-sets we agree or disagree with. What we know for certain is that these experiences will shape our thinking one way or another, presenting us with a real-time opportunity to govern ourselves well and to steward the family in a healthy and lasting way.

I am picturing some of you reading this right now and lamenting, "It would have been a break for me to have an occasional traumatic event or crisis in my family of origin or even today in my nuclear family. Crisis was/is constant in my world …" My heart goes out to you. This is why the first Family Legacy Protocol in the model is EQ—emotional intelligence. Having a way to discover and heal from these wounds and undo the ingrained ways of thinking that perpetuate dysfunction is vital in a day-to-day reality.

Governing well in the face of the rejection and abandonment, the misunderstandings and judgments, the unmet expectations, or worse yet, the physical, emotional, and sexual abuse or the carnage of an alcoholic home is paramount to the success of current and future generations of the family line.

When we do, we change the gene expression in our DNA and create new genetic programming for our generations to come. If we can make the changes prior to conception, our prodigy will carry a new program and mind-set into their offspring.

Thus, it creates generations of children a little healthier and better able to overcome life's challenges. Ultimately, given they know how to take personal responsibility and continue to self-govern well, the likelihood of them becoming wise builders of families, businesses, and communities in their own right increases exponentially—healthy cultural architects influencing for good in the gates of culture.

MISSION Definition, Value, and Framework

Definition

The MISSION is an intentional way for family to steward the most challenging times in life together, as one.

In so doing, the family will avoid many of the arrows and wounds that fly furiously in times of crisis and model a healthy way for the children to handle crisis to further repel these perilous soul wounds. Finally, in these emotionally tender times, the soil of the heart is fertile for creating deep and lasting legacy imprints for generations to come, both good and bad.

The MISSION is a way to wisely navigate the rough waters of family crisis and opportunity. The practices provide a framework for how everyone can show up productively during these seasons of challenge in ways that will minimize the destructive potential of these experiences, replacing them with life-giving, legacy-shaping, heart-connecting experiences together as a family.

You may choose to activate a Family Legacy MISSION in the following kinds of circumstances:

- death of a loved one, whether expected or unexpected
- sickness or injury, including mental health, addiction treatment or recovery
- wedding or divorce
- home purchase
- bankruptcy or financial distress
- major transition—new job, retirement, family move, new school, and so on
- new business
- empty nest
- new birth or adoption
- moral failures
- criminal behavior
- change or shift around spiritual beliefs
- goals or achievements—training and competing in a triathlon, finishing a university degree, weight loss
- vacations or travel
- more ...

A Family Legacy MISSION could also include a family cause-based MISSION (e.g., starting a nonprofit for pancreatic cancer research or building a school or orphanage as a missionary project in honor or remembrance of a family member).

Value

In times of high stress, deep grief, frantic uncertainty, and rapid change, people need the support and structure of a process to navigate through the turbulent waters. Families, businesses, and organizations are shaken in these times, and having a plan for bringing everyone together with clear roles can keep the ship upright and moving forward.

The Family Legacy MISSION Protocol Framework

M—Momentary
I—Intentional
S—Specific
S—Supportive
I—Intervention
O—as One
N—in response to Need

Momentary
(moh-muh n-ter-ee)

adj.—lasting for a brief amount of time

The MISSION is temporary in length and application. The family determines at the time of MISSION launch how long the mission will last. On average, it lasts between thirty and ninety days, sometimes more and sometimes less. There is a beginning and an end to a MISSION. Not everyone may be able to participate in every family MISSION. If you are in, then you are all in. If you can't be all in for the piece that you commit to, pass on that MISSION or make your commitment to participate appropriate to the capacity you actual have and follow through. Follow-through builds and ensures trust among members and gets the job done efficiently.

Intentional
(in-ten-shuh-nl)

adj.—done with intention or on purpose; designed, willful, deliberate

You launch a family MISSION on purpose. It requires agreement and accountability for family team members who are choosing to participate in any given MISSION. For best results, members will have simple and clearly defined roles and expectations designed for them. Handling things in times of need can be stressful, overwhelming, and uncertain. The peace, certainty, and confidence that having a plan brings are amazing, and they come at the price of being intentional.

These practices don't have to be complicated and difficult, but they do have to be intentional. An intentional effort that is focused and well defined is powerful.

Like any important mission, there is a price to pay. Family members should be mindful in weighing the costs before making the commitment to participate in any given MISSION

Things to address when considering personal involvement in a MISSION include the following:

- creating capacity to serve in your already busy schedule.
- rearranging other priorities to give yourself adequately to the MISSION
- facing potential emotional challenges that surface
- dealing with the discomfort gracefully
- the degree to which you choose to put the needs of others before your own for a season
- extra or unexpected financial expenses for equipment, attorneys, funeral homes, travel, gas …
- outlay of physical energy required for the MISSION—to clean, to pack and move a home, to meet with doctors, to give transport, and so on
- who will accept the role of MISSION commander
- how your unique gifts and strength can best be used

Specific
(spi-sif-ik)

adj.—precise, detailed, explicit qualities or characteristics

All the important details of the MISSION are discussed, determined, assigned. and agreed upon. Specifically! The family isn't just winging it. It's not about just randomly showing up and making things better. After all, what specifically does "better" mean? How will we measure if it is actually better or not better? What criteria will we set to ensure that the MISSION is successfully completed?

The who, what, when, where, why, and how of the MISSION need to be determined and communicated to all. As many of the important details as possible will be determined at the time of MISSION launch (see tools). Changes and audibles must also be determined and communicated in a specific manner for the clarity and inclusion of all. Doing so will also minimize potential misunderstanding and conflict.

Supportive
(sup·port/sə'pôrt/)

verb

1. bear all or part of the weight of; hold up
2. give assistance to, encourage, enable to function or act

The atmosphere of the Family Legacy MISSION from start to finish is one of support. The MISSION is not a time to argue, criticize, blame, position, or take. It is a time to offer help, comfort, and backup to those we love.

When you face the most difficult and challenging parts of life, will you have family who can carry you when you are out of strength? Will they bear part of the weight that you are lifting as you navigate the waters of divorce, death, natural disaster, and sickness? Where will you get assistance when you don't know what to do? Family, as designed, is there for one another when more is required from a member than they have the capacity for on their own. The Family Legacy MISSION is all about coming together in a spirit and attitude of love and support for one another as a family.

When those in your family face a crisis, do they look to one another? Do they look to you? Do you look to them? Do you show up with love and service or with blame, shame, and guilt?

The unconditional love and support of family is a great treasure and priceless gem.

Intervention
(in-ter-ven-shuh n)

verb—to intercede, to involve, to occur or be between two things

The family MISSION occurs between two things, in between the time of need or crisis and the time of living the new normal. For example, a MISSION is activated after a job firing or geographic transfer and is complete when the new job is in place and the move to a new city is finished.

- in between a divorce or a death and the healthy new normal
- in between the loneliness crash of an empty nest and a new rhythm for life
- in between a business or moral failure and restoration
- in between a diagnosis and an end of treatment
- in between the crash of a car accident and things getting back to normal
- in between the start of triathlon training and crossing the finish line

This is a strategic time for modeling how to love, serve, trust, communicate, problem-solve, and be a good family member. How we steward ourselves and our families in these times is critical.

One, Oneness
(wuhn-nis)

noun—the quality of being one; unity of thought, feeling, belief, aim, etc.; agreement; concord; a strong feeling of closeness or affinity; union

Strong families stick together in good times and bad. A win for one is a win for all. A challenge for one is an invitation to lock shields and partner as appropriate to overcome that challenge together, as one.

Does your family show up as one and in the fight together? Not all do. Many people are left to face a crisis alone. They are isolated from the family and afraid of the criticism, blame, and shame that they fear is waiting for them in the words of those designed to be their inner circle of safety and support.

Sometimes the crisis is not external but rather an internal crisis, directly involving family members, complicating further this idea of addressing the challenge as one with the whole family.

It is possible to come together and address any circumstance together as one, if you choose to remember that the battle is outside of us. Even when the challenge is between us, it is not you against me; it is us against the problem. We are on the same team, the same body fighting for what is good, right, and just for us and all we love. We come together as one against the enemies of our soul, against our own misaligned mind-sets, and we fight ... not each other but the problem. Whether an external threat or an issue among family members, the way forward in peace is together as one!

In the end, *it's worth it.*

- enjoying the fun of engaging as a family
- living purposefully by helping one another grow, heal, overcome, and thrive
- experiencing the love, peace, and joy of family
- feeling the connectedness and belonging that comes when winning together
- expressing and receiving gratitude from those closest to you
- supporting the healing of one another, leading to longer and healthier lives
- passing on of important life lessons, practices, and solutions
- gaining the strength of intact families who persevered through challenges and helped one another live their dreams
- equipping our children with experiential knowledge of how to do family

One can put one thousand to flight, but two can put ten thousand to flight. There are exponential resources available when we come together as one to address life opportunities and challenges in the family.

Need

(need)

noun

1. lack of something deemed a necessity; an urgent want deemed necessary
2. necessity arising from the circumstances of a situation or case
3. a situation or time of difficulty

Sometimes life can live you. Human beings are amazingly resilient, most of the time. In my profession as a minister, I saw many examples of individuals and families in need.

I've experienced many painful and traumatic things in my life, as I shared in chapter 3 of this book. There have been many times of need in the lives of each person in my family. You likely have firsthand experience with need in your family as well.

Great challenges are also great opportunities. They provide opportunities to heal, grow, and connect, along with so many others. Coming together as a family unit when facing tough times deepens love and implants legacy deep into the hearts and minds of all involved, especially our children.

Here are important questions for you to consider:

Q: What traumatic events or crisis did my genetic donors experience?
Q: How did they address them?
Q: What were the healthy and unhealthy mind-sets that resulted from those experiences?
Q: How have those mind-sets surfaced in you or others, and what has resulted?
Q: What crisis have you experienced in your life?
Q: What are the circumstances of great need currently in your family of origin?
Q: In your nuclear family?
Q: How will you choose to engage your family around the crisis or opportunity?
Q: What harmful mind-sets are being formed by family members as a result of crisis?

Q: How will your legacy be impacted by these events and mind-sets?
Q: What would be different if you approached these crisis and opportunities as one with your family by launching a family MISSION?
Q: What holds you back from taking action and launching one?
Q: What are you doing to teach and equip your children to know how to walk through times like these over their lifetime?

Tips for Environment and Execution

As you prepare to take your family through the Family MISSION Protocol, please review the sections in chapter 4. Following the guidelines is essential for getting the most out of the exercises for the benefit of your family. In addition, here are a few additional tips for successful execution.

Environment and Execution

- The MISSION Protocol, by design, happens in times of stress on the family. Depending on your family, you may choose to conduct this protocol privately with only family or inner circle relationships. Decisions need to be made on a timeline. A clear, detailed, and well-communicated plan must be executed. If necessary, have participants join by phone or digital app, as it is important to include all participants in the MISSION launch meeting.
- Remember to use the EQ tools from chapter 5: empathetic listening, speaking the truth in love, fact/story, the Family Social Covenant, and so on. Governing yourself well is vital to stewarding the family during this time.
- The MISSION Protocols are essentially a series of questions that must be discussed and answered together as one that will result in the formulation of an action plan addressing the details of the MISSION.
- You will also find a list of Family Legacy Tools for the exercises in chapter 11. Download them at www.culturalarchitets.org. In addition, you may want to order workbooks for everyone to keep everyone's collective work in one place for easy use and reference.

- In preparation, review the entire exercise ahead of time so that you know what to expect.
- Allow enough time for each person to fully answer the questions or perform the exercise.
- Be willing to draw out the thoughts and feelings of participants as they are processing the work and sharing.
- Make sure everyone gets their time to share or be the focus of the family equally and as needed.
- It is vitally important that you keep the environment safe for everyone. Do not allow criticism, sarcasm, cynical remarks, rude comments, and so on. This is not the time or the place for that. Make sure that no one pays the price for being vulnerable.
- Stay open to how things will play out.
- Deal with things as they come up.
- Appoint a good notetaker to capture accurately the things being said and agreed to.
- You will want to make copies of the MISSION blueprint once completed for everyone participating.
- Schedule a MISSION brief, a regular meeting or conference call on a regular and predetermined frequency to share progress, updates, changes, needs, decisions, and so on.
- Reach out for help if you get stuck, don't know what to do, or if things go astray.
- You may decide to join the Family Legacy monthly subscription for additional support, attend a workshop, take an e-course, or request coaching and facilitating support.

MISSION Protocols

The experiential exercises for the Family Legacy MISSION Protocol below are straightforward, detailed, and thorough. They are designed to do the thinking for you and provide a clear path forward during a time of family crisis. They will assist you in organizing, delegating, and communicating the details of the MISSION for the family members who are involved.

Remember, we are here to help you if you find leading these exercises to be difficult. Contact our office and talk with one of our coaches, make arrangements for us to lead your family through the exercises, or attend one of our workshops, conferences, or e-courses. Don't skip the exercises. They are included for a reason.

I have written a brief description of each of the experiential exercises below. You will understand the purpose and value of the exercises as you read. You will want to go to our website to download the editable PDF Family Legacy Protocol Tools for each exercise to walk you through the execution of each one step-by-step. www.culturalarchitects.org

MISSION Protocol Descriptions

MISSION Exercise 1—MISSION Blueprint (Preparation and Planning)

The purpose of this exercise is to provide the family with a mechanism to quickly and thoroughly move from a family crisis event into a detailed and organized plan of action together as one. The idea here is that of a special operations military-style mission in response to a time of urgent family need. The exercise is literally the completion of the MISSION Blueprint Preparation Tool. Whoever decides to take the lead in this exercise is called the commander. The commander may want to invite a few others to help in the completion of the blueprint, but it is not required.

For those of you who have a faith orientation, I recommend that you start this entire process with prayer, surrendering and dedicating this entire process to God.

The MISSION Blueprint Preparation Tool will guide you through the process of putting all the details together quickly. The tool will address the who, what, when, where, why, and how of the MISSION and address things such as follow:

- Who is assuming the role of commander of this family MISSION?
- What is your contact information?

- What is the estimated time of duration for this MISSION (thirty to ninety days)? Projected start date is _____, and projected end date is _____.
- Is permission needed to engage in this MISSION (e.g., the person(s) in crisis)?
- Who will secure permission from them? By when?
- What is the purpose of this MISSION?
- What is the official code name for this family MISSION?
- What are the outcomes you see for the successful completion of this MISSION?
- Where are things at right now? Describe what "is" as of right now in this moment.
- How will we get there from here?
- What is needed for the MISSION? List the detail as you understand it:
    - activities
    - resources
    - money
    - prayer
    - advice
    - wisdom
    - roles
    - skills
    - labor
    - transportation
    - projects
    - events
    - professional support (pastor, therapist, doctor, coach, real estate, attorney)
    - complete brain dump of what is needed for the MISSION
- What further research or insights do we need for this MISSION?

The tool addresses several additional details in preparation for the MISSION launch gathering.

Every MISSION will only be as effective as the preparation and planning of the blueprint. Don't take any shortcuts here.

MISSION Exercise 2—MISSION Launch (Gathering and Assignments)

The purpose of this exercise is to officially launch a MISSION by the commander calling a gathering, where they will share the blueprint and engage family members and other potential participants to assign tasks, roles, and functions, along with specific actions that each will commit to as a part of this MISSION

The MISSION Launch Tool will guide you through the launch step-by-step and address things such as follows:

- the official name of this MISSION
- the purpose of the MISSION
- MISSION blueprint walk-through by commander
- resources needed for the MISSION
- gaining agreement for the primary means of communication (Ask and decide.)
- the obstacles present
- solutions that we are missing
- assignments—who's in and what each one will do specifically
- care to not overload anyone
- care to include everyone who is willing and able in appropriate ways
- distributing the assignments once completed to all involved
- more

The commander will bring the launch gathering to a close by clearly communicating the expectations around the MISSION brief (regular ongoing communication) and addressing anything that remains unclear or undecided. Once the launch is complete, there is an official active MISSION.

You may be asking, "Why is this so formal?" The answer to that question is that by adding a measure of order and formality to this process, it intrinsically adds a measure of seriousness with a heightened level of clarity around expectations and, ultimately, a more effective Family Legacy MISSION.

The MISSION Launch Tool will guide you through this exercise each step of the way.

MISSION Exercise 3—MISSION Brief (Regular Briefing Meeting)

The purpose of this exercise is to provide the family with a process for regular briefing meetings for the stewardship of the MISSION, keeping everyone up to speed with developments. The commander is responsible for the regular briefing meeting, called the MISSION brief. This is the ongoing communication between all MISSION participants that keeps everyone on track and in the know. This is also the place where opportunities arise to support one another, address any balls that have been dropped, add new tasks, comfort one another in setbacks, and celebrate wins. It is the regular opportunity to learn from the journey, to connect with family members, and to be strengthened with support for what lies ahead.

First things first. The commander will need to communicate the following:

- The MISSION briefs scheduled: day_____ dates_____ time_____.
- The estimated length of time for the briefs (thirty to forty-five minutes is standard).
- The means of communication: conference call____ digital app____ in person____.
- Who is invited to the brief?
- Who is the notetaker for the brief?
- The basic agenda to follow for each MISSION brief is:
    - MISSION brief open (commander officially opens the brief, prayer optional)
    - roll call (who's in the brief)
    - MISSION report from each member (commander facilitates)
        - What is the status of your individual commitment since our last brief?
        - What worked?
        - What didn't?
        - What next? Commitment of specific individual action before the next brief.
        - Support needed? What help or support is needed by member? Response.
        - Focused input from other MISSION members on each report.

- MISSION learnings and lessons (open discussion—commander leads)
  - What are we learning about ourselves and our family in this MISSION?
  - How do these lessons apply to the family moving forward?
- MISSION affirmations and acknowledgments
  - Commander opens the floor for members to affirm and acknowledge one another.
- MISSION brief dismissal (commander officially closes the brief, prayer optional)

Depending on your family and the level of detail you prefer, a private Facebook group or other platform like it may be a helpful way to stay connected to one another in between MISSION briefs.

- Post weekly commitments and progress to keep everyone informed.
- Encourage one another.
- Celebrate, honor, and support the commitments of your family members.
- Have a little fun together.
- Provide inspiration to each other.
- Give MISSION updates.
- Communicate changing circumstances.
- Reach out for additional support.

The MISSION brief, if done well, will be the rudder of the MISSION ship. It will be a regular instrument reading and course correction for where things are at, what's next, what are we are learning, and how are we doing.

The MISSION Brief Tool will guide you through each step of the way.

MISSION Exercise 4—MISSION Wrap Up and Debrief

The purpose of this exercise is to provide the family with a process to purposefully steward the final MISSION outcomes and debrief to capture the lessons learned and the growth experienced and to express gratitude to all who participated. Finally, an intentional legacy connection and recognition of lasting learnings bring everything to completion in what I call the MISSION Wrap Up and Debrief.

Every MISSION is momentary and has a clear start and end date. For the crisis that may not be resolved at the time of the preplanned end date, two things can happen. First, the mission can be extended as is for up to ninety days, with or without a brief respite of seven to fourteen days. Second, a new MISSION can be launched with the appropriate modifications that reflect the current status and needs of the crisis and participating members. Launching a new MISSION would mean repeating the exercises in the protocol.

The wrap-up and debrief is an important exercise for the purpose of deeply implanting the lessons and takeaways from the experience into the hearts and DNA of every participant. By focusing on the outcomes, lessons, and learnings of the MISSION in an authentic and vulnerable way, the family is drawn together in gratitude, respect, and sense of identity. It is the emotional implantation of the experience that remains sticky in the lives of members, especially in the children.

The Basic MISSION Wrap Up and Debrief Agenda

- MISSION final report out by the commander
    - specific results of the MISSION
    - highlights for you as the commander
    - expression of gratitude and thanks specifically by name by commander
- MISSION learnings and lessons (open discussion, commander leads)
    - lessons about ourselves and our family in this MISSION
    - applications to the family moving forward
- MISSION legacy connections
    - commander opens the floor for members to connect this experience to family identity, character, and purpose
- MISSION affirmations and acknowledgments
    - commander opens the floor for members to affirm and acknowledge one another
- MISSION celebration
    - The feast! No celebration is complete without some great food.
    - The fun! Play a game, go for a swim, or anything your family considers to be fun.
    - Share the love. No matter the outcome, you came together as one.

- Remember to appoint a notetaker to capture this for posterity. It is important for the generations to come to have a written record of the family MISSION. Can you imagine what it would have been like for your parents or grandparents to have gone through this and passed down a written record of this journey? What a meaningful sharing of life experience, wisdom, love, and learning. By keeping a written and digital copy of your family MISSIONs, you will equip generations to come with a value and model for doing family together as one in times of crisis.

By following this simple structure, family members will have clarity, accountability, and connectedness. Importantly, this simple structure can also be taught to our children and become a better way to do family for generations.

Once again, go to our website to download the editable PDF Family Legacy Protocol Tools for each exercise to walk you through the execution of each one step-by-step. www.culturalarchitects.org

Chapter 10
Family Legacy Impartation

How to intentionally impart the most important things so your legacy endures.

The purpose of the Family Legacy Impartation Protocol is to provide an end-of-life, intentional process for creating an enduring legacy by passing on the most important things in life to our children and grandchildren while teaching them how to do the same. It is a mechanism for passing on the legacy so that it continues to be passed on.

What are the most important things in life to be passed on to our families?

Beyond all the loving memories, experiences, and lessons learned with family, at the end of life, what really matters? After much thought, I believe the answer to this question is as follows:

- the wisdom of a life lived
- the parental blessing of a father and mother
- the heavenly blessing
- the stuff that can't go with us

In order to finish well, it is also important for us to reconcile any unfinished business with God, people, and the responsibilities we have been stewarding. And finally, to deliver the Family Legacy Covenant to the next generation.

In my experience, most families do a poor job in nearly all these areas. High-net-worth families tend to more thoroughly address passing on the stuff because they have a lot and desire to steward it well. In addition, more resources and attention are given to the material aspects of a family legacy in our culture. There's a long line of lawyers, financial planners, investment portfolio managers, business partners, and philanthropic enterprises who all have a personal interest in supporting families in making decisions with their stuff.

But where is our focus when it comes to living life in a way that passes on family identity, core values, mission, and character? Where is the urgency to ensure that our families have experienced and understand how to do family effectively by instilling simple, intentional core protocols and practices that impart the family wisdom, blessing, and stuff thoughtfully? When do we invest into ensuring our family line is successful, our children are equipped to lead at the gates of culture, and they are empowered to lead others in doing the same?

Urgency that leads to intentional action around life's most important things is what families need today. Urgency or the "want to" isn't enough. We have what we are committed to, not what we want. We make time for whatever we truly value. There are no guarantees that anyone will know exactly when their life here on earth is about to end and transition to life in eternity. Some people are given that privilege, while others are not. Accidents happen. Sudden and unexpected deaths occur. It's not like we can pick a day on a calendar and put our things in order before a certain deadline.

Or can we?

Yes, actually, we can. We have the ability to set a deadline for ourselves by choosing a date on the calendar and taking the time, energy, and heart to complete the Impartation Protocols. We can, but will we? The choice is ours to make. The responsibility to prioritize and complete legacy work lies on each individual's shoulders.

You may be saying, "I'm only thirty-five or forty-five years of age. I've got plenty of time to do this." Maybe you do and maybe you do not. However, you do have today. Why not put these vital pieces of your legacy together now and record them both in writing and by video? You can easily update them every year or two as needed. Set a deadline of the next sixty days and get it done. We've created a map and tools to help. If you are nearing end-of-life transition, it is even more urgent that you get your legacy work completed now for the good of your family.

If not now, then when?

If not by using the Family Legacy Impartation Protocols, then how?

If *you* don't do this with your family and teach them to do it with theirs, then who will?

And what will be diminished or even lost to your family line, your community, even lost to the world if you choose to not intentionally live and leave your legacy?

The time for action is now.

Impartation Definition, Value, and Framework

Definition

The Family Legacy Impartation Protocol is a thoughtful, intentional, and systematic process for meaningfully imparting the most important aspects of life and legacy to our children and grandchildren. It is the "how to" pass on a legacy in an end-of-life context. Through a set of exercises, tools, worksheets, and checklists, you will be equipped to compile a written and video Legacy Cache for your family. By preparing this now, you ensure that your legacy will endure in the event of an accidental or early death. Should you be graced with a long life, you will also be prepared for a powerful impartation by sharing this Legacy Cache face-to-face with your family. Having addressed this protocol will also empower you to make the most of the story times in the other five Legacy Protocols.

Value

According to our Creator and Designer, the value of wisdom is incomparable. It is beyond compare or placing a value on it.

The writer of Proverbs grasps at language to properly and adequately communicate how precious and immense the treasure of gaining wisdom actually is. It seems the best he can do is to say that it is more valuable than any treasure on this earth. "Above all, seek wisdom."

Let that sink in.

As wisdom increases, a great treasure is imparted ... it is a more valuable commodity than gold and gemstones, for there is nothing you desire that could compare to her ... Wisdom extends to you long life in one hand and wealth and promotion in the other. (Proverbs 3:14–16 TPT)

Those who find true wisdom obtain tools for understanding the proper way to live, for they will have a fountain of blessing pouring into their lives. (Proverbs 3:13 TPT)

Wise people are builders. They build families, businesses, communities. And through intelligence and insight, their enterprises are established and endure. Because of their skilled leadership, the hearts of people are filled with the treasures of wisdom and the pleasures of spiritual wealth. (Proverbs 24:3–4 TPT)

Framework

The Family Legacy Impartation Protocol framework prioritizes life's most important aspects and provides a pathway to see them implanted deep into the hearts and DNA of the next generation.

Intentionally imparting ...

- the wisdom
- the blessing
- the stuff
- the unfinished business
- the Family Legacy Generational Covenant

The Wisdom

Intentionally passing on your life's lessons, insights, and revelations on a myriad of topics so that your children and family line can receive the benefits from them and, in turn, give them away to benefit others is an amazing gift. Doing this by using the protocols and tools makes it easy as you compile a written and video cache for posterity. We walk you through step-by-step.

The Blessing

Patterned after the biblical concept of blessing, this protocol is dad and or mom's last and best truth bomb, spoken in love for the good of the children. It is the last loving observations, affirmations, advice, pronouncements, assessments, consequences, hopes, and governing activities of the head of the family.

This protocol is the parent's last and best expression from the reservoir of their entire life experience with specific children for their greatest good in fulfilling their life purpose. We focus on two primary aspects of the biblical practice of blessing. First, the loving truth telling from parents to each child. The biblical idea of blessing may include the good, the bad, the ugly, and the consequence of life choices. It may also include approval, reward, and guidance for the future. Second, the declaration of God's blessing on an individual child He has identified to best steward His own purpose and design in each specific family line.

The Stuff

This protocol is not a detailed road map for the traditional passing on of financial wealth, property, and assets. Most of what is offered in the marketplace to families around family legacy addresses wealth transfer and for good reason. By all means, find and use qualified financial and legal professionals to cover the bases here. There is so much available in the marketplace for these services, and while very important, they are not what I am primarily addressing in this protocol. Frankly, material wealth transfer without a coinciding transfer of wisdom, character, values, and purpose is simply not enough to shape culture well or leave an enduring and eternal family legacy to the glory of God. We must thoughtfully transfer both to our generations.

While this protocol does address who gets what to some extent, the clearer focus is the why behind the intentional impartation of the stuff. It is more about who gets what and why. What does the stuff mean or represent to the one passing it on and the one receiving it? What does the item say about their character? What is the story, the purpose, and the emotional connection attached to the stuff that is being given to a new steward? This part of the protocol creates a much deeper emotional implant and value for ongoing family legacy.

The Unfinished Business

This section may be better titled "The Finished Business." It is important that we impart finished business to our children and not unfinished business. It is much sweeter to impart the order, clarity, ease, and purpose of finished business than to impart the bitter chaos, uncertainty, hardship, and aimlessness of unfinished business to those we love.

Practically speaking, how do we sift through all of life's responsibilities and distractions to uncover the few essentials, the most important things, according to our Designer, to finish when the time for our heavenly promotion has come?

We have created several tools to assist you to do just that—worksheets that will help you tie up all sorts of loose ends in relationships, in finances, with stuff, and with the responsibilities that you steward. All of them have an intentional legacy connection included in the process.

The Family Legacy Generational Covenant

In order to ensure that that the purposes of God in our family line and our family legacy are imparted to generation after generation, we have designed an intentional process to officially charge the next generation with this sacred honor. In so doing, the stewardship of continuing the Family Legacy Protocols is placed squarely on the shoulders of the next generation.

The impartation protocol done well will ensure a profound and lasting family legacy for generations to come. As our generations are shown how to build families, businesses, and communities, they will also have what they need to shape culture after God's design from the inside out.

Four Guidelines for Successfully Imparting Your Legacy

When you think about imparting the most important things in life in an end-of-life context to your family, what kinds of emotions emerge inside of you? Few things are more emotional and emotionally diverse for the entire family as the combination of life and death, fear and uncertainty, regret and gratitude, grief and celebration, love and loss, and the purpose of life itself that present themselves at end-of-life transition.

Whether that transition is sudden and unexpected or not, what is the most valuable way that the family can experience the impartation protocols for their benefit and the benefit of an enduring family legacy?

Whether you are sitting down to execute the Family Legacy Impartation Protocols in writing and on video or in a face-to-face family gathering, there are four vitally important guidelines to follow as you determine the manner in which you show up in delivering them. In other words, how you do what you are doing.

- Be intentional.
- Be clear.
- Be authentic.
- Be truthful and loving.

Be Intentional

It is likely that the biggest challenge you will face in carrying out the Impartation Protocols is making the time, focus, decisions, energy, heart, and follow-through required to put words to paper, record the video, and deliver them face-to-face. Will you choose to value the family legacy enough to engage self-discipline and complete the work?

This may also be the biggest challenge for putting the entire Family Legacy Model and protocols into practice. Will you place enough value in creating an enduring family legacy that has the power to build families, businesses, and communities to find the self-discipline and intentionality to do the work? Will you put a deadline on the calendar to complete them? Will you invest whatever it takes to build a legacy that will bless your family and shape culture from the inside out over time? Will you say no to other things so that you can say yes to imparting your legacy?

If your answer is "Yes, I will," then be intentional with your calendar, your effort, and the work it takes to complete the protocols. It takes what it takes, and it's worth it in the end. If you get stuck, reach out to our office for the support of a Family Legacy coach. Join our monthly subscribers and get the tools and coaching you need to get unstuck. Join our weekly Family Legacy webinars and ask your questions. It may take some grit to get your legacy in order.

Be Clear

Say what you mean and mean what you say. Be specific with your communication. Share exactly what you are thinking, feeling, and deciding. The clarity you provide will bring the greatest benefit to your family by helping them more fully understand you, your wishes, your perspectives, your purposes, your requests, and your decisions.

If you don't fill in the specifics and are silent or unclear on them, your family will be left to decide for themselves what you meant. Frankly, this is where many arguments and misunderstandings happen as each family member fills in the blanks with their own stories and typically from their own self-interests.

Capturing your legacy in writing, on video, and by face-to-face gatherings provides a clear and lasting record for generations to come. We have provided many tools and protocols to assist you in bringing the clarity needed as you implement the protocols. Again, if you get stuck, reach out to us. We are here to help!

Be Authentic

Do you! Be yourself as you articulate, record, and deliver the impartation protocols. If you feel like cracking a joke, do it. If you are overcome with emotion, let it be seen. If you get choked up, don't redo the recording. If you get upset, be upset. If you are sad, relieved, concerned, grateful, or determined, then be that. *Be real. Be vulnerable.*

Recognize that the impartation protocol is happening in an end-of-life context and deserves the sobriety and sincerity that such an impactful experience intrinsically has within it. The emotion that you authentically reveal will create a deep and lasting emotional implantation in the DNA of your family. This will also go a long way in ensuring a lasting legacy.

Be Truthful and Loving

Remember that the power of life and death is in the tongue. Words contain great power for good and bad. It is important that you choose to saturate your words with truth and love as you convey them. This is a time of speaking the truth you have stored up inside of you from a whole life of experience and a time to say whatever you have to say in love.

To speak the truth without love can deeply wound your family. To speak lovingly without truth can fall short of creating the new awareness needed for real transformation in your family. It is not an either/or choice. It is possible to speak both truthfully and lovingly for the highest possible good. Both are needed to give our generations the best chance at successfully fulfilling their own life purpose as well as God's purposes for the family line.

Following these simple guidelines as you perform the Impartation Protocols will provide the optimal environment for a powerful passing on of life's most important things to your family legacy.

Imparting the Wisdom

Think about this. Arguably, the wisest man who ever lived, King Solomon took the time and effort to listen, learn, and live and compile for his children a written record of the wisdom that he had accumulated for their benefit. Anyone who reads the Proverbs in the Bible and puts them into practice is also a beneficiary of Solomon's efforts.

Solomon imparted his best and most practical wisdom on a wide variety of relevant topics, including the following:

- love
- marriage
- family
- parenting
- business
- sexuality
- relationships
- leadership
- being a good neighbor
- conflict resolution
- being a good listener
- work habits
- financial stewardship
- self-control
- physical health
- emotional health
- spiritual health
- life and death
- power of words
- building communities
- good and bad character
- perils of foolishness
- warnings of alcoholism
- consequences of sexual perversion
- legacy planning
- friendship
- wealth creation
- wealth transfer
- poverty
- prosperity
- social justice
- longevity
- sustainability
- healing
- more

In fact, one of the characteristics of the Spirit of God is that He is a Spirit of Wisdom. The Bible makes many references to the "Spirit of Wisdom" being upon or within a person. Jesus, Mary, Daniel, Joshua, as well as craftsmen, artisans, and skilled workers of varied types were said to have been given a Spirit of Wisdom. Truthfully, every person who has the Spirit of God inside of them has wisdom living there. The important question is whether that person chooses to access, grow in, and become one with the Spirit of Wisdom.

Solomon didn't write volumes of graduate-level academic or theoretical content. He took what his father, David, had taught him, along with what he learned himself from God and boiled this life wisdom down to practical, short sayings, poetic verse, and direct observation that could be easily understood and put into practice—*if* the hearer had "ears to hear and a heart to understand," if the hearer had a respect for the Designer's words and ways. If the hearer would simply obey, then prosperity, blessing, and long life were within their grasp.

Solomon did this first and foremost for his own children and his legacy. How amazing would it be for your father to share and record a written treasure trove of his own personal life wisdom for you and your children? Priceless!

I believe that one of the best things we can do for our family legacy is to read, meditate on, and practice the wisdom found in the book of Proverbs. For decades, I have read a chapter of Proverbs a day. Lesli and I practice this together daily even now. I look forward to it. It is life to me.

In recent years, I have experienced more than wise words on paper and proven principles to follow. I have regularly sensed God's Spirit of Wisdom walk with me and teach me. He connects so many dots of understanding all at once as revelation knowledge unveils truth that brings clarity, trust, and confidence—not just for me but for my family, friends, and clients that I train and coach.

All of that to say that when it comes to the most important things in life to impart to our generations by way of family legacy, wisdom tops the list according to our Designer.

We can only give away what we have received, so get wisdom. And then give it away. Get wisdom from God's Word and God's Spirit and then intentionally give it away to your family, your friends, and all those you influence. In so doing, you teach them how to do the same.

Here are four important keys to imparting the wisdom for an enduring family legacy:

- Get wisdom. Read the Proverbs daily. Cultivate ears that hear and a heart that understands. Ask questions of parents and family heads. Be a learner.
- Live wisdom. Walk with the Spirit of Wisdom. Put wisdom into practice intentionally with accountability. We must live it to give it.
- Share wisdom. Share wisdom by telling stories day by day and during the Family Legacy Protocols.
- Impart wisdom. Compile and record wisdom (written, verbal, and video) and then literally pass it on.

Get Wisdom

Don't overcomplicate this. The wisdom of God is cloaked in simplicity.

It starts with a decision to respect the Lord, the Designer, enough to give His words and ways proper authority. Follow that with a decision to cultivate a desire to hear and understand God's wisdom in the Proverbs and the entire Bible. Eat and digest His Word daily, allowing the Holy Spirit to lead you into revelation and truth. Surrender to His leadership. Decide to agree with Him. Allow Him to transform what you believe in your heart. "As a man thinks in his heart, so is he." Ask Father questions and listen to His responses. Remember to practice Rule 51. Take advantage of moments with family heads; ask them good questions and then listen.

Live Wisdom

Again, keep it simple. Abide and obey.

First, choose to abide in and with Holy Spirit through every part of your daily life in a conversational and learning mode. Ask Him questions, listen for His responses, receive them and agree with Him, and do this continually. This is one of the secrets of praying without ceasing. This is the reality of "walking by the Spirit" or "living in the Spirit," who is by very nature wisdom. The other secret of praying without ceasing is to pray in the Spirit.

Second, choose to obey what you hear the Holy Spirit saying to you and teaching you. Put into practice the words of wisdom from the scriptures and from what you hear as you abide in Him. Just do it! Choose to get out of resistance and accept that what the Spirit of Wisdom is saying to you is loving, true, good, and meant to prosper you and to bless you and your family for generations to come.

Share Wisdom

If you get wisdom and live wisdom, then people will see the results of wisdom in your family, your business, your relationships, and your character. However, it is when you share wisdom by telling stories that connect to those results that your family and friends can experience wisdom firsthand—unless, of course, they are getting and living wisdom on their own, which is the ultimate goal.

Everyday life is overflowing with opportunities to share a story of some aspect of wisdom with those you are doing life with. A car ride to soccer practice becomes an opportunity to share the wisdom from your own life around work ethic, integrity, teamwork, friendship, or any number of other topics. Watching a newscast becomes an opportunity to share the wisdom from your own life about poverty, politics, helping the poor, social justice, generosity, or the perils of sexual impurity. Choose to make the most of every opportunity that daily life gifts you to pass on stories of wisdom.

And occasionally, an opportunity in daily life presents itself, and you must choose to seize it instead of letting it slip through your fingers.

That's exactly what happened in late autumn 2018 for my family. We purchased a plane ticket for my father to return to his hometown to spend some precious last days with an uncle and close friend, Dale. Travel is difficult for my father, and money was tight. Nevertheless, he was determined to invest his time and energy into reminiscing and connecting with this lifelong friend. He made the journey to properly say goodbye.

Dale, a Korean War vet, was given only a few months to live. While he was in no pain, he had stopped eating and chose to accept his transition gracefully and purposefully. He had visitors from all over the country calling and visiting him at his home to share their love and appreciation for him. My father was not going to miss out on his turn. Neither were Lesli and I, and neither were my

Family Legacy Impartation

kids. Many times, over the years living away from my hometown and family members, I chose work, business, convenience, or other priorities over making the journey home to participate in important family time. Not this time!

My wife and I and three of our kids jumped in the car to meet them at Dale's home and join in these important last moments together this side of eternity, alongside my dad.

Dale was upbeat and all smiles as we all gathered around him in his recliner. Dad sat on the floor at Dale's feet, leaning back on the recliner near Dale's legs.

He told stories, and we listened. We asked questions, and he answered. We expressed our love and gratitude for him, and he received it and reciprocated. And we laughed and laughed and hugged and laughed and cried.

> Where is your favorite place in the world to visit and why?
>
> What is one of the funniest things that ever happened to you?
>
> What was it like growing up or in the war?
>
> What did you learn from those experiences?
>
> What have you seen? Heard? Experienced that was important or impactful to you?
>
> Along with all sorts of questions, I asked Dale at one point that afternoon, "What's the most important wisdom that you gained in life?"

Dale paused and then tearfully proceeded to say, "Be kind to everyone. Know and love Jesus the way I do."

"I am at total peace, looking forward to seeing Joyce, your mother, Cal, and everyone else who's there waiting for me." Such simple and powerful wisdom coming from a decorated Korean War vet whose life expectancy as a forward observer in the war was next Tuesday.

"What did you learn in the military?" I asked.

"I was trained as a flame thrower, but what I learned was honor, courage, team, family, obedience, servitude, protection, character, and love."

I was so grateful to have that time with Dale and my family. I'm grateful my wife and children experienced it with me. I didn't get that same time with my brother Reece, who was killed in a car accident at age twenty-five, leaving a wife and two small children. I didn't get that time with my mom, who passed quietly and surprisingly in her sleep in Florida.

I sadly had not chosen to make the intentional time and effort to do something so simple yet so powerful ... so inexpensive yet so priceless ... so temporary yet so eternal ... so easy to do and yet so easy not to. I missed the day-to-day opportunities to ask for wisdom from them and to deeply listen.

How do you share wisdom in the day-to-day?

- Make a decision to be intentional and *show up* today ready to receive and share wisdom with others.
- Ask a good question of the one you want to share wisdom with. For example, what do you see as important for success in life, marriage, or business? How or why do you think that man ended up breaking the law and going to prison? What does good parenting look like in your eyes?
- Listen to their responses and ask follow-up questions to draw out more of their thinking.
- Once you see where their thinking is at, ask them if they would like to know what you have learned about the subject through your life experience.
- Share an example from your life on the subject and what you learned, saw, and experienced.
- Ask if what you are sharing makes sense and if they have any questions.
- Finally, where able, tie a bow on the conversation with a reference to a proverb.

Sharing stories of wisdom in the flow of day-to-day life is a profound practice. Intentionally establishing routines, rituals, and practices where we can share wisdom is equally or even more powerful. This is why following the Family Legacy Protocols are so effective for passing on legacy. The protocols provide a mechanism for imparting wisdom by sharing stories of wisdom over meals, ventures, gatherings, and at end of life.

Impart Wisdom

My uncle Paul made an intentional video of my grandfather Carlyle answering several important life questions as he neared his reward at age ninety-six. I got to hear and learn from His life wisdom. It was profound ... precious ... enduring. Thanks, Paul!

Compiling and recording a written, verbal, and video cache of wisdom for your family intentionally is another important way to share wisdom in a way that will impact generations to come.

In late October 2017, I took the kids on a Family Legacy Venture to see my dad in Auburndale, Florida. I had prepared them as detailed in chapter 8 of this book. I wanted to create the environment and opportunities for my dad to pass on his legacy to us.

We ate good food around the table for hours and told one another our life's stories of victory and defeat, joy and sorrow, challenges and achievements.

> We cooked together.
> We laughed together.
> We swam together.
> We played together.
> We played guitar together.
> We dreamed together.
> We learned together.
> We traveled together.
> We talked together.
> We listened together.
> We laughed some more together.
> We cried together.
> We may or may not have smoked cigars together.

My dad said through tears and chuckles that he was telling us some stories he had never told anyone before ... that he couldn't believe that we were talking so openly and sharing so vulnerably. He was deeply moved emotionally.

I remember asking my father to share with us all from his storehouse of life wisdom, and he did not disappoint. I'll share a few of the nuggets with you. You must understand, my father is one of my life heroes. He is a humble man with great character and wisdom, now in his mid-eighties.

What he said: "You want to change your life ... change your friends."

What I heard: his secret of transformation and making a change.

What he said: "You have to surround yourself with the right people."

What I heard: a core value of our family and a secret to success.

What he said: "Empathy is walking in another person's shoes with full understanding."

What I heard: empathy and serving others is an important part of our family identity.

What he said: "You have to treat people right."

What I heard: a core value of our family to value people and honor them rightly.

What he said- remember, he was a banker: "Don't spend more than you make."

What I heard: how to think about finances and a simple key for staying out of debt.

What he said: "I would never have made it through losing Reece and your mom without my faith in the Lord. I don't know how people can make it without their faith."

What I heard: the family secret to enduring and overcoming the worst life has to throw at you is faith in Jesus.

This opportunity for me and my children to hear and receive wisdom from my father was an intentional activity during one of our Family Legacy Ventures. It happened on purpose.

Here are two more simple tools for intentionally receiving and intentionally imparting wisdom. It can and should work both ways. We can only give away what we have received.

Note: The experiential exercises in the wisdom section are simply the completion and execution of the tools included below and in the Family Legacy Protocols Toolbox on our website. The tools are self-explanatory and happen both over time and in an event. For example, you will gather wisdom day to day in an ongoing manner using the tools, and you will eventually impart that wisdom to your family in one or more of the following ways:

- written compilation completed and put in safe storage in case of unexpected death and (or) imparted at an appropriate time
- video record completed and put in safe storage in case of unexpected death and (or) imparted at an appropriate time
- at a Family Legacy Encounter Weekend
- at an end-of-life impartation face-to-face

Family Legacy Wisdom Treasure Hunt Tool

King Solomon told anyone listening to seek wisdom like you were seeking hidden treasure. There is hidden treasure in the life experiences and lessons learned inside of your parents and grandparents. Inside of others who have gone before you lay the treasures of wisdom waiting for you to discover and receive by doing three amazingly simple yet profound things.

1. Ask a good question.
2. Listen to understand the answer.
3. Put it into action in your own life.

Ask a good question:

- What is your life purpose?
- How did you discover your life purpose?
- What are your core values? The six to ten most important values in your life and why?
- What lessons did you learn about forgiveness?
- What lessons did you learn about stress?
- What have you learned from your experiences?
- What are the most impactful experiences you have had in your life and why?
- What are some of the oldest and most interesting stories you remember about family generations back?
- What are some of the biggest mistakes that you made in your life?

- What did you learn from them?
- What are some of the most difficult challenges you had in your life?
- What did you do?
- What did you learn from them?
- What is the life wisdom in these experiences?
- What would you do differently in your life if you could?
- What regrets do you have in life and why?
- What are some of your biggest achievements or successes?
- What did it take to make those happen?
- What did those experiences teach you?
- What are some of the most important things you've learned about …
  - relationships
  - parenting
  - trust
  - work and career
  - marriage
  - divorce
  - family
  - friendship
  - business
- What are some of the most valuable lessons you have learned about money and finances?
- What is the life wisdom you've gathered regarding building a healthy family?
- What is the life wisdom you've gathered regarding religion and faith?
- What is the life wisdom you've gathered regarding government and politics?
- What is the life wisdom you've gathered regarding education and learning?
- What is the life wisdom you've gathered regarding business and work?
- What is the life wisdom you've gathered regarding entertainment and fun?
- What is the life wisdom you've gathered regarding the media?

Choose to deeply listen for the purpose of understanding. Gather the answers and the wisdom like you would gather the jewels and gold bars into a treasure chest to keep them. I recommend that you record in writing and by video so that you can keep the treasures of wisdom that you have found. Journal the learning during or after a powerful conversation. Pull out your smartphone and record your conversations.

Choose to put wisdom into practice by applying them in your own life day by day. Ask for God's help. Just do it! When it's time to make a decision, review your treasure chest full of insight, intelligence, understanding, and wisdom and then follow the advice in making your decision.

Family Legacy Wisdom Impartation Tool

Choose to be prepared to share the wisdom you have to give when the time is right by thoughtfully completing the following exercise. Whether you share your wisdom one-on-one while fishing, with the whole family gathered around you in a Family Legacy Encounter, or at an end-of-life family gathering by compiling your life wisdom in writing and (or) by video, you will be ready and ensure that your family benefits from your life lived.

Imparting the Wisdom

What are the most important pieces of wisdom you want to pass on to your children and the generations that follow? After each of the topics below, thoughtfully, prayerfully share from the treasures of wisdom that are stored inside of you.

Potential topics based on areas King Solomon addressed in the book of Proverbs:

- love
- family
- parenting
- business
- sexuality
- relationships
- leadership
- being a good neighbor
- conflict resolution
- being a good listener
- work habits
- financial stewardship
- self-control
- physical health
- emotional health
- spiritual health
- life and death
- power of words
- building communities
- good and bad character
- perils of foolishness
- warnings of alcoholism
- consequences of sexual perversion

- legacy planning
- friendship
- wealth creation
- wealth transfer
- poverty
- prosperity
- social justice
- longevity
- sustainability
- healing
- more

I strongly encourage you to make both a written and video record of all the Impartation Protocols. By writing them out first, you can more completely and easily share them on video. This is also important to do so that in case of an unexpected death, there is a recorded legacy in place for your family.

For what it's worth, here are just a few of my biggest life lessons of wisdom I choose to pass on.

While there are multiple volumes of detail underneath each one of these pieces of wisdom, I choose to state them simply, emphasizing both being and doing. Enjoy!

- Abide and obey as one with God and your spouse.
- Family is the primary purpose for life by design.
- Choice.
- Seek wisdom.
- Simplicity.
- Kindness.
- Intentionality.
- Love.
- Learn.
- Lead.
- Serve.
- Grow.
- Listen.
- Forgive.
- Work.
- Rest.
- Trust (God, others, and myself).
- Believe—choose to agree with God.
- Know.
- Be known.
- Persevere.
- Laugh.
- Feel.
- Self-govern.
- Faithfulness.
- Stewardship.
- Integrity.
- Keep agreements.
- Create.
- Play.
- Worship.
- Pray.
- Authentic.
- Vulnerable.
- Be.

Imparting the Blessing

The second piece of the Family Legacy Impartation Protocol is the intentional passing on of the blessing. Like many of the other protocols, our construct of passing on the blessing is founded on the wisdom of our Designer and His example to us found in the Bible.

The fact is words have power. The Bible teaches us that the words pouring out of our mouths come from the overflow of what is in our hearts. We are also instructed that even the power of life and death are in our tongues. Our words filled with the power of what is in our hearts have lasting influence over those they are spoken over. This is a profound reality.

The magnitude and significance of speaking powerful words of blessing over our children and families at the end of life should not be underestimated. They are a vital part of building and imparting a lasting family legacy.

As I mentioned earlier in the chapter, our practice of this protocol focuses on two primary aspects of the biblical practice of blessing.

First, the loving truth telling from parents to each child. This idea of blessing may include the good, the bad, the ugly, and the consequence of life choices. It may also include approval, reward, and guidance for the future. It is delivered in love and for the highest good in supporting each child to most fully complete their individual life purpose.

Second, the declaration of God's blessing on an individual child He has identified to best steward His own purpose and design for each specific family line.

God identified Himself as the God of Abraham, Isaac, and Jacob and made sure that Jacob (Israel) passed on this aspect of the blessing to one of his sons, Joseph. It is important to our Designer that His people understand God's purposes through a family line. He specifically identified that family line all the way to Jesus Christ, God's own Son.

Practically speaking, we have the blessing of the parents upon each child, and we have what I call the heavenly blessing upon the one child who God recognizes as the chosen primary steward of His purposes for the family line in each generation.

The Blessing

The parental blessing is giving the last and best truth in love bomb before end of life in hopes that what is spoken will become a mirror to the recipient and, in some way, move them forward in fulfilling their life purpose. It is a sober offering of a whole life of experience and the most important words the hearer needs to hear from the speaker before they can speak no more.

The blessing is both the truth telling of parents and God's blessing of His heavenly purpose for the family line.

I don't believe that God plays favorites; we are all his favorite. However, I do see that He is a rewarder of those who seek, know, and obey Him. For those children who best steward God's design and purpose for the family line, His way is to support that stewardship with a special blessing and supernatural empowerment. This blessing is directly linked to His big design and purpose in the bigger picture through each family line.

Examples of both blessings are found in the scripture when Israel (Jacob) blesses his sons in Genesis 49:1–33 (NIV):

> Then Jacob called for his sons and said: "Gather around so I can tell you what will happen to you in days to come. "Assemble and listen, sons of Jacob; listen to your father Israel. "Reuben, you are my firstborn, my might, the first sign of my strength, excelling in honor, excelling in power.
>
> Turbulent as the waters, you will no longer excel, for you went up onto your father's bed, onto my couch and defiled it. "Simeon and Levi are brothers—their swords[a] are weapons of violence. Let me not enter their council, let me not join their assembly, for they have killed men in their anger and hamstrung oxen as they pleased. Cursed be their anger, so fierce, and their fury, so cruel! I will scatter them in Jacob and disperse them in Israel. "Judah,[b] your brothers will praise you; your hand will be on the neck of your enemies; your father's sons will bow down to you. You are a lion's cub, Judah; you return from the prey, my son. Like a lion he crouches and lies down, like a lioness—who dares to rouse him? The scepter will not depart from Judah, nor the ruler's staff from between his feet,[c] until he to whom it belongs[d] shall come and the obedience of the nations shall be his. He will tether his donkey to a

Family Legacy Impartation

vine, his colt to the choicest branch; he will wash his garments in wine, his robes in the blood of grapes. His eyes will be darker than wine, his teeth whiter than milk.[e]

"Zebulun will live by the seashore and become a haven for ships; his border will extend toward Sidon. "Issachar is a rawboned[f] donkey lying down among the sheep pens.[g] When he sees how good is his resting place and how pleasant is his land, he will bend his shoulder to the burden and submit to forced labor. "Dan[h] will provide justice for his people as one of the tribes of Israel. Dan will be a snake by the roadside, a viper along the path, that bites the horse's heels so that its rider tumbles backward. "I look for your deliverance, Lord. "Gad[i] will be attacked by a band of raiders, but he will attack them at their heels. "Asher's food will be rich; he will provide delicacies fit for a king. "Naphtali is a doe set free that bears beautiful fawns.[j]

"Joseph is a fruitful vine, a fruitful vine near a spring, whose branches climb over a wall.[k] With bitterness archers attacked him; they shot at him with hostility. But his bow remained steady, his strong arms stayed[l] limber, because of the hand of the Mighty One of Jacob, because of the Shepherd, the Rock of Israel, because of your father's God, who helps you, because of the Almighty,[m] who blesses you with blessings of the skies above, blessings of the deep springs below, blessings of the breast and womb. Your father's blessings are greater than the blessings of the ancient mountains, than[n] the bounty of the age-old hills. Let all these rest on the head of Joseph, on the brow of the prince among[o] his brothers.

"Benjamin is a ravenous wolf; in the morning he devours the prey, in the evening he divides the plunder." All these are the twelve tribes of Israel, and this is what their father said to them when he blessed them, giving each the blessing appropriate to him.

The Death of Jacob

Then he gave them these instructions: "I am about to be gathered to my people. Bury me with my fathers in the cave in the field of Ephron the Hittite, thirty the cave in the field of Machpelah, near Mamre in Canaan, which Abraham bought along with the field as a burial place from Ephron the Hittite. There Abraham and his wife Sarah were buried, there Isaac and his wife Rebekah were buried, and there I buried Leah. The field and the cave in it were bought from the Hittites.[p]"

When Jacob had finished giving instructions to his sons, he drew his feet up into the bed, breathed his last and was gathered to his people.

Jacob's example provides us with important guidelines for the way he imparted the blessing. The Impartation Protocol reflects them.

- He knew his time was close and was prepared.
- He gathered them all together.
- He pronounced the blessing face-to-face in the open.
- He urged them to listen.
- He starts with the oldest out of respect for design.
- He was decisive, and things shifted in the moment.
- He blessed each one according to the blessing appropriate to him.
- He gave his last burial wishes.

The substance of his parental blessings is also reflected in the Impartation Protocols, including the following:

- identity statements
- acknowledgments of character strengths
- acknowledgments of character flaws
- affirmations
- life purpose declarations
- business advice
- truth telling in love
- curses and punishment
- leadership roles within the family
- assignment of responsibilities
- cultural engagement
- foretelling of upcoming battles and winning strategy advice

Interestingly, Jacob had imparted his stuff (land, assets, and wealth) at an earlier time, prior to the final blessing and before his time of death. This is by design. It is also why in the Family Legacy Protocols we recommend imparting the stuff separately from the parental and heavenly blessings.

Jacob's heavenly blessing to Joseph in Genesis 49:22–26 was distinct in substance from the parental blessings to his brothers and included the following:

- identity statements
- acknowledgment of Joseph's good stewardship and fruitfulness to God's purposes for the family line historically
- prophetic declaration of Joseph's fruitfulness in the future
- historical accounts of Joseph's battles and victories
- recognition that God's hand was upon Joseph
- recognition that God actively shepherded Joseph
- acknowledgment that God's choice in Joseph was rock solid
- acknowledgment that Jacob's God also helped Joseph
- declaration that God's blessing was on Joseph
- declaration that all of Jacob's blessings rested on Joseph
- recognition of Joseph's responsibilities as the "prince among his brothers"
- a multigenerational heavenly blessing to Joseph's sons Ephraim and Manasseh (Genesis 48), making it clear who the purposes of God for the family line would be stewarded by

The heavenly blessing is giving God's blessing to the one God has chosen to be responsible for His purposes. God's big mission in a family line has a blessing for supernatural empowerment to accomplish it. It is important that we recognize who He has chosen, to agree with His choice, and to intentionally pass on the heavenly blessing to them.

A word of caution: if you know that you are carrying the heavenly blessing for your family line, carry it with great humility and great confidence. Joseph knew as a teenager through a series of dreams that God had plans for him in stewarding the heavenly blessing for his family line. He let everyone know about the dreams when he received them. However, he was the eleventh in the birth order of twelve sons of Jacob. His brothers got jealous of Joseph's dreams and of their dad's favor of Joseph over them. This jealousy led to a very hard road for Joseph of abandonment, slavery, false accusation, and imprisonment. But God used all of this to eventually promote Joseph as the second in command to the Pharaohs of Egypt.

Joseph then used his authority to save his entire family line in a time of great famine. He would later say to his brothers, "What you meant for harm, God used for good."

I believe that God would have prepared Joseph no matter how he handled sharing the dreams and his awareness of his role in carrying the heavenly blessing. However, a little humility and sensitivity to his brothers may have had a different outcome for both his and his brothers' journeys along the way. I believe that every child in Jacob's family had a purpose for life that was also significant in God's big plan. There was simply something different that Joseph was identified to steward.

Signs that you are carrying the heavenly blessing for your family line:

- clarity and articulation of God's mission on your family line
- awareness and confidence God chose you to steward that mission
- demonstrated faithfulness to God and the mission
- track record of supernatural empowerment for mission results
- a track record of abiding and obeying in vibrant relationship with God
- an appetite for getting, living, and sharing God's wisdom
- awareness of who God is choosing in your generations to steward the mission after you
- prioritizing the intentional preparation and impartation of the mission, along with the heavenly blessing to God's next faithful steward in your family line
- the actual impartation of the mission and the heavenly blessing to the next generation(s) by speaking them over the recipients

What if you are uncertain if you are carrying the stewardship of God's mission for your family line? First, ask God who is carrying it for your family line and listen for His answer. Second, examine who in your family line is demonstrating the bullet points listed above. If you can identify them, work with them to maximize God's purposes. Help them understand and succeed. If you cannot identify them, ask God for His heavenly blessing on you to more faithfully understand and steward His purposes. Receive what He gives you and begin putting the bullet list above into practice with His help.

A Personal Example

Two things happened when I was twelve years of age that initiated my own awareness that God had something different for me to steward in my family line. I had an encounter at church camp where the Lord showed me my life purpose of serving leaders of leaders to love God with all their hearts and to demonstrate the kingdom of God as cultural architects, shaping culture from the inside out.

Not long after that encounter, my grandfather Carlyle prayed for me at the altar of my childhood church and specifically spoke the heavenly blessing that he carried over me for God's purposes to be stewarded in the generations. It has been a lifelong journey to understand and carry this assignment. I have been tested by all sorts of trials and difficulties. Yet I believe God has used them all to shape me and for my good and the good of His purposes.

In some ways, it's in the last few years that I have embraced the deeper responsibilities and implications of these experiences. While I have given my life to what I heard as best as I was able, I now have the clarity and confidence to finish strong, especially in my family. The Family Legacy Model and protocols are a harvest of the seeds planted long ago.

Our family motto inscribed on our newly created Bixby family coat of arms captures three other important aspects of God's purpose for our family legacy: "Love, Learn, Lead."

Note: The experiential exercises in the blessing section are simply the completion and execution of the tools included below and in the Family Legacy Protocols Toolbox on our website. The tools are self-explanatory and happen both over time and in an event. For example, you will craft parental and heavenly blessings over time using the tools, and you will eventually impart those blessings to your family in one or more of the following ways:

- written compilation completed and put in safe storage in case of unexpected death and (or) imparted at an appropriate time
- video record completed and put in safe storage in case of unexpected death and (or) imparted at an appropriate time
- at a Family Legacy Encounter Weekend
- at an end-of-life impartation face-to-face

Crafting the Parental Blessing Tool

The purpose of this tool is to help you craft specific parental blessings for your children and grandchildren, patterned after how these blessings appear in the scriptures.

Instructions:

- Keep it simple.
- Follow the six-step process below.
- Write them down and (or) record them on video.
- Deliver them in person, face-to-face if at all possible.

One: Put yourself in a calm, comfortable state and say a prayer requesting God's help in this process. Give yourself uninterrupted time and space.

Two: Reread Genesis 49 where Jacob blesses his twelve sons.

Three: Review the guidelines and substance sections in chapter 10 above and take them into account as you prepare the parental blessings.

Four: Craft the individual parental blessings for each child or grandchild by mindfully determining from your heart the most important truths for your generations to hear from you that will have the greatest likelihood of supporting them in fulfilling their life purpose and mission.

Write down the names of each of your children, and then after each name, work through the bullet list below and write down notes of the things that come to mind for them. You may or may not have something written for each person and each bullet point. This serves as a guide for you to follow in crafting the parental blessings.

The substance of parental blessings in scripture is reflected in the Impartation Protocols and include the following:

- identity statements
- acknowledgements of character strengths
- acknowledgements of character flaws
- affirmations
- life purpose declarations
- business advice
- truth telling in love
- curses and punishment
- leadership roles within the family
- assignment of responsibilities
- cultural engagement
- foretelling of upcoming battles and winning strategy advice

Names of children and (or) grandchildren and your notes for each one below.

Name	Notes
1.	
2.	
3.	
4.	
5.	

More as needed:

Five: Write down each name again and then craft a complete parental blessing statement from the notes you've made above.

Name	Crafted Parental Blessing
1.	
2.	
3.	
4.	
5.	

More as needed:

Six: Deliver the blessings by either reading them while recording yourself on video or in a face-to-face gathering of family. The video recording is to ensure that you impart the parental blessing even if there would be an unexpected death. If you find yourself in a known end-of-life scenario, you may want to deliver the blessings face-to-face.

Remember, our Family Legacy coaches are here to assist you at any point along the way as you implement the protocols. Don't hesitate to reach out for support.

Crafting the Heavenly Blessing Tool

The purpose of this tool is to help you craft a specific heavenly blessing for the child you have identified as God's choice in stewarding His purposes for your family line, patterned after how this blessing appears in scripture.

Instructions:

- Keep it simple.
- Follow the six-step process below.
- Write your work down and (or) record them on video.
- Deliver the heavenly blessing in person, face-to-face if at all possible.

One: Put yourself in a calm, comfortable state and say a prayer requesting God's help in this process. Give yourself uninterrupted time and space.

Two: Reread Genesis 49:22–26, where Jacob blesses Joseph.

Three: Review the heavenly blessing substance section in chapter 10 and take them into account as you prepare the heavenly blessing.

Four: Craft the individual heavenly blessing for the child by mindfully determining from your heart, in consultation with God, the most important things God has for them to empower them as they faithfully steward God's purposes in the family line.

Write down the name of the one identified and then work through the bullet list below and write down notes of the things that come to mind. You may or may not have something written for each bullet point. This serves as a guide for you to follow in crafting the heavenly blessings.

Jacob's heavenly blessing to Joseph in Genesis 49:22–26 was distinct in substance from the parental blessings to his brothers and included the following:

- identity statements
- acknowledgment of Joseph's good stewardship and fruitfulness to God's purposes for the family line historically
- prophetic declaration of Joseph's fruitfulness in the future
- historical accounts of Joseph's battles and victories
- recognition that God's hand was upon Joseph

- recognition that God actively shepherded Joseph
- acknowledgment that God's choice in Joseph was rock solid
- acknowledgment that Jacob's God also helped Joseph
- declaration that God's blessing was on Joseph
- declaration that all of Jacob's blessings rested on Joseph
- recognition of Joseph's responsibilities as the "prince among his brothers"
- a multigenerational heavenly blessing to Joseph's sons Ephraim and Manasseh (Genesis 48), making it clear who the purposes of God for the family line would be stewarded by

Name Notes

Five: Craft a complete heavenly blessing from your notes above.

Name the heavenly blessing.

Six: Deliver the heavenly blessing by either reading it while recording yourself on video or in a face-to-face gathering of family. The video recording is to ensure that you impart the heavenly blessing even if there would be an unexpected death. If you find yourself in a known end-of-life scenario, you may want to deliver the blessing face-to-face.

Remember, our Family Legacy coaches are here to assist you at any point along the way as you implement the protocols. Don't hesitate to reach out for support.

Stewarding our families as God designed so that our generations are equipped with the character to lead at the gates of culture requires the parental and heavenly blessings of parents. It just does.

Imparting the Stuff

The third piece of The Family Legacy Impartation Protocol is the intentional passing on of the stuff.

As I mentioned earlier in this chapter, this protocol is not the traditional road map for the passing on of financial wealth, property, and assets. Our focus is not on investment strategies, the creation of legal instruments, or evaluating the tax implications of how you structure these decisions.

There is so much available in the marketplace for these services, and while very important, they are not what I am primarily addressing in this protocol. Frankly, material wealth transfer without a coinciding transfer of wisdom, character, values, and purpose is simply not enough to shape culture well or leave an enduring and eternal family legacy to the glory of God. We must thoughtfully transfer both to our generations.

This is one of the biggest concerns today among those tasked with the enormous transfer of wealth that's taking place in families. Will my children have the character, the wisdom, and the will to faithfully steward the wealth they are receiving? Will it ruin them? Will they squander it? Will they fulfill the purpose of the family line as they steward what they are being entrusted with? The answers to these questions had better not be guesswork. Prayerfully and thoughtfully pass on the stuff with wisdom to those whose character will most faithfully steward them.

While this protocol does address who gets what to some extent, the clearer focus is the why behind the intentional impartation of the stuff. It is more about who gets what and why. What does the stuff mean or represent to the one passing it on and the one receiving it? What does the item say about their character? What is the story, the purpose, and the emotional connection attached to the stuff that is being given to a new steward? This part of the protocol creates a much deeper emotional implant and value for ongoing family legacy.

While your will or trust may address many of the same items in terms of who gets what, this piece of the Impartation Protocol supplements those items with the heart and the why underneath the transfer. The protocol is designed to give greater understanding and ownership of the purpose and stewardship of the items for a more powerful family legacy and cultural impact.

Personal Example

On another recent Family Legacy Venture to Florida to visit my father, we had one evening set aside for him to impart some stuff to all of us with the story of the why behind the stuff and its connection to the family legacy.

After a grilled steak and homemade mac and cheese dinner full of good questions, authentic answers, and lots of laughs, we cleared the table and waited to receive what my father had thoughtfully prepared to give to each of us, along with the story and legacy connection of each item.

He pulled out a gift bag that was filled with several large sealed envelopes and a few personal items. One by one, he handed out an envelope, starting with my oldest son, and had each of them open the envelopes one at a time. As they did, he took the time to talk about the item inside, what it was, why it was meaningful to him, why he was giving it to them, and made a legacy connection between all of that and how it was important in their lives moving forward. It was profound and relatively simple.

Dad gave out his employee award certificates and told the stories about what it required to earn them and how they represented different character qualities, such as empathy, faithfulness, kindness, trustworthiness, and a strong work ethic. He connected how doing the right thing and treating people right were so important for success in life and career. He encouraged us to be good leaders with good character. All of this was done intentionally, and it was a little emotional—exactly as it should have been for a lasting imprint of the family values and legacy on the hearts of his generations.

Dad did this with a few other items as well. This wasn't an end-of-life, give it all away as the end approaches context. This was a family venture where we took a focused time to impart some stuff, along with the stories of why and the intentional legacy connection.

He gave me a few items that have rich meaning to me and to our legacy. He gave me my mother's Bible, his IHSAA Football Officials Hall of Fame Award, and one of his favorite books on leadership. All of these items are profound symbols to me for what they represent in my father's life, my life, and the life of my children.

My mother was the spiritual leader in our home. Her hunger for God and her simple life of devoted obedience has impacted me forever. Her Bible contained her personal notes and handwritten prayers. The underlined and highlighted verses tell her story of faith and simplistic obedience to God. They explain her joy in the face of the challenges of multiple brain surgeries, limitations in her quality of life, and periods of isolation and recovery. I saw her reading that very Bible all the years I knew her. It is a priceless treasure that continues to speak to me. Now, it is speaking to my children and our family legacy through the simple and powerful intentional passing on of the stuff after a family venture vacation dinner.

The Family Legacy

My dad and I have a long history of connecting and learning through athletics. When I was a boy, my father would take me with him to high school football games all over Iowa on Friday nights. It was larger than life for me to be on the sidelines as he officiated games on the field. He was inducted into the state Hall of Fame for his efforts, while I was instructed in how to connect with your son, how to teach him about effort, team, leadership, integrity, and playing by the rules. There were so many lessons he taught me in the car, on the sidelines, in the locker room, and at dinner after the games. It is a priceless memory of how he invested in me. All of those lessons continue to shape me along with my children as we look upon that award and connect the story of what it represents to us.

His choice to pass on a book on leadership that tells the true life story of Ed Thomas, a high school football coach, hit my heart. On June 24, 2009, Thomas was shot and killed in his Parkersburg, Iowa, football team's weight room by Mark Becker, one of Thomas's former players who struggled with mental illness. How Thomas lived, the impact he made on the lives of young men and families in that community, and the lasting legacy he left speak so loudly to me around my own life purpose and the Bixby family legacy. Now they speak to my children as well.

Note: The experiential exercises in the stuff section are simply the completion and execution of the tools listed below and found in the Family Legacy Protocols Toolbox on our website. www.culturalarchitects.org. The tools are self-explanatory and happen both over time and in an event. For example, you will complete the tools over time, and you will eventually impart stuff to your family in one or more of the following ways:

- written compilation completed and put in safe storage in case of unexpected death and (or) imparted at an appropriate time
- video record completed and put in safe storage in case of unexpected death and (or) imparted at an appropriate time
- at a Family Legacy Encounter Weekend
- at an end-of-life impartation face-to-face

This is not a complicated or even a complex thing to do. It is simple. Our tools will walk you through how to impart the stuff by simply addressing the following four things as you prepare to impart the stuff.

- the specific possession(s) being given to designated people or organizations prior to or upon a death
- the location of the item
- the emotional why, story, and purpose for giving it to them
- the relevant insights on how to steward it well and connection to family legacy

The tools for imparting the stuff are available in the Family Legacy Toolbox on our website. www.culturalarchitects.org

___ Specific Gift of Personal Items: List specific possessions you want to leave to designated people or organizations upon your death, the location of the item, the emotional why and purpose for giving it, and any relevant insights on how to steward it well. Complete the Family Legacy Imparting the Stuff Form No. 1.

___ Vital Personal Information: This information includes your social security number, safety deposit box information, location of important papers, the name of your accountant, and other important information. Complete the Family Legacy Imparting the Stuff Form No. 2.

___ List of All Bank Accounts: List the details of all personal bank accounts, who is receiving what, the emotional why and purpose for giving it, and any relevant insights on how to steward it well. Complete Family Legacy Imparting the Stuff Form No. 3.

___ List of All Investment and Non-Bank Accounts: List the details of all personal investment and accounts other than bank accounts, who is receiving what, the emotional why and purpose for giving it, and any relevant insights on how to steward it well. Complete Family Legacy Imparting the Stuff Form No. 4.

___ List of Non-Liquid Assets: If you have pieces of furniture, artwork, books, stamp collections, jewelry, cars, properties, or other items that are particularly valuable, they should be included in a written list so these items don't end up in a yard sale or worse. List specific possessions you want to leave to designated people or organizations upon your death, the location of the item, the emotional why and purpose for giving it, and any relevant insights on how to steward it well. Complete Family Legacy Imparting the Stuff Form No. 5.

The Unfinished Business

Once you have finished the wisdom, the blessing, and the stuff pieces of this protocol, it's time to address any unfinished business. The unfinished business includes putting things in order, including your legal, financial, familial, personal, material, digital, medical, business, and other responsibilities. It is also time to make sure that any unfinished business between you and God and you and people is properly addressed for a strong finish.

It is important that we impart finished business to our children and not unfinished business. It is much sweeter to impart the order, clarity, ease, and purpose of finished business than to impart the bitter chaos, uncertainty, hardship, and aimlessness of unfinished business to those we love. Finished business is a force multiplier for family legacy. Finishing the business by putting things in order will allow your family to put their attention on more important aspects of the family legacy than on resolving the unfinished business.

When I think about finishing well in life, I think of the apostle Paul and Jesus. Paul wrote, "I have fought the good fight, I have finished the race, I have kept the faith." I think of Jesus, who was able to say that He had completed everything the Father had given Him to do. His last words on the cross were, "It is finished!"

What does it look like in our own lives to be able to say, "It is finished"? How exactly do we complete all we have been given to do in this life so that we have no unfinished business? The simple answer? Abide and obey out of love. Live in the Spirit and do His will in partnership with Him as one. Be intentional and get it done.

Personal Example

One lazy afternoon while at my father's house on another Family Legacy Venture, he bumped my arm and said, "Come with me." He showed me how to get into his house in the event that something would happen to him where he wasn't able to let me in. It was a little eerie yet comforting at the same time.

He then walked me into the back bedroom of his home and to his desk. He had pulled up on his computer an asset sheet with his financials on it. He went through it with me line by line, just as he had with my sister, explaining the necessary details for each one—what it was, where it was, and so forth. He reminded me that he had sent my sister and me both a copy of his will and all the details around that.

He took the time to show me where some of the family archives were, including family photo albums, important documents, sentimental items like the obituary articles from the paper for brother Reece and Mom. He showed me his University of Iowa Hawkeye stuff, his golf clubs, his awards, his football officiating Hall of Fame award, and his high school scrapbooks that contained his athletic achievements.

He told me how he wanted to be cremated like Mom and how everything is prepared and paid for at the funeral home. He told me that he wanted his ashes taken back to his home in Waterloo, Iowa. How he has a place prepared beside Mom at the cemetery and how he has seen that all is taken care of.

I was feeling this weird tension between grief and gratitude. On the one hand, I couldn't bear to think about me going through this when he's gone, the heavy loss and sadness that day would carry …

Yet I was grateful to celebrate his life with him in a way and relieved to know where things were, what to do, where to go, how he wanted it to be. Everything had been put in order. What a gift.

He shared with me his thinking around choosing to live in Florida. He and Mom dreamed of retiring where it was warm after many cold Iowa winters. And he is needed there … friends, neighbors, travelers on the Florida toll roads where he works as a toll collector that need a warm smile and kind words.

He told me why he continues to work into his early eighties. He enjoys the work, the people, and being useful to others. He also wants to save all the money he can to pass on to his family, and as long as he is healthy, he enjoys it. Even at his age, he is a multiyear recipient of the employee awards at the Florida Toll Road Department.

Out of the entire week with Dad, those three or four hours of irreplaceable time with my dad are among the most impactful, intimate, and enduring moments of my entire life. They will live on as vivid memories saturated with love and wisdom for the rest of my life and beyond for generations. I felt deep gratitude, love, and appreciation that he had gone to the effort to finish his business in this way. His example has inspired me and demonstrated to me how to make this happen in my life for my children. I want to do the same for you.

We have created numerous tools contained in the Legacy Cache to walk you through step-by-step how to practically put these things in order and ensure you are indeed passing on the legacy of finished business.

Unfinished Relational Business

In addition to the unfinished business that needs to be put in order before we die so that it can be stewarded well, two other areas are of the highest importance to address. They specifically focus on relationships.

Any unfinished business between you and God.

Any unfinished business between you and others.

Some of the most painful and devastating wounds in life are the wounds in relationships that do not get resolved. When they are unresolved at time of death, the pain is both taken to the grave and buried alive, on the one hand, and left to live on above ground on the other. These unresolved and unhealed wounds get into our DNA and are passed down to our generations as a part of their genetic legacy. Resolving the unfinished business in key relationships is a critical part of finishing well and passing on a healed family legacy.

While you can access the complete set of tools for finishing your business with God and others online, here are some of the basic questions to answer for yourself. Your answers will form the blueprint for your next action steps.

> What will it take for you to have total peace with God?
>
> What will it take for you to have total peace with others?
>
> What relationships are not in order?
>
> What will it take, as much as it depends on you, to put them in order?
>
> Do you hold any unforgiveness toward God?
>
> Will you forgive Him now?
>
> Do you hold any unforgiveness toward another person? Who? What?

Will you forgive them now?

Do you need to ask forgiveness of God?

Do you need to ask forgiveness of another person? Who?

Is there anything that you have left unsaid to God or others? What?

Is there anything that you have left undone toward God or others? What?

What specific action will you take on the above items?

When will you take action on the above items?

What support will you need to ensure that you finish the relational business above?

Remember, if you would like the support of others or of our Family Legacy coaches to come alongside of you to ensure the successful completion of the work above, please contact our office or visit our website to see the resources we have to help you every step of the way.

We have created numerous tools contained in the Family Legacy Toolbox to walk you through step-by-step how to practically put the unfinished business in order and ensure you are indeed passing on the legacy of finished business.

Note: The experiential exercises in the unfinished business section are simply the completion and execution of the tools listed below and found in the Family Legacy Protocols Toolbox on our website. www.culturalarchitects.org The tools are self-explanatory and happen both over time and in an event. For example, you will complete the tools over time, and you will eventually address and impart the unfinished business to your family in one or more of the following ways:

- written compilation completed and put in safe storage in case of unexpected death and (or) imparted at an appropriate time
- video record completed and put in safe storage in case of unexpected death and (or) imparted at an appropriate time
- at a Family Legacy Encounter Weekend
- at an end-of-life impartation face-to-face

___ Funeral, Burial, Cremation, Memorial Service, and Related Instructions: Do you want to be buried or cremated? How do you want to be remembered at your final services? Who do you want to officiate, sing, or eulogize? Failure to put your wishes in writing can cause not only dissension in your family but maybe even lasting family animosity. Your grieving family may have difficulty knowing what to do. Decide for them and give them a plan to follow. Complete the Family Legacy Unfinished Business Form No. 1.

___ List of People and Organizations to Be Notified of Your Death: Complete Family Legacy Unfinished Business Form No. 2.

___ Digital Footprint Information: Computer, Email, Cell Phone, Social Media, Cloud Storage, Digital Apps, and other Passwords: Upon your death, especially if it's sudden and unexpected, you will want someone to have access to and be able to close your various online social media and other accounts; check messages on your home and cell and notify callers of your death; check your emails and let senders know of your death and then close the accounts; and so on. Complete Family Legacy Unfinished Business Form No. 3.

___ List of All Loans and Mortgages: Your heirs or executor will need this information to settle your debts. Complete Family Legacy Unfinished Business Form No. 4.

___ List of All Credit Card Accounts: Your heirs or executor will need this information to immediately close the accounts to protect your estate from identity theft as well as to arrange for payments of all outstanding balances. Complete Family Legacy Unfinished Business Form No. 5.

___ Detailed Child Care Instructions: Whoever will be caring for your child or children after your death will need detailed information about their diet, medical needs, school information, extracurricular activities, and so on. Complete Family Legacy Unfinished Business Form No. 6.

___ Home Utility and Service Providers: Your heirs or executor will need to know the name and account information for all home utilities, phone service, television service provider, internet access, and so on to either close the accounts or change the name on the account. Complete Family Legacy Unfinished Business Form No. 7.

___ Ownership of Pet(s) upon Death: Make certain that your pet(s) have a good home when you die by designating in writing who will be undertaking their care upon your death. Complete Family Legacy Unfinished Business Form No. 8.

___ Pet Care Instructions: The person caring for your pet(s) upon your death will need detailed care information, including feeding instructions, medication schedule, exercise and grooming requirements, the name of their vet, and so on. Complete Family Legacy Unfinished Business Form No. 9

___ List of All Insurance Policies: In addition to cashing in any life insurance, burial, or similar policies in force at the time of your death, your heirs will need a written record of all of your other insurance policies so they can be canceled and any unamortized premiums already paid returned to your estate. Complete Family Legacy Unfinished Business Form No. 10.

___ Business Bank Accounts: List the details of all business bank accounts, who is receiving what, the emotional why and purpose for giving it, and any relevant insights on how to steward it well. Complete Family Legacy Unfinished Business Form No. 11.

___ List of Business Loans, Credit Cards, and Other Debts: Your heirs or executor will need this information to settle your estate and to close accounts or to continue to run the business. Complete Family Legacy Unfinished Business Form No. 12.

___ Business Digital Footprint (computers, phones, etc.): Whether your business will be closed, sold, or run by your heirs, your heirs or executor will need to be able to access your work email, phone, and other messaging devices as to be able to access any work-related website, social media accounts, and so on. Complete Family Legacy Unfinished Business Form No. 13.

___ Work/Business Notification List: Leave a list of the people/organizations to be notified in the event of your death, including associates, customers, vendors, landlords, and so on. Complete Family Legacy Unfinished Business Form No. 14.

Other Important Legal Matters

You will need actual legal documents for the following items on the checklist that are not provided by Family Legacy. Consult an attorney or use a service like Legal Zoom.

____ Healthcare, Living Will, and Advance Directives: Every adult should have written documents appointing a trusted person to make health care and end-of-life decisions on their behalf in the event they are unable to make those decisions themselves. These documents let your family and doctors know what kind of medical treatments you do or do not want near the end of life. This includes decisions for things like the use of CPR, breathing tubes, nutrition/hydration, and other common lifesaving interventions.

____ Power of Attorney for Finances: This is a person you designate to make financial decisions for you and your estate if you are incapacitated and no longer able to voice your wishes while you are still alive.

____ Will or Trust: A legal instrument or document you write in order to give your assets, money, or property to people or organizations once you die.

Your life team and contact information for your family as the steward of your responsibilities when you are finished:

Role	Name	Phone	Email
Attorney			
Notary			
Financial advisor			
Medical doctor			
Family member			
Executor			
Godparents			
Banker			
Business contact			
Insurance agent(s)			
Funeral/memorial director			
Pastor or priest			

By completing the tools provided in the workbook or online, you will create a written legacy. I encourage you to also create a video legacy by reading and talking through your completed written legacy on video. This provides a solid Legacy Cache for your family in the case of an early or unexpected death.

If you are committed to passing on a powerful family legacy in your children and grandchildren, one that will equip and empower them to lead well in their families, businesses, and communities and in our culture, then you will make time to finish well by finishing your business.

The Family Legacy Generational Covenant

The final piece of the Family Legacy Impartation Protocol is the Family Legacy Generational Covenant. This covenant is an intentional conveying upon the next generation the responsibility of stewarding the family legacy faithfully in their lifetime. It is also a practice designed to be repeated with each generation to ensure this stewardship of legacy endures.

A covenant is the highest form of agreement between two or more parties, based on the biblical example and definition. God made a covenant with Abraham that was transferred to Isaac, then to Jacob, and so on. We have the old and new covenants in the scriptures. An agreement between God Himself and man. A covenant is a sacred promise or agreement that all parties who choose to be involved will do what they have agreed to do for generations.

It is an all-in, whatever it takes, no turning back, and no giving up agreement between parties. Biblically, covenants were sealed with the shedding of blood; or in other words, "On the promise of my life, I will keep this covenant, and so will my entire house (family)."

God's idea of covenant is sobering, life-giving, and powerful. The Family Legacy Generational Covenant is patterned after the same idea of making a sacred promise to do what all parties are agreeing to do with the intensity of an all-in, whatever-it-takes commitment that includes the generations to come. It is a deep and sober commitment from the heart to build and steward the family legacy faithfully and for the purposes and glory of God.

The Family Legacy Generational Covenant exercise is simply the completion and execution of the tool.

Explanation

When God wanted His chosen family to remember something important, He attached an action or a practice to it to create a trigger that reminded them of the significance of that thing. God instituted various ceremonies, festivals, feasts, holy days, symbols, practices, sacraments, ordinances, and protocols so that the meaning underneath these containers could be conveyed to everyone and passed on from generation to generation as His legacy.

Communion, baptism, Passover, and the bar mitzvah are all examples of ways that God formalized important spiritual truths and practices into containers that could be duplicated and passed on for generations in a way that could be understood and continued.

This is what the Family Legacy Generational Covenant is about. It is an intentional practice of formally making a lasting covenant between parent(s), their children, and God to ensure the stewardship of the family legacy in perpetuity for the glory of God. No one is compelled to make this covenant. Family members have the opportunity to choose in.

Before you are tempted to minimize the power of agreement, consider that God has chosen to govern all creation, to relate to humankind, even to put our inheritance along with His own credibility all in the framework of agreements and covenants. Making an agreement is a big deal.

The Family Legacy Generational Covenant is also a covenant between families. It is an agreement between your family and God, who by very nature is a family (Father, Son, Holy Spirit). It is a sacred choice to faithfully steward your family identity, purpose, values, and sovereign design. It is an agreement entered into by choice and made with everyone else in the family who is choosing "in" to this responsibility with you.

The Family Legacy Generational Covenant Tool

The Ceremony

The purpose of the ceremony is to emphasize the importance of faithfully stewarding the family legacy while gaining the commitment and agreement of the next generation to continue in the protocols and to do the same with their children.

The Family Legacy Generational Covenant ceremony should take place face-to-face with the entire family once the family has been introduced to the protocols contained in the Family Legacy Model. It may be especially impactful when it is time for the ones who have been carrying the main responsibility for the legacy work to pass that primary responsibility on to someone else. End of life would be one good time for the ceremony.

Another effective time to hold the ceremony is at the end of the Family Legacy Encounter Workshop where we spend the better part of three days with a single family, walking them through all the protocols. By the time the family has engaged in the learning experience and knows how to execute the protocols, a family covenant before God to prioritize and carry out the protocols faithfully is a powerful culmination of the encounter.

It may also be a good idea to record on video the ceremony as a leader and keep with the other legacy content for use in the event of unexpected death.

Instructions

Leader:
Gather the family in a semicircle with the parent(s) standing out in front of the family facing them. Determine which parent will lead the covenant.

Leader:
"God in Heaven, we the __(Last name)__ family have gathered before you to make a sacred covenant with each other and with You (Father, Son, and Holy Spirit).

"Whereas, by Your good, wise, and eternal design, You have set us in this family from before the foundations of the world, and

"Whereas, Your design for our family line is to bring glory and honor to Your great name and to advance Your eternal kingdom by shaping culture from the inside out, and

"Whereas, You have bestowed upon our family line Your character, Your love, Your purposes, and Your power to accomplish this in agreement with Your design, and

"Whereas, You have made known to us the design for how to live and leave a powerful and enduring family legacy in Your Word, and

"Whereas, the Family Legacy Protocols are patterned after and in full agreement with Your design,

"All who are willing to join in this decree, repeat after me."

> "I choose to be a wise builder." (Repeat.)
>
> "I commit to building our family, our businesses, our community, and our culture." (Repeat.)
>
> "And through intelligence and insight," (repeat)
>
> "Together as one with You and this family," (repeat)
>
> "Our enterprises are established and endure" (repeat)
>
> "For the glory of our King and His kingdom." (repeat)
>
> "So be it!" (Repeat.)

Leader:

"Knowing that You are a good Father and that You keep Your covenants to always do Your part in ensuring that Your legacy is fulfilled in our family line, we now offer our agreements in our Family Legacy Generational Covenant with You.

"All who are willing to join in this covenant, repeat after me."

> "I commit to wholeheartedly engage in the faithful stewardship of my family legacy regularly." (Repeat.)
>
> "I agree to give my best effort to practice the Family Legacy Protocols personally," (repeat)
>
> "with my family of origin" (repeat)
>
> "and with my own children." (repeat)
>
> "I agree to reach out for help and support in keeping this covenant when challenged." (Repeat.)
>
> "I commit to equipping my children and grandchildren to use the Family Legacy Protocols," (repeat)
>
> "and to instruct them to do the same." (repeat)

"I choose to live and leave a powerful and enduring family legacy to the glory of God." (Repeat.)

"I commit to help other families understand and use the protocols as God directs me." (Repeat.)

Leader:
A closing prayer from the heart would be appropriate here.

The Family Legacy Model Protocols

Family Legacy EQ—how to treat and to love each other

Family Legacy Identity— character, values, purpose, coat of arms, painting, song

Family Legacy Rituals—regular, intentional sharing of food, fun, wisdom, story, and coaching

Family Legacy Ventures—the learning adventure that connects and offers growth

Family Legacy MISSION–the strategic blueprint for handling a crisis together as one

Family Legacy Impartation—passing on the wisdom, the blessing, the stuff, the unfinished business and the covenant

Chapter 11
The Family Legacy Toolbox

Download the free, editable PDF Family Legacy Protocol Tools to walk you through the execution of each exercise step-by-step. www.culturalarchitects.org

Family Legacy EQ Tools

    Personal Investigator EQ Tool

    Family Legacy Social Covenant EQ Tool

    Healthy Communication Empathetic Listening EQ Tool

    Healthy Communication Speaking the Truth in Love EQ Tool

    OOOH NO! EQ Tool

    Fact/Story EQ Tool

    Love Without Hooks EQ Tool

    Powerful/Powerless EQ Tool

    The Personality Profile Comparison EQ Tool* (This tool reports are available for a small fee.)

Family Legacy Identity Tools

    True Identity Tool

    Family History Tool

    Family Genetic History Tool

Family Generational History Tool

Inner Healing Tool

Family Personality Profile Tool* (This tool and the reports are available for a small fee.)

Family Identity CVP Tool (Character, Values, Purpose)

Family Coat of Arms Tool

Rule 51 Tool

Choice to Believe Identity Tool

Family Legacy Coach Approach Tool

Family Legacy Ritual Tools

Ritual Launch Tool

Ritual Agenda Tool

Ritual Advance Planning Tool

Ritual Coaching Tool

Ritual Idea Tool

Family Legacy MISSION Tools

MISSION Blueprint Preparation Tool

MISSION Launch Tool

MISSION Brief Tool

MISSION Wrap Up and Debrief Tool

Family Legacy Venture Tools

Venture Launch Tool

Venture Advance Planning Tool

Venture Agenda Tool

Venture Service Project Tool

Venture Book Discussion Tool

Venture Coaching Tool

Venture Experience Module Tool

Venture Legacy Tool

Family Legacy Impartation Tools

Wisdom

Family Legacy Wisdom Treasure Hunt Tool

Family Legacy Wisdom Impartation Tool

Blessing

Crafting the Parental Blessing Tool

Crafting the Heavenly Blessing Tool

Stuff

Specific Gift of Personal Items

Vital Personal Information

List of All Bank Accounts

List of All Investment and Non-Bank Accounts

List of Non-Liquid Assets

Unfinished Business

Funeral, Burial, Cremation, Memorial Service, and Related Instructions

List of People and Organizations to Be Notified of Your Death

Digital Footprint Information

List of All Loans and Mortgages

List of All Credit Card Accounts

Detailed Child Care Instructions

Home Utility and Service Providers

Ownership of Pet(s) upon Death

Pet Care Instructions

List of All Insurance Policies

Business Bank Accounts

List of Business Loans, Credit Cards, and Other Debts

Business Digital Footprint (Computers, Phones, Etc.)

Work/Business Notification List

The Family Legacy Generational Covenant Tool

Other Important Legal Matters

You may need actual legal documents for the following items on the checklist that are not provided by Family Legacy. Consult an attorney or use a service like Legal Zoom.

Health Care, Living Will, and Advance Directives

Power of Attorney for Finances

Will or Trust

Chapter 12
Family Legacy Solutions:
Training, Coaching, Subscription, E-courses and Resources

To learn more, visit our website
www.culturalarchitects.org

The Family Legacy Training

Family Legacy Sermon, Keynote, or Conference Presenter

Family Legacy Training for Pastors, church staff, small group leaders - 3 hrs. (Introduction)

Family Legacy Pastor/Small Group Leader Certification: two days live training or E-Course training

Family Legacy Conference 12 hours total

- Friday evening
- Saturday all Day
- Saturday evening
- Sunday morning

Family Legacy School- 12-2 hour sessions, 24 hours total plus homework

- Format 1: Three 8 hour days
- Format 2: Twelve weeks 2 hours per week
- Format 3: Twelve months 2 hours per month
- Format 4: Build your own 24 hours total

Family Legacy Coach Approach to Family- 2 days / 16 hours

Family Legacy Camp- 5 days- multiple families

Family Legacy Encounter- one family, one weekend, one unforgettably life and legacy changing experience   2 and 1//2 days. This is our premiere training for fast and lasting family legacy transformation.

The Family Legacy Coaching Services

All coaching is done by ICF Certified and Family Legacy Certified coaches via online video or by phone. Inquire about in person coaching.

*Family Coaching is a ministry reduced in price from other CA Coaching services.

Single Session- Immediate support for times of crisis or occasional family coaching support.

Partner Package- 3 sessions- Limited one-on-one access to a coaching partner for your Family Legacy journey.

Guide Package- 8 sessions - Full one-on-one access to an expert coach to guide you through the six Family Legacy protocols.

Mentor Package- 12 sessions- Complete one-on-one Mentor Coach access for a six-month Family Legacy Journey.

Custom Packages- As needed 12 or more sessions, multiple family members, specific family challenges, full day in person, etc.

Become a certified Family Legacy Coach

Family Legacy Coach Certification*

Join the Family Legacy coaching staff

Life and Business Coaching from a Cultural Architect ICF Certified Coach available in our regular coaching packages on the Coaching page of our website. www.culturalarchitects.org

Subscription

"The Family" Family Legacy by Cultural Architect's monthly Subscription.*

Family Legacy weekly programs and live webinars*

- ▫ week one- interview with a special guest
- ▫ week two- Randy and Lesli teaching on The Family Legacy Protocols, exercises, tools
- ▫ week three- Family Legacy Coaching call in
- ▫ week four- Family Legacy Q/A and Testimonies

60 tools and exercises from the book

60 tool and exercise How To Videos* (*only available to Family subscription members)

Six Secrets of Legacy Leadership Training*

Periscope 360- a unique annual learning, goal setting, and planning video training series*

coaching tips

facilitating tips

testimonies

free assessments

new content added regularly

The Family Legacy E-Courses

Family Legacy Individual Protocol E-Courses (video training / tools / workbook)

EQ Protocol 1
Identity Protocol 2
Ritual Protocol 3
Venture Protocol 4
Mission Protocol 5

Impartation Protocol 6

The Complete Family Legacy E-School

Introduction, Protocols 1-6, coaching and facilitating tips, tools and forms-
12- two-hour sessions, 24 hours total

Church small group license for the Complete Family Legacy E-School course

Family Legacy Pastor and Small Group Leader Certification E-Course.

Family Legacy E-School + Pastor/Small Group Leader E-Certification course

NOTE: churches and small groups require:

license to use Family Legacy E-School videos

leader who has completed Pastor/Small Group Leader Certification live or E-Course

Each family/couple/person in a small group needs a:

Family Legacy Book

Family Legacy Small Group Workbook

Tool videos are helpful and available through annual Family Legacy Subscription

The Coach Approach to Family E-course

More...

Resources

The Family Legacy Best Selling Book

Free Tools for book exercises

VLOG

Testimonials

Videos

Assessments

Family Legacy Subscription

Cultural Architect Podcasts webinar- The latest and best of what's happening with Cultural Architects

- Weekly
- week one- interview with a cultural architect
- week two- teaching from Cultural Architects
- week three- live coaching webinar for Cultural Architects
- Week four- Cultural Architect Q/A and testimonies

Family Legacy Merchandise

Family Legacy Creative Services – Coat of Arms Design, Family Song, Family Painting

Family Legacy Small Group Workbook

The Historymaker Journal- Journeys of Faith and Character